On Beauty and Measure

THE COLLECTED WRITINGS OF JOHN SALLIS
Volume III/2

ON BEAUTY AND MEASURE

Plato's Symposium *and* Statesman

John Sallis

Edited by S. Montgomery Ewegen

Indiana University Press

This book is a publication of

Indiana University Press
Office of Scholarly Publishing
Herman B Wells Library 350
1320 East 10th Street
Bloomington, Indiana 47405 USA

iupress.org

© 2021 by Indiana University Press

All rights reserved
No part of this book may be reproduced or utilized in any form or by any means, electronic or mechanical, including photocopying and recording, or by any information storage and retrieval system, without permission in writing from the publisher. The paper used in this publication meets the minimum requirements of the American National Standard for Information Sciences—Permanence of Paper for Printed Library Materials, ANSI Z39.48–1992.

Manufactured in the United States of America

First printing 2021

Library of Congress Cataloging-in-Publication Data

Names: Sallis, John, 1938- author. | Ewegen, S. Montgomery, editor.
Title: On beauty and measure : Plato's Symposium and Statesman / John Sallis ; edited by S. Montgomery Ewegen.
Description: Bloomington, Indiana, USA : Indiana University Press, 2021. | Series: The collected writings of John Sallis | Includes bibliographical references and index.
Identifiers: LCCN 2021008040 (print) | LCCN 2021008041 (ebook) | ISBN 9780253057952 (hardback) | ISBN 9780253057969 (paperback) | ISBN 9780253057983 (ebook)
Subjects: LCSH: Plato. Symposium. | Plato. Statesman.
Classification: LCC B395 .S238 2021 (print) | LCC B395 (ebook) | DDC 184—dc23
LC record available at https://lccn.loc.gov/2021008040
LC ebook record available at https://lccn.loc.gov/2021008041

Contents

Part I. Plato's *Symposium*

1. Introduction (172a–173e) — 3
2. Phaedrus / Pausanias / Eryximachus (174a–188e) — 17
3. Aristophanes / Agathon (189a–197e) — 29
4. Socrates (Diotima) (198a–212a) — 42
5. Alcibiades (212b–223d) — 59

Part II. Plato's *Statesman*

1. Introduction — 71
2. Initial Divisions (257a–259d) — 84
3. The Mathematical Comedy of Animals (259e–268e) — 95
4. The Myth of Cosmic Revolutions (269a–276e) — 110
5. Paradigms (277a–291c) — 120
6. The Weaver of the Πόλις (291d–311c) — 131

Editor's Afterword — 141
Bibliography — 143
Index — 145
Index of Greek Terms — 149

ON BEAUTY AND MEASURE

Part I.
Plato's *Symposium*

Lecture course presented at Boston College, Chestnut Hill, Massachusetts
Fall 2011

1. Introduction (172a–173e)

THE CONCERN OF the present inquiry is Plato's dialogue the *Symposium*.[1] Our goal is *to read* this text—or, perhaps better, to begin to learn *how to read* this text. For reading such a text is no simple matter at all, if indeed, rather than simply assimilating it to our ready-made preconceptions, we want to open ourselves to it such that it can engage us and evoke our wonder—which, for the Greeks, was the very beginning of philosophy.[2]

We will need to read slowly and carefully. Like Nietzsche—and, indeed, perhaps even more so—Plato is a teacher of slow reading.[3] We will need to read carefully, with utmost attentiveness, to every turn in the text, to every theoretical, mythical, and dramatic nuance.

This dialogue, above all, will force us to give up thinking that Plato's texts consist primarily of so-called logical arguments, and to abandon the belief that whatever does not belong to these arguments can safely be ignored, or at least be passed quickly by as if it were a mere ornament. For not only is there, strictly speaking, no logic in Plato's *Symposium*—nor, for that matter, in any other Platonic dialogue, since it was Aristotle who first invented logic[4]—but there are also *mythical* elements that inform the discourse, that give it added, or even different, sense. For example, there are the various myths, such as those about lovers who endure the descent into Hades in search of their beloveds (*Symp.* 179d). Additionally, there are deeds (ἔργα) that contribute to what a dialogue makes manifest: for example, when drunken Alcibiades puts a wreath around the head of Socrates (*Symp.* 213e), or when Aristophanes gets the hiccups (*Symp.* 185c).[5]

Owing to all of this, we as slow readers must—insofar as we can—weigh every nuance, every turn, no matter how subtle, for in the Platonic dialogues there are virtually no insignificant details. These are texts in which everything counts, wherein everything contributes to the manifestation that the dialogue as a whole accomplishes.[6]

---

1. The translation consulted and sometimes quoted is by Benardete (2001). However, many translated passages are the author's own.
2. [Editor's Note: See *Theat.*, 155d; see also *Met.* 982b12.]
3. [Editor's Note: See sec. 5 of the preface to Nietzsche's *Morgenröthe*.]
4. [Editor's Note: See Sallis (2012), 26.]
5. [Editor's Note: The significance of these textual moments is explored in later chapters.]
6. [Editor's Note: See Sallis (1975), 1–5.]

* * *

In the *Timaeus*, there is an injunction about beginning. It occurs near, though not quite at, the beginning of Timaeus's first discourse: "With regard to everything, it is most important to begin at the natural beginning" (*Tim.* 29b). In keeping with this injunction, we shall begin with the title of the dialogue presently under consideration: the *Symposium*. We note immediately that this is a unique title, for the majority of Plato's dialogues are named for a character who speaks within the dialogue—for example, the *Theaetetus*, the *Protagoras*, the *Meno*, and the *Gorgias*. Some other texts have a theme as their title—for example, the *Republic*, the *Laws*, and the *Statesman*. But only the *Symposium* is named for an *event* represented in the dialogue.

What kind of event is a "symposium"? The word συμπόσιον comes from συμπίνω, which means "to drink together." The event in question, then, is a *drinking party*. Very near the beginning of the text, two other words are used to describe the event. The first word is συνουσία, which means "being-together"—as, for example, at a party. However, this word can also have a sexual sense;[7] and, indeed, Greek symposia often included sexual activity. (The flute girl who typically attended such get-togethers[8] was often expected to provide not only musical, but also sexual, entertainment.) The other word used at the beginning of the text to describe the event is σύνδειπνον, which refers to a common meal or a banquet. We will see as the text unfolds that the participants in Plato's *Symposium* will indeed enjoy a meal—although Socrates himself will miss about half of it.

Despite these other important nuances, the party is primarily a *drinking* party. After the meal, the participants make libations to gods, daimons, and heroes, and they sing songs in praise of gods: then, as the dialogue says, they "turned to drinking" (*Symp.* 176a). As a result, wine figures prominently in the dialogue, as does the god most closely associated with wine, Dionysus.[9] In the figure of this god, the Greeks recognized the sense of elation, sociality, and well-being induced by wine, but also the frenzy and even madness that it could produce. In Euripides's *Bacchae*, for example, Dionysus is portrayed with the Maenads, who were

---

7. See, for example, *Symp.* 206c, where it refers to the being-together of a man and a woman that results in the birth of a child.

8. [Editor's Note: See *Symp.* 176e.]

9. Wine was considered a symbol of Greek culture. Most of the wine was fairly sweet and very potent (15–16%). It had bits of grape and vine debris in it, so the first step in preparing it was to pour it through a sieve. The only time it was drunk unmixed was in the libation to gods and daimons at the beginning of a drinking party. Otherwise, it was always mixed with water—about two parts wine to five parts water—and thus was not very strong and could be drunk in fairly large quantities. The wine (unmixed) would first be chilled in a wine cooler (ψυκτήρ); then it would be mixed with water in a large mixing bowl (κρατήρ); then it would be poured either directly into the drinking cups (ἔκπομα) or into a jug that a slave would carry around.

bands of women frenzied with wine who roamed the countryside. They uttered cries and waved wands topped with pine cones, and would attack wild animals, tearing them to pieces and eating their raw flesh.

Dionysus was the only god whose parents were not both gods: he was the child of Zeus and the Theban princess Semele.[10] The great dramatic festival in Athens, the Lenaia, was held in honor of Dionysus. Such a festival is what provides the occasion for the drinking party depicted in Plato's *Symposium*, which occurs on the day after the solemn celebration (with sacrifices) of the tragic poet Agathon's winning, with his first tragedy, the prize that accompanied the festival. The drinking party is a continuation of the previous day's celebration.

The next word we read after the title is the name of the narrator, Apollodorus, who narrates the entire account of the drinking party to some unnamed companions. The dialogue consists entirely of Apollodorus's account, except for a couple of brief remarks made by one of the (anonymous) companions near the beginning of the text. Apollodorus's name means "gift of Apollo": thus, his serving as narrator indicates that another god, Apollo, also figures in the dialogue.

Who is Apollo? Most important in this regard is his epithet "Phoebus." The Greek word φοῖβος (from φαός/φῶς) means "bright," "light," "radiant," and "shining." In being associated with light, Apollo is also associated with truth (ἀλήθεια), for it is in the light that things become visible such that they show themselves as they truly are. Apollo is also a master musician who plays the lyre; indeed, there was a famous musical contest between Apollo and the satyr Marsyas, to which we will later find reference in the *Symposium* (215b ff.). Apollo is also a healer, and is the god who gave humans the art of healing—an art carried on by his son Asclepius, god of physicians. (One of the characters at the drinking party—namely, Eryximachus—is a physician.)

It is also very important to note that pronouncements of Apollo's were given through the Delphic Oracle. This was the most famous oracle in Greece, often consulted when there were important questions to be settled. There is also, of course, a very important connection between the Delphic Oracle and Socrates. In Plato's *Apology*, Socrates tells of how Chaerephon went to Delphi and asked the oracle if there was anyone wiser than Socrates (*Ap.* 21a). The priestess answered that there was no one wiser. At first, Socrates was puzzled. Since he was aware that he was not wise, he could not understand how the god could make such a pronouncement, since gods do not lie—least of all this god, the very god of light, manifestation, and truth. Then, Apollo's pronouncement became the provocation for Socrates's questioning of others in the search for someone wiser than he. In this way, Socrates called the god and his pronouncement into question—an action that borders on the kind of excess that the Greeks called ὕβρις: overweening

---

10. [Editor's Note: See Hesiod, *Theogony*, 940 ff.]

pride, even outrage. (Later in the *Symposium* [175e], Socrates will once again be charged with ὕβρις.) Eventually, through his questioning of others, Socrates came to interpret the pronouncement as meaning that he was wiser in that he knew that he did not know (*Ap.* 21d). As a result, his questioning of others became a continual confirmation of the god's saying. Thus, Socrates's practice—that is, his *philosophizing*—is prompted and sustained by the Delphic pronouncement: hence, Socrates, as philosopher, has a decisive connection with the god Apollo.

But who is Apollodorus, the narrator of the *Symposium*? Apollodorus shows up in Plato's *Apology* as one of those willing to give money to secure Socrates's acquittal or release (*Ap.* 38b). In the *Phaedo*, we learn that he was present on the day of Socrates's death. We also learn that he was the most emotional of those present, for when Socrates finally drank the potion (φάρμακον), he completely broke down in tears: "But Apollodorus, who hadn't stopped weeping even during the whole time before, at that moment really let loose with such a storm of wailing and fussing that there wasn't a single one of those present whom he didn't break up—except, of course, Socrates himself" (*Phd.* 117d).

At the beginning of the *Symposium*, Apollodorus describes his relation to Socrates: "It is scarcely three years now that I have been spending my time with Socrates and have made it my concern on each and every day to know whatever he says or does" (*Symp.* 172c). He goes on to say that, before he attached himself to Socrates, he ran around aimlessly and, in truth, was miserable. Through the first pages of the *Symposium*, it becomes clear that Apollodorus is a rather blunt, almost rude fellow. He accuses his companion of being miserable, even without knowing it. He gives an indication regarding what kind of people the companions are by pejoratively describing their kind of λόγος as that of the rich and the moneymakers. In turn, the companion refers to Apollodorus's nickname, μανικός ("mad").[11]

So, Apollodorus, this gift of Apollo, rages in frenzy like one who is mad—almost as though he were more on the side of Dionysus than of Apollo. This tension between his name and his character anticipates the fact that in the drinking party, the story of which he narrates, there is tension, interchange, and conflict between the two sides represented by Apollo and Dionysus.

* * *

We turn now to the first line of the *Symposium*:

> In my opinion, I am not unprepared for what you ask about; for just the other day—when I was on my way up to town from my home in Phaleron—one of

---

11. Some editors read μαλακός here, which means "soft," "gentle," "mild"; however, μανικός (i.e., "mad") seems more likely in view of Apollodorus's self-description that immediately follows: μαίνομαι καὶ παραπαίω—"I rage and fall out" (*Symp.* 173e)—as when drunk in a Bacchic frenzy where one loses one's senses.

my acquaintances spotted me a long way off from behind and called, playing with his call: "Phalerian," he said. "You there, Apollodorus, aren't you going to wait?" And I stopped and let him catch up. And he said: "Apollodorus, why, it was just recently that I was looking for you; I had wanted to question you closely about Agathon's party—the one at which Socrates, Alcibiades, and the others were then present at dinner together—to question about the erotic speeches." (*Symp.* 172a–b)

To begin with, we must attend to the first two words of the text: δοκῶ μοι—literally, "I seem to myself" (i.e., to be not unprepared regarding what you ask about). It is not a matter of Apollodorus simply holding an *opinion*, carrying it around in his head. Rather, it is a matter of a *seeming*, an *appearing*, and in this case one that is reflexive: a seeming *to himself*. The words δοκέω, δόξα, and δοξάζω are often translated (as above) by some form of the word "opinion." However, it is important to note that these words do not mean "opinion" in the modern sense: rather, they always have reference to an *appearing*, a *seeming*, a *looking*. One has an opinion (δόξα) about something—one opines (δοξάζω) about it in a certain way—*because* the thing itself seems, appears, or looks that way. In other words, opinion is always correlative to an appearing. It is perhaps closer to the Greek if we speak of "having a view" (of something). However, the translation of δοκέω and its cognates as "opinion" is so firmly established that we will retain it in what follows, but always while remembering its precise sense as delineated above. Unless we keep this sense in mind, we will never understand the importance of what these words name. That importance is evident in the fact that it is precisely a discussion of δοξάζω that forms the very first step in the discourse that Socrates will report having received from Diotima, a discourse that is usually considered to be the culminating discourse of the dialogue.[12]

As seen above, Apollodorus says that just the other day, as he was *going up* to the city from his home in Phaleron, an acquaintance spotted him from behind and called to him to wait. Phaleron is the old harbor of Athens, which lies six miles southwest of the city proper, at the point on the sea nearest to the city. Phaleron became less important as a port after the establishment of Piraeus as the main harbor of Athens (in the beginning of the fifth century BCE). Like Piraeus, Phaleron was joined to the city by a wall that ran between them. In going from the harbor in Phaleron up to the city, one walked along and inside the Phaleric Wall.[13] Apollodorus says that he was *going up* (in)to the city. "Going up" translates the word ἀνιών (from ἄνειμι), and one must be careful to note the upward directionality of this term. He was "going up," he says, "(in)to the city": εἰς ἄστυ.

---

12. [Editor's Note: Diotima's speech is analyzed in detail in chap. 4.]
13. Piraeus, for its part, was joined to the city by two parallel walls (i.e., the "Long Walls"), and one walked between them.

Ἄστυ is the name by which the Athenians commonly referred to their city. It refers specifically to the upper city, in distinction to the harbors and the outlying countryside.

Now, these words given near the opening of the *Symposium* unmistakably echo the opening words of Plato's *Republic*: "I went down [κατέβην] yesterday to the Piraeus" (*Rep.* 327a). The *Republic* begins with a *going-down* from the city to the harbor: it begins, that is, with a κατάβασις, a descent. The *Symposium*, for its part, begins with a *going-up* from the harbor to the city: it begins, that is, with an ἀνάβασις, an ascent. Furthermore, in the *Republic*, Socrates (accompanied by Glaucon) starts back up toward the city, only to be caught from behind and detained by Polemarchus (*Rep.* 327b). In the *Symposium*, Apollodorus (this constant companion of Socrates's) is called from behind and is detained. We soon learn that the one who detains him is Glaucon (*Symp.* 172c).

Yet, Apollodorus quickly agrees to what Glaucon requests—namely, that he tell him about the drinking party. More literally, Apollodorus agrees to tell him "what the λόγοι were" that took place at the party (*Symp.* 173e). It is important to note that, in fact, Apollodorus will tell more than simply what the λόγοι were. He will also tell of actions and gestures—that is, ἔργα, deeds—many of which convey significance (especially when they occur between persons involved in an erotic relationship). It is also important to note that Glaucon's remark that he was looking for Apollodorus "just recently" installs a temporal interval from the beginning of the dialogue. When Apollodorus explains that the party took place long ago, a longer temporal interval is inserted reaching from long ago when the party took place up to the time of Apollodorus's conversation with Glaucon and even still farther to the present time when Apollodorus recounts that conversation to his companions.

In any case, once Apollodorus agrees to tell of the drinking party, he and Glaucon set out walking, going up to the city. Now, this upward directionality, this ascent, is of enormous significance (as is the descent in the *Republic*). Here, at the outset of the *Symposium*, an ascent is initiated in *deed*, and it is an ascent that will be underway throughout the narrative that constitutes the rest of the dialogue. Moreover, in the speeches that Apollodorus will relate, certain ascents will be carried out in λόγος. Thus, this ascent *in deed* images and prepares the ascents that will be carried out in λόγος at the drinking party, preeminently in the speech given by Socrates.[14]

---

14. One final point of comparison with the beginning of the *Republic* can be made here: In the *Republic*, as in the *Symposium*, there is reference at the outset to a meal. In the former, there is reference to a meal at Polemarchus's house (*Rep.* 328b)—a meal that, as it turns out, never happens. In the *Symposium*, there is the banquet at Agathon's, a banquet where, less ascetically than in the *Republic*, the meal will actually take place. Even those who are uninvited (namely, Aristodemus), as well as those who come very late (namely, Socrates), are allowed to eat their fill.

Apollodorus says that the person who called him from behind (namely, Glaucon) was "playing with [ἅμα] his call," for, when he called, he said, "Phalerian, you there, Apollodorus, aren't you going to wait?" (*Symp.* 172a). How, by calling him in this manner, was Glaucon *playing* (παίζων)—that is, jesting, joking, even mocking? Several views have been proposed as to what the playing or the joke is, all of which are perhaps operative to some degree. To begin with, it has been noted that Glaucon uses here a legal style of address, beginning with a description derived from the name of Apollodorus's domicile and only then calling him by his name.[15] This can be taken as announcing that a kind of legal process—perhaps even a trial—is about to occur. One could say that Apollodorus is playfully put on trial here in a way that images how Socrates will later—though less in jest—be put on trial by Alcibiades (see *Symp.* 176a and 215a ff.).

The reference to Phaleron (i.e., calling Apollodorus "Phalerian") could also be seen as a mild insult, owing to the fact that the harbor areas were considered seedy places, and the people who lived in them were not of the higher classes. Further, calling him "Phalerian" could also be taken not only as an insult, but as a somewhat vulgar one. The words φαληρεύς/φάληρον are derived from φαληρός, meaning "having a patch of white" or "white-crested," and ultimately derive from the word φάλος, meaning "white." The word φάλος looks and sounds almost identical to the word φαλλός,[16] a word that designates not only the male organ, but also the huge sculpted images of it that were carried along in Dionysian processions as an emblem of the generative powers in nature.

The vulgar joke, together with Glaucon's description of the speeches at the drinking party as "erotic speeches" (*Symp.* 172b), announces the main theme of the dialogue: namely, ἔρως (love). What do the Greeks understand by ἔρως? In Homer, it is not yet the name of a god, but refers only to the powerful impulse that drives lovers. One sees this, for example, in Book XIV of the *Iliad*, where Hera has plotted to lure Zeus to make love to her by pretending that she is about to go off to some remote place. As Zeus says to Hera, "Hera, there will be a time afterwards when you can go there as well. But now, let us go to bed and turn to love-making [φιλότητι]: for never before has love [ἔρος] for any goddess or woman so melted about the heart inside me, broken it to submission, as now" (*Il.*, 315 ff.). One sees this also in Book XVIII of the *Odyssey*, where Penelope, awaiting the return of Odysseus, appears before the suitors: "When she, shining among women, came near the suitors, she stood by the pillar that supported the roof with its joinery, holding her shining veil in front of her face, to shield it, and a devoted attendant was stationed on either side of her. Their [i.e., the suitors'] knees gave way, and their hearts were enchanted

---

15. See Hopkins (2011), 287.
16. Ibid.

with love [ἔρῳ], and each one prayed for the privilege of lying with her" (*Od.* XVIII, 210 ff.).

In Hesiod, on the other hand, ἔρως is presented as a god. In fact, ἔρως is said to have come into being at the beginning, preceded only by Chaos and Earth, and is said to be "the most beautiful of the immortal gods, who in every man and every god softens the sinews and overpowers the prudence of the mind" (*Th.*, 120–122).

In the Classical period, ἔρως designated both love (especially sexual love, distinguished from friendship [φιλία], though the border between these is not rigid), *and* the god Ἔρως, usually considered the god of love.[17] There is a tacit connection between these two designations, for, if one is driven by passionate love, it is because one has been overcome by the god. (In Roman times, and again in the neoclassicism of the eighteenth century, this connection is reduced to pictures of Venus and Cupid, the latter as an infant whose arrows set humans aflame with love.)

In the *Symposium*, then, there are not only the gods Dionysus and Apollo, but also, and even more prominently, the god Eros. In fact, virtually the entire dialogue will be devoted to speeches in praise of Eros: that is, *erotic* speeches. The *Symposium* is the only dialogue devoted to speeches in praise of a god.

Narrative Frame

The *Symposium* belongs to a group of nine Platonic dialogues that are narrated, rather than directly performed.[18] However, whereas most narrated dialogues simply involve a narrator who is introduced and then tells the story—for example, Socrates in the *Republic*—the narrative frame of the *Symposium* is much more complicated.

To begin with, Apollodorus is the narrator who tells the story to some unnamed companions:

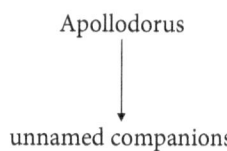

However, just a few days before, Apollodorus had told the same story to Glaucon. So, he begins his narrative by telling about telling the story to Glaucon—namely,

---

17. To be sure, there are other gods closely associated with love, especially Aphrodite (with whom Eros was portrayed as a near-constant companion).

18. *Phaedo, Theaetetus, Parmenides, Phaedo, Charmides, Lysis, Euthydemus, Protagoras,* and *Republic.* Four of these—namely, *Theaetetus, Parmenides, Phaedo,* and *Symposium*—are narrated by someone other than Socrates.

about how he was stopped by Glaucon as he was going up to the city. He then tells the story to the unnamed companions as he told it to Glaucon—or, more precisely, by recounting (i.e., actively remembering) his telling of the story to Glaucon:

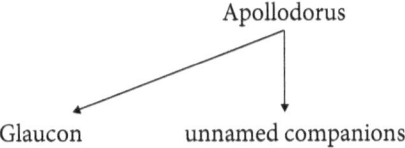

Yet (Apollodorus tells his companions), Glaucon revealed that he had already heard the story from some (unnamed) other who had heard it from someone named Phoenix. However, it seems that this other had told the story badly, since, on the basis of what was said, Glaucon was unaware that the event took place so long ago—indeed, when he and Glaucon were mere boys—that Apollodorus could not have been present:

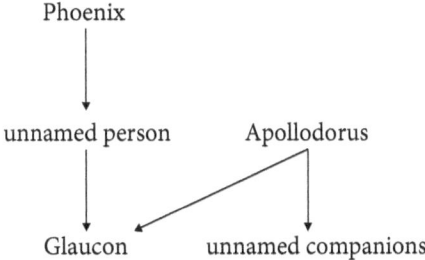

Apollodorus next says that Glaucon then asked him whether he had heard about the party from Socrates. Apollodorus says (that he said to Glaucon) no: rather, he heard it from the same person who told Phoenix, namely, Aristodemus, who had been present at the party. Apollodorus says that he checked with Socrates about some points, and that Socrates confirmed what Aristodemus had said:

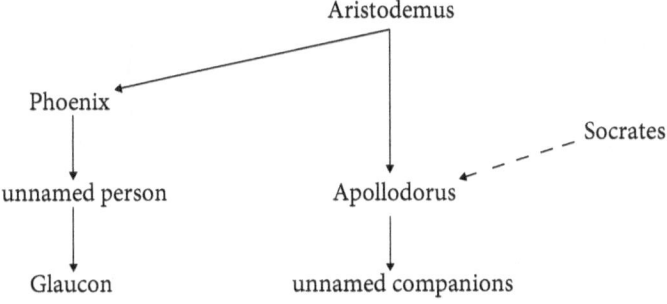

Apollodorus tells his companions that he told Glaucon that the original narrator, Aristodemus, was short (σμικρός).[19] He also says that he always went along barefooted—like Socrates himself—and was very much in love with Socrates.

The whole story depends, then, on Aristodemus's remembrance of the event (though some points were confirmed by Socrates). It depends also upon Apollodorus's remembrance of what he was told by Aristodemus. Hopefully, he remembers it better than Phoenix and the unnamed narrator did. In fact, the account of the event that the unnamed companions (and so, we ourselves) receive depends *doubly* upon Apollodorus's remembrance: that is, it depends both on what Aristodemus told him and on his telling the story to Glaucon, the recounting of which is his telling of the story to the unnamed companions:

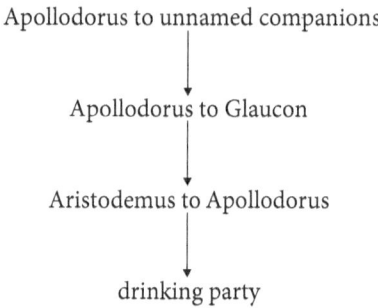

Now, there are some grounds for suspecting that the remembrances may be somewhat lacking. For example, at one point, Apollodorus says, "Now, Aristodemus scarcely remembered all that each and every one of them said, and I in turn do not remember all that he said [οὔτε πάνυ ὁ Ἀριστόδημος ἐμέμνητο οὔτ' αὖ ἐγὼ ἃ ἐκεῖνος ἔλεγε πάντα]" (*Symp.* 178a). Also, immediately after the first speech (by Phaedrus) is recounted, Apollodorus tells his companions that he told Glaucon that "he [Aristodemus] said that [. . .] after Phaedrus there were some others that he scarcely could recall [οὐ πάνυ διεμνημόνευε]; he passed them over and told of Pausanias' speech" (*Symp.* 180c). All of this points to a certain deficiency on the part of the narrative retelling.

Quite remarkably, Aristodemus does not recount his own speech. Presumably he gave one, since he was cordially invited in (after he arrived uninvited) and included in the party, and was told to sit next to Eryximachus. Does this mean, then, that he forgot his own speech, or even forgot that he had given a speech? Even further, he says that the speeches he omitted were by persons sitting between Phaedrus and Pausanias, and yet we know that he was sitting next to Eryximachus!

---

19. The word σμικρός means both short in stature and lowborn. Xenophon, in his *Memorabilia*, calls Aristodemus "the dwarf" (τὸν μικρὸν) (*Mem.*, I. IV. 2).

How is one to understand this elaborate dramatic frame? What is its significance for the dialogue as a whole? Two points must be mentioned that, at this stage, remain necessarily preliminary. First of all, the dramatic frame consists of the above schematized recollective structure. Aristodemus remembers the event in order to narrate it to Apollodorus; Apollodorus remembers Aristodemus's narration in order to narrate it to Glaucon; a few days later, Apollodorus remembers his narration to Glaucon in order to narrate it (that is, repeat it) to his companions. Thus, what is presented in the dialogue—namely, the speeches and the happenings at the drinking party—is presented through a complex web of remembrances. It is perhaps worth noting that there are stories (μῦθοι) told in other Platonic dialogues according to which all presentation, and hence all knowledge corresponding to something's being presented, is achieved through a kind of remembrance.[20] So, one might suppose that the recollective structure of the *Symposium* images a certain connection between remembrance and knowledge.

Second, another effect of the dramatic frame is to stress that the narration about the drinking party is *far removed* from the event itself—that is, the narrative λόγος is remote from the actual event (i.e., the particular speeches and deeds) of which it tells. The λόγος (of Apollodorus) is, as we will see, far removed *in time* from the actual event. Why this had to be the case is understandable from the historical context (to which we turn below). But with the emphasis on this distance, there is perhaps also a reference to the more fundamental *difference* that sets λόγος apart from actual things, events, and deeds. In this case, we would need to ask: Why is this difference so significant for the *Symposium* that it has to be signaled by this dramatic frame?

Historical Situation

When did the *Symposium* occur? What is its dramatic date? And what was happening in Athens at that time?

There are two dramatic dates at play in the *Symposium*: the date of the dramatic frame (i.e., Apollodorus's narration), and the date of the drinking party itself. The date of the party is known: it was at the time when Agathon's first tragedy won the prize at the Lenaia. There is ancient testimony (given by Athenaeus) that this occurred in 416 BCE.[21]

From Apollodorus's remarks to Glaucon, we know that the narrative takes place many years later, since "it has been many years since Agathon resided here" (*Symp.* 172c). It is known that Agathon left Athens around 408 BCE with his love Pausanias and went to live at the court of Macedonia. Since Socrates was executed

---

20. [Editor's Note: See *Phaedrus*, 246a ff.; see also *Meno*, 81d.]
21. [Editor's Note: See Athenaeus, 345.]

in 399 BCE and is spoken of within Apollodorus's narration as still being alive (as is Agathon, who died about the same time), the date is approximately 400 BCE.

During the 430s BCE, tensions and threats of war between Athens and Sparta (and their respective allies, the Athenian Alliance and the Peloponnesian League) had been increasing. One of the first trouble spots was Potidaea (on the Chalcidice peninsula). This city belonged to the Athenian Alliance and yet was a colony of Corinth's, who was allied with Sparta. In 432 BCE, Athens ordered that the Potidaeans expel all Corinthian officials. Attempts at negotiation were unsuccessful, and the Potidaeans sent envoys to the Peloponnesian League, who extracted a promise of support against Athens. Joined by two thousand men from the Peloponnesian League, Potidaea revolted against Athens. The Athenians defeated this force and laid siege to Potidaea. (Later in the *Symposium*, Alcibiades will explain that he and Socrates fought in Potidaea [*Symp.* 219e ff.]—presumably in this very battle.)

After the siege of Potidaea, there were serious efforts to avoid war. But shortly thereafter, Thebes (an ally of Sparta's) attacked Athens's ally Plataea, a celebrated site owing to the fact that the Greeks had defeated the Persians there in 478 BCE. As a result, the Peloponnesian War began (in 431 BCE). Athens had supreme naval power (consisting of three to four hundred ships), but the Spartan infantry was superior to the Athenian ground forces, which largely consisted of farmer-soldiers rather than a professional military. Pericles's strategy was to attack Peloponnesian territory with his navy, but to avoid engaging the Spartan hoplites. Thus, he ordered farmers in Attica to move into Athens (inside the Long Walls), so that when the Spartans came to ravage the countryside, there would be no one and nothing there. As the war continued, Sparta attacked Attica, and the Athenian navy attacked coastal areas of Pelop; and in 427 BCE, the Spartans destroyed Plataea. Meanwhile, the plague had broken out in Athens and claimed the life of Pericles.

Around this time, the Athenians became involved in Sicily. Their purpose was to aid their allies there against the encroachments of Syracuse, to cut off export of grain to Pelop, and ultimately to bring Sicily into the Athenian Empire. Finally, in 421 BCE, negotiations led to the Peace of Nicias. It was around this time that Alcibiades appeared on the scene. His aim was to reactivate the war; and, at his instigation, the Athenians attacked the island of Melos (in Cyclades) in 416 BCE. When the Melians refused to join the Athenian Alliance, the Athenians killed all the Melian men and sold the women and children into slavery.

This brings us to the time of the drinking party, which was a time when Athens was at the height of its power and enjoyed peace (at least temporarily). But it was also the time when the Athenian invasion of Sicily—the largest military expedition in Athens's history, and the most disastrous—was being planned. Eventually, Athens suffered catastrophic defeat, which was the major factor in their eventually losing the war. By 405 BCE, Athens had lost several battles and was under siege. In 404 BCE, Athens was defeated and the Long Walls were destroyed. The Thirty (a puppet government) was established, ushering in a reign of terror. This brings us to the dramatic date of the textual frame.[22]

There was a particular event in 415 BCE (one year after the party) that is of great significance. Just before departure of the fleet to Sicily, under the command of Alcibiades and Nicias, two crimes of impiety were committed. First, there was the mutilation of the herms (ἑρμαῖ), which were low marble pillars on which there was a statue of the face and phallus of Hermes. These stood beside many houses and public places, often marking their boundaries. The ships were ready to sail to Sicily when, on a single night, nearly all of the city's herms were smashed. Second, there was the profanation of the Eleusinian Mysteries. A parodic performance of these mystery rites, without the proper priests present, took place in private homes of many of the city's rich young men, including Alcibiades. Regarding all of this, Thucydides writes the following in *The Peloponnesian War*:

> Their preparations were underway, but then, of all the stone herms in the city of Athens (the square-cut type, following local custom), most had their faces mutilated during a single night. No one knew who the perpetrators were, but there was a search for them with large rewards out of public funds, and they voted in addition that whoever wished, if he knew of any other sacrilege that had occurred, was to give information with impunity, citizen, foreigner, or slave. They took the matter seriously; it looked like an omen for the voyage, and furthermore as though it had been done as part of a conspiracy for revolution and the overthrow of the democracy. So, information came in from certain metics and servants not about the herms but concerning mutilation of some other statues as acts of drunken sport on the part of young men, and, in addition to this, that scurrilous celebrations of the Mysteries were being held in private homes; they accused Alcibiades. Taking up the charges were those who especially resented Alcibiades for standing in the way of their assured ascendancy over the people, and in the belief that by removing him they would rise to the top they exaggerated them and raised the cry that both the Mysteries and the mutilation of the herms were connected with the overthrow of the democracy, and that none of this had been done without his complicity, adducing as evidence the undemocratic licentiousness of his conduct in general. (Thuc. VI, 27–29)[23]

---

22. One should especially note the contrast between the historical situation of the drinking party and that of Apollodorus's narration of it: at the time of the party, Athens is at the height of its power, while at the time of Apollodorus's narration, Athens is defeated and controlled by its greatest enemy.

23. As Lattimore notes, citing Aristophanes's *Lysistrata* (1093–1094), the herms had their φαλλοί mutilated in addition to their faces.

A situation of fear and panic resulted, and many were accused (often by unreliable witnesses) and executed, or fled into exile. Among them were Phaedrus and Eryximachus.

Alcibiades went ahead with the expedition to Sicily, but then was called back to stand trial almost as soon as the ships had sailed. However, Alcibiades escaped and went to Sparta, and gave the Spartans all of Athens's military secrets. He, more than anyone else, was responsible for Athens losing the war. Nonetheless, in 407 BCE, there was an amnesty of sorts, and he was allowed to return to Athens, where he pleaded innocence regarding the charges against him, without objection. In 404 BCE, he was murdered somewhere in Asia Minor.

It is significant that all of this had happened between the time of the drinking party and the time when Apollodorus gives his narrative about it. At the time of the drinking party itself, Athens was at the height of its power. There was temporary peace—although, largely through the instigation of Alcibiades, the Athenians were about to undertake the disastrous invasion of Sicily. On the eve of this venture, hysteria would erupt in Athens in reaction to the mutilation of the herms and the profanation of the Mysteries, for which Alcibiades (and eventually Eryximachus and Phaedrus) would be accused. By the time Apollodorus narrates the story (around 400 BCE), Athens is defeated and completely controlled by Sparta. Alcibiades is dead, and Eryximachus and Phaedrus have been executed or driven into exile. Agathon and Pausanias have gone off to Macedonia. Only Socrates and Aristodemus are still alive and living in Athens—and Socrates, of course, not for long.

2. Phaedrus / Pausanias / Eryximachus (174a–188e)

APOLLODORUS, GIFT OF Apollo, agrees to tell the story from the beginning, as it was told to him by Aristodemus. Aristodemus said that he came upon Socrates freshly bathed and wearing shoes, which he seldom did. Aristodemus asked him where he was going, having become "in this way beautiful" (*Symp.* 174a). Already, in the time of Homer, it was customary to bathe before a meal, though it seems that this may not have been Socrates's usual practice, since comic poets made fun of him as "unwashed."[1] Clearly, then, this was a very special occasion. Indeed, Aristodemus mentions that even wearing shoes, as Socrates was doing here, was something that Socrates seldom did. (Much later in the *Symposium*, Alcibiades will portray him as going barefoot even under severe winter conditions at Potidaea [*Symp.* 220b].) But now, when Aristodemus comes upon Socrates, the latter is freshly bathed and well-shod as he prepares to go to dinner at Agathon's house.

Thus, Socrates has become, according to Aristodemus, "in this way beautiful [οὕτω καλός]." What does this word καλός mean? It is broader in significance than simply "beautiful," meaning also "fine," "fair," and "noble," though it is also important to distinguish it from "good."[2] To begin opening up the deeper meaning of the word καλός, one can turn to two words with which Socrates describes the beautiful in the *Phaedrus* (250 d–e): namely, the two superlatives ἐκφανέστατον and ἐρασμιώτατον.[3] The word ἐκφανέστατον derives from the words φάος ("light") and φανός ("bright," "shining"). Ἐκφανής means "shining forth," and the superlative form ἐκφανέστατον means "most shining forth." (It is related to φανερός, which means "open to sight," "visible," "manifest.") Ἐρασμιώτατον, for its part, derives from ἔρως / ἐράω ("love"), the adjectival form of which is ἐράσμιος ("lovely"). The superlative form ἐρασμιώτατον means "most lovely"—that is, what is most worthy of love. Taken together, then, this would mean that the beautiful, as both ἐκφανέστατον and ἐρασμιώτατον, is what most shines forth or manifests itself so as to be open to sight, and in such a way as to be most worthy of love.

Socrates says that, in order to go to dinner at Agathon's, he has got himself up beautifully "in order that beautiful I may go to a beauty" (*Symp.* 174a).

---

1. [Editor's Note: See Aristophanes, *Birds*, 1284.]
2. In this sense, it is like the German word *schön*.
3. On this, see Sallis (1975), chap. 3, sec. 2c.

Agathon was a young and exceptionally handsome man. He displays his nobility when Aristodemus arrives uninvited, pretending that he had tried to invite him on the previous day and welcoming him to the party nonetheless (*Symp.* 174e). Socrates mentions that Agathon is young, and that the day before his wisdom could be seen "shining forth [ἐκφανής] before thirty thousand Greek witnesses" (*Symp.* 175e). Also, he is the beloved of Pausanias—that is, he is the one who, in Pausanias's eyes, shines forth as the loveliest.

So, Agathon is beautiful, and Socrates has dandied himself up beautifully in an effort to be a match for him. This already suggests that there will be a contest between Socrates the philosopher and Agathon the tragic poet. Indeed, later, after Socrates demeans his own wisdom and magnifies that of Agathon's, Agathon will accuse him of being hubristic (*Symp.* 175e).[4] Then, Agathon will say to Socrates that "a little later you and I will go to court about our wisdom, with Dionysus as judge" (*Symp.* 175e). Yet, one wonders: Would Dionysus be a fair judge of this contest? Would he not rather be decisively on the side of the tragic poet Agathon? And what precisely is the relation of Socrates the philosopher to Dionysus? (We shall return to these considerations below.)

Socrates asked Aristodemus whether he would be willing to go uninvited to the feast, so that they could "alter and lead astray [i.e., corrupt] the proverb 'the good go uninvited to the feast of the good'" (*Symp.* 174b). Here, Socrates is playing on the name Agathon (ἀγάθος), which means "good." But how is Socrates altering, let alone leading astray or corrupting, the proverb? He is doing so by interchanging the words "beautiful" (κάλος) and "good" (ἀγάθος)—specifically, by substituting the word "beautiful" for the word "good." In light of this substitution, the question becomes: What is the relation between the beautiful and the good such that this substitution leads astray or corrupts the proverb?

Socrates says that Homer not only corrupted the proverb, but committed ὕβρις against it—that is, he *assaulted* it. Homer, in the *Iliad*, has Menelaus go uninvited to a feast of Agamemnon's (*Il.*, 17.587). This amounted to a case of the worse going uninvited to a feast of the better. Thus, Homer substituted *worse* for *good*—and this was an assault in that it enacted corruption as such, which occurs precisely when the worse comes to replace the better.

Aristodemus then says to Socrates that, if he were to go along, it would be more as Homer says than as Socrates has said:

> Worthless   going (uninvited) to the feast of a wise man
> (uneducated:
> φαῦλος)

---

4. In the Athenian law courts, ὕβρις was a personal assault or insult. The word also refers to any outrageous act committed out of a sense of excessive pride.

Moreover, Aristodemus is short, barefooted, and presumably has not bathed, since he is washed by Agathon's attendants after he arrives at the party (*Symp.* 175a). In a word, he is not *beautiful*, not even in the way that Socrates has gotten himself up to be. Nor, for that matter, is Socrates himself beautiful, even though he has made himself up beautifully *in this way* (that is, by bathing and putting on shoes). Socrates was renowned, and indeed ridiculed, for his ugliness. Even Alcibiades, in praising Socrates near the end of the *Symposium*, compares him to the sileni and the satyrs (*Symp.* 215b), who were quite ugly indeed. Thus, instead of the beautiful going to the feast of a beauty, the two nonbeautiful men go to the feast of a beauty. And so, *in deed*—though, to be sure, not in *word*—Socrates substitutes nonbeautiful for beautiful, which is almost as reprehensible (or hubristic) as Homer's substituting worse for good. *In deed*, the good—namely, Agathon himself—will (as mentioned above) charge Socrates with ὕβρις as soon as he arrives at the feast of the good.

Still further in this direction, although Socrates is not beautiful, he has made himself up so as to be *in this way* beautiful. Thus, he is neither simply beautiful nor simply nonbeautiful, but is rather *in between*:

So: a man in-between (i.e., beautiful and not-beautiful) } goes invited (yet deferred) to the feast of the beautiful

This situation images, from afar, the relation of ἔρως to the beautiful as Socrates will later describe it (*Symp.* 199b ff.).

As Socrates and Aristodemus walked on toward Agathon's—in other words, as they were approaching "the good"—Socrates "somehow turned his thought [τὸν νοῦν] to himself" and told Aristodemus to go on ahead (*Symp.* 174d). When Agathon sends a servant boy to bring Socrates to the party, Socrates has retreated onto a neighbor's porch, where he stands and refuses to come along. When hearing about this, Agathon calls the behavior "strange [ἄτοπόν]"[5] (*Symp.* 175a), to which Aristodemus replies, "No, no—leave him alone. He has this habit [ἔθος].[6] Sometimes he moves off and stands stock still wherever he happens to be. He will come at once, I suspect. So do not try to budge him, but leave him alone" (*Symp.* 175b).

What was Socrates doing during this time? He never says—not even when Agathon, making an erotic approach to him, tries to tease it out of him (*Symp.* 175c–d). But one might suspect that it has to do with the circumstance that he is approaching the good (Agathon), or at least the place (that is, the palace) of the good.[7] This approach presumably calls somehow for him to turn his thought to himself—that is, to look within himself and perhaps to take the measure of

---

5 Literally, "out of place."
6. The word ἔθος means "habit" or "custom," but can also mean "abode" or "place."
7. Cf. *Rep.* 516b: "the good in its χώρα."

himself in order that he not exceed that measure in an act of ὕβρις. For it is with ὕβρις that the good (namely, Agathon) charges him, and Agathon foretells that what is at issue in this charge—namely, wisdom—will be decided in a court where Dionysus will be the judge (*Symp.* 175e).

Curiously, immediately after the name of the good is explicitly mentioned, a decision is made against Dionysus: namely, he is banished from the party. Those present agree not to indulge in heavy drinking, and Eryximachus dismisses the flute girl, who otherwise would have offered Dionysian music (and perhaps sexual entertainment). The Greek flute (αὐλός) was associated with Dionysian cults and was used in worship of Dionysus. (Such a flute was played by the satyr Marsyas, a companion of Dionysus, about whom more will be said later).[8] In this manner, Dionysus is banished; and yet, those present at the party banish him precisely because they were all drunk the night before—that is, because they were overcome by him!

Then Eryximachus makes his proposal—or rather, he pushes forward the proposal he takes up from Phaedrus, his beloved: they are all to produce hymns or paeans (ὕμνους καὶ παίωνας)—that is, festive or solemn songs—to ἔρως. As Eryximachus puts it, "It seems to me fitting that each of us, starting from the left, make a λόγος as beautiful as he can praising ἔρως" (*Symp.* 177d). Thus, they will make beautiful λόγοι in praise of ἔρως.

Phaedrus will begin, since he is "father of the λόγος." Socrates, presumably looking around, observes that none would vote against this proposal, and says regarding himself that "I claim to know about nothing but erotics" (*Symp.* 177e). The question is this: How is this claim of Socrates's to be squared with his attestation in the *Apology* that his wisdom (of which the Delphic Apollo had spoken) consists in knowing only that he does not know (*Ap.* 23b)? Is it the case that knowing about ἔρως amounts somehow to knowing the limits of one's wisdom?

* * *

Phaedrus's Speech (178a–180b)

Phaedrus begins—as he had proposed—with praise of the god: Eros is a great and wondrous (θαυμαστός) god. This, he says, is shown by the fact that he is among the oldest, and this, in turn, is shown by the fact that there are no parents who precede him. As testimony, Phaedrus cites, first of all, Hesiod: "Hesiod says that Chaos came first: 'Then, thereafter, broad-breasted Earth, always the safe seat of all, and Eros.' After Chaos, he says, there came to be these two, Earth and Eros" (*Symp.* 178b). His point is that before Earth and Eros, there was nothing

---

8. [Editor's Note: See part 1, chap. 5 of the present volume.]

but chaos—no gods or other beings that spawned him and so would be older. It is important to note that, when Phaedrus repeats what he cited from Hesiod, he omits the phrase "always the safest seat of all"—and perhaps he omitted still more in the citations, since there is further elaboration of this phrase that may have belonged to the text (i.e., all "the immortals who lived on snowy peaks of Olympus . . .").[9]

According to Phaedrus, as the oldest and greatest god, Eros is the cause of our greatest good, bestowing it upon us. Continuing, Phaedrus says that, for humans who intend to *live beautifully* (καλῶς), what should govern their lives is neither blood ties, honors, nor wealth, but love. Thus, one sees that, in this beautiful speech about Eros, Phaedrus immediately forges a connection between eros and beauty (namely, the beautiful life, which is bestowed by Eros). Phaedrus explains that love induces "shame in the face of shameful [or ugly] things, and honorable ambition[10] in the face of beautiful things [τὴν ἐπὶ μὲν τοῖς αἰσχροῖς αἰσχύνην, ἐπὶ δὲ τοῖς καλοῖς φιλοτιμίαν]" (*Symp.* 178d). In other words, love's gift is that it drives men *away* from certain things—namely, those that are shameful or ugly—and moves them *toward* other, beautiful things.

In order to show how love bestows the greatest good, Phaedrus speaks of it as bearing not only on the beautiful life, but also on the beautiful death. He proceeds to tell three stories (μῦθοι) of lovers who were willing (in some sense) to die for the one they loved. First, he speaks of Alcestis, whose husband Admetus was told by Apollo that the Fates were on the point of cutting his thread of life, but that he (Apollo) had gotten them to agree that if someone would die in Admetus's stead, he would be allowed to live. Admetus set about trying to find someone to die in his place. First, he went to his elderly parents, but they refused to die for him. Then he went to his friends, but all refused. Finally, his wife Alcestis offered to die for him. Though deeply saddened at the thought of losing such a good wife, he accepted her offer—and as he stood by weeping, she died.[11] Recalling this story, Phaedrus goes on to say that the gods so admired her deed that they sent her soul back up from Hades.

Next, Phaedrus tells the story of Orpheus, which differs from the previous story in an important sense. Orpheus went down to Hades in order to bring back up his deceased wife, Eurydice. However, the gods only showed him a phantom of his wife, and did not give her genuine self back to him—for he had not dared to die (as Alcestis had), but rather contrived to go down into Hades alive.[12]

---

9. One wonders, parenthetically, what accounts for the omission. What is the significance of suppressing the role of the *Earth* as the safest seat—that is, as the basis, the foundation, of life, and even, perhaps, of the gods?

10. Φιλοτιμία· literally, "love of honor."

11. [Editor's Note: See Hamilton (2013), 238.]

12. [Editor's Note: See Ovid, *Met.* X, 71.]

Finally, Phaedrus speaks of Achilles. The story of Achilles has the beloved, rather than the lover (namely, Patroclus, who is already dead), die for the sake of his lover. Achilles kills Hector (who had killed Patroclus), even though he had been told that if he did this he would surely die. The gods so admired Achilles's deed that they sent him up to the Isle of the Blest.

What the three stories show is that, when love is so strong that one is willing to die for it, the gods bring it about that one can ascend to a new life, whereas if one is too soft to die for one's beloved (like Orpheus was), then there is only a sham ascent, and no subsequent return to life.

Two points must be considered regarding Phaedrus's speech. First of all, in all three of the mythic tales to which Phaedrus refers, both Apollo and Dionysus are involved. Regarding the story of Alcestis: because of a quarrel with Zeus (who had killed his son Asclepius), Apollo was forced to serve as a slave in a mortal household for a year. The household was that of Admetus, and it was in order to show his friendship to Admetus that Apollo told him of his impending death.[13] Thus, Apollo was instrumental in setting up the situation in which Alcestis died for her husband. In his account, Phaedrus says that the gods brought her up from Hades. However, according to the μῦθος, it was Heracles who went to Hades and rescued her.[14] He did this in order to compensate for the outrage of having gotten roaring drunk—on wine, no doubt—in the house of Admetus at the very time of the funeral. Regarding the second story, it is important to note that Orpheus, the musician, was devoted to Apollo. (Like Apollo, he played the lyre masterfully.) He was so devoted to Apollo that he came to address the morning sun by his name.[15] In the end, however, Orpheus died by being torn to pieces by the Maenads, the female worshippers of Dionysus.[16] Finally, regarding the story of Achilles, one notes that Achilles died from an arrow (piercing his heel) that was shot by Paris, whose hand was guided by Apollo (or even by Apollo in the guise of Paris).[17] However, his ashes were placed in an urn that had been given to his mother Thetis by none other than Dionysus.[18]

Second, all three stories make reference to an *ascent*, a going-up from Hades or to the Isle of the Blest. In this way, Phaedrus's speech lays out a mythical basis from which the later speeches, also more and more about ascents, will arise—such that, in a sense, the entire dialogue, arising from this mythic basis, will not only tell about, but also will enact, ascent. In this manner, Phaedrus is truly "the father of the λόγος" (*Symp.* 177d).

---

13. [Editor's Note: See Hamilton (1942), 238.]
14. [Editor's Note: See Pseudo-Apollodorus, *Bibliotheca*, 2.6.2.]
15. [Editor's Note: See Eratosthenes, *Catasterismi*, xxiv.]
16. [Editor's Note: See Pausanias, *Description of Greece*, 9.30.5; see also Ovid, *Metamorphoses*, 11.1.]
17. [Editor's Note: See Hamilton (1942), 278.]
18. [Editor's Note: See Homer, *Od.*, 24.73 ff.]

Indeed, in its very form, Phaedrus's speech already enacts a kind of ascent. At the outset, it is totally immersed in the narrative structure: "First of all, as I say, he said that Phaedrus began his speech at somewhat the following point [. . .]" (*Symp.* 178a). But as the speech proceeds, it rises above this narrative structure (e.g., "I say that he said that Phaedrus began . . ."), so that at the end of his speech (e.g., "So this is how *I* assert that Eros is the oldest . . ." [*Symp.* 180b]) the first-person pronoun refers neither to Apollodorus nor Aristodemus, but to Phaedrus himself. Thus, both in form and in its mythic content, Phaedrus's speech is one of ascent, of *going-up*. And we recall that as Apollodorus is telling Glaucon about this speech, they themselves are underway, going up to the city.

* * *

Once Apollodorus has narrated Phaedrus's speech, and in such a way that finally it is as though Phaedrus himself were speaking, he continues: "He [i.e., Aristodemus] said that Phaedrus made some such speech, and after Phaedrus there were some others that he could not entirely remember; he passed them over and told of Pausanias' speech [λόγος]" (*Symp.* 180c). There is no indication whatsoever who these others were or what they said. When, in his speech, Pausanias refers back to what has been said, he refers (at least according to Apollodorus) *only* to Phaedrus, and does not even mention the others. This gap again signals the separation—that is, the distance, the difference—between Apollodorus's narrative and the actual event. But it also calls attention to the seating order:

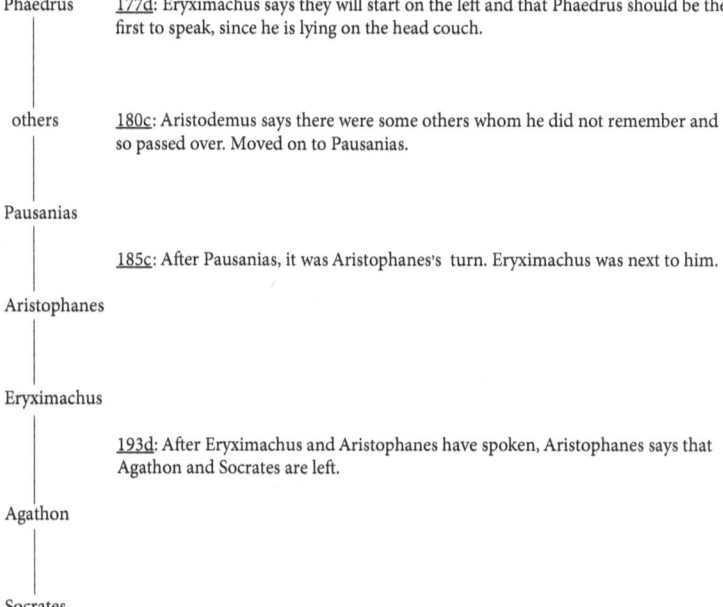

Pausanias's Speech (180c–185c)

Pausanias is next to speak. He begins by addressing Phaedrus critically: "Phaedrus, it seems to me that the way the λόγος has been presented to us is not beautiful" (*Symp*. 180c).[19] Yet, the task set at the beginning was to present a beautiful λόγος in praise of ἔρως. Thus, Pausanias is saying, in effect, that Phaedrus has not really succeeded in carrying out the task that, precisely through his initiative, was set.

Then, however, Pausanias moderates his criticism. If Eros were one, he says, then the speech would be beautiful; however, Eros is not one, and so it is necessary to say first which Eros is to be praised. In order to distinguish between the two kinds of Eros, Pausanias develops the link between Eros and Aphrodite, a link that is already present in the μῦθοι regarding Eros. (Here, one sees how the μῦθοι form a supporting basis for the λόγοι.) Aphrodite is the goddess most closely associated with the power of love, with fertility, and with beauty. Eros was portrayed as constantly accompanying her, and sometimes even as her son.[20] Hesiod calls her "a tender and beautiful goddess," also saying that "Eros and beautiful Desire [ἵμερος] were her attendants both at her birth and at her first going to join the family of the gods" (*Th*. 92 ff.).

Pausanias goes on to say that there are two Aphrodites, and thus also two Erotes. On the one hand, there is the Aphrodite to whom the name "Uranian" is applied, and on the other hand, the Aphrodite who is called "Pandemus." Historically, there were in fact these two names for Aphrodite: Οὐρανία ("heavenly") was a cult name for her on Cyprus and in Corinth, and Πάνδημος ("common to all the people") was a name (or epithet) used for her in Athens and some other cities. Pausanias goes on to elaborate the distinction between these two Aphrodites. Uranian Aphrodite is the daughter of Uranos the Titan and has no mother; she is also the older and, according to Pausanias, partakes only of the male. Pandemian Aphrodite, who is the younger of the two, is the daughter of Zeus and Dione, and partakes of both male and female.

According to Pausanias, Pandemian Eros is the one that worthless people (οἱ φαῦλοι)[21] have as their love. Such people, being only concerned with the sexual act, are no less in love with women than with boys, are in love with their bodies rather than with their souls, and are in love with the stupidest sort of people. But Uranian Eros, like Uranian Aphrodite, partakes only of male, and not of female: in other words, it is the love of boys (pederasty), and it involves no ὕβρις (in the legal sense).[22] Pausanias declares that those who have made pederasty a

---

19. More literally, Phaedrus says that it has been presented "not beautifully [οὐ καλῶς]."
20. [Editor's Note: See, e.g., *Phaedr.*, 242d.]
21. This is the same term that Aristodemus applied to himself before he and Socrates set out to join the get-together (*Symp*. 174c).
22. That is, it involved no physical assault.

disgrace did so in view only of Pandemian lovers. But the eros linked to Uranian Aphrodite is otherwise, for it aims at producing ἀρετή (i.e., virtue or excellence) in the beloved. As Phaedrus says, "Thus, for the sake of virtue alone is it wholly beautiful [πάντως γε καλόν] to grant one's favors. This is the love of the Uranian goddess" (*Symp.* 185b).

Four points about Pausanias's speech need to be considered. First, one notes that Pausanias is the lover of Agathon. In Plato's *Protagoras*, they are portrayed as being present at the great gathering of sophists at the house of Callias. In particular, they are pictured as lying together on a couch near the sophist Prodicus. Agathon is there described as still quite young,[23] of good birth and upbringing, as very καλός, and as Pausanias's "beloved boy" (παιδικά) (*Prot.* 315d–e). In Xenophon's *Symposium*, Pausanias is called "the lover of the poet Agathon" (Xen. *Symp.* 8:32). Once we are aware of this erotic connection, it is evident that Pausanias's speech is a deed of self-justification, perhaps directed primarily at his beloved, Agathon. In effect, his speech explains how the love of boys (and hence his erotic relation to Agathon) can be something beautiful, something καλός. The problem, according to Pausanias, is just that people fail to realize that there is such a thing as Uranian eros, and falsely identify all pederasty as Pandemian eros.

Second, a considerable portion of Pausanias's speech is devoted to a discussion of law, specifically law about eros. Law about eros is, in effect, law intended to *control* eros, to keep it under control, to prevent its unruly, wild, hubristic, destructive—that is, *Dionysian*—moment from erupting. In some cities (such as Elis), the gratification of lovers is declared by law to be καλός. In other cities (such as Ionia), it is declared by law to be shameful or ugly (αἰσχρός), and thus to be the very opposite of καλός. But in Athens, the law regarding eros is finer and more subtle, and is such as to promote a testing of whether lovers love beautifully and love what is lasting, such as good character (ἦθος). In all these cases, the legal control of eros is linked to λόγος, specifically to the capacity for λόγος. In Elis, gratification is legalized because the people "are incapable of speaking [οὐ μὴ σοφοὶ λέγειν]" and so could not easily persuade the young (*Symp.* 182b). In Ionia and other places where people live under barbarians, pederasty (and philosophy) are condemned by law. Though Pausanias relates this to tyranny, there is also an issue of λόγος here, for a barbarian is precisely one who does not speak Greek, and so does not speak intelligibly or intelligently. In Athens, on the other hand, where the λόγος is highly cultivated, much finer and more subtle laws prevail. The basic question that is raised by the entire discussion of law is whether or not eros submits to the control of law. Can its Dionysian side be kept under control by law? Or does this unruly moment resist or escape control? Even if repressed, does the Dionysian eventually return?

---

23. The dramatic date of the *Protagoras* is some fifteen years earlier than that of the *Symposium*.

Third, in Pausanias's speech, the banishment of Dionysus is very much in force. Beyond the initial measures (e.g., no heavy drinking, no flute girl), Pausanias has sought in his speech to distinguish a kind of eros (namely, the Uranian) that would be immune to Dionysus. And yet, traces of Dionysus remain in both of the Aphrodites in terms of which he understands the two kinds of eros. In the case of the Pandemian Aphrodite, she is said to have Zeus and Dione as parents. (Dione was sometimes identified as a consort of Zeus's, though she was later displaced by Hera.) There are numerous extant Greek vases that show Dione as being in the circle of Dionysus. Moreover, a fragment of a lost play by Euripides even identified her as the mother of Dionysus[24]—which would make Pandemian Aphrodite the sister of Dionysus! But even the Uranian Aphrodite has, beneath the surface, a connection with an unruly, destructive moment, as is evident if one looks to the context of her birth. To be sure, she has no mother and is born from the foam. But, after Earth came forth, she gave birth to Uranos. Together they spawned the Titans, whose leader was Cronus. Then hatred erupted between Earth and Uranos, and she persuaded Cronus to take a sickle she had made and castrate his father Uranos. His male organ was thrown into the sea, foam appeared around it, and from the foam Aphrodite was born.[25]

Fourth, even if a trace of Dionysus remains within it, Pausanias's speech does have the effect of elevating a certain kind of eros—namely, that which is καλός—above the common eros. It is significant that this eros is called Uranian, since οὐρανός means "sky" or "heaven."[26] Thus, from the mythic basis, Pausanias's speech ascends above the common, ugly eros, going up to a heavenly eros that is καλός—just as, in the stories told by Phaedrus, those who died for their love ascended (as from Hades), and just as, continuing his narrative, Apollodorus is, with Glaucon, going up to the city.

* * *

The moment Pausanias finishes his speech, Apollodorus (narrating from a distance) makes a very obvious pun—one that almost works in English—and even calls attention to it: "With Pausanias's pausation—the wise teach me to talk in such balanced phrases . . ." (*Symp.* 185c). The pun is, in Greek, Παυσανίου δὲ παυσαμένου. The verb παύω (of which παυσαμένου is the participle) means "to stop" or "to cease." The pun helps us to notice that Pausanias does in fact pause—indeed, he ceases talking entirely, and is the only character who says nothing else

---

24. See Cancik, 2:62. See also Euripides, *Dramatic Fragments*, 169.
25. Hesiod, *Theogony*, 188.
26. Οὐρανία, the epithet for Aphrodite, is also the name of one of the nine Muses. The Muses give men the gift of song, which lifts their spirits. Οὐρανία is the Muse of astronomy. This, too, contributes to the upward directionality of the speech.

for the entire remainder of the dialogue. Why such silence? Perhaps it is because he, having (with his speech) performed his deed of justifying himself in the eyes of his beloved Agathon, has nothing further to say.

After Pausanias stops speaking, it is Aristophanes's turn to speak. However, there is an interruption of the rigorously established order—something that, like the Dionysian, is unruly and resistant to control. Yet, this interruption comes not in the guise of Dionysus himself, but rather as a comic interruption, befitting the comic poet Aristophanes. Aristophanes has the hiccups and so cannot present his λόγος. One could even suppose that, while Pausanias was speaking about laws meant to control eros, the listeners might have been distracted by the sound of hiccups issuing from Aristophanes's mouth. But now Eryximachus, the omniscient physician, gives him a remedy for stopping the hiccups, telling him to hold his breath for a long time, then gargle with water, and then make himself sneeze. Meanwhile, Eryximachus takes his place as the next speaker, thus upsetting the original order.

Also, there is another interruption, or rather incoherence, in the order—namely, a missing speech. Earlier (cf. *Symp.* 175a), Agathon seated Aristodemus next to Eryximachus. After both Aristophanes and Eryximachus have spoken, Aristophanes remarks that only two are left: namely, Agathon and Socrates. Thus, Aristodemus must be sitting between Aristophanes and Eryximachus, and yet, there is no mention whatsoever of his speech.

Eryximachus's Speech (185e–188e)

Eryximachus proposes to complete the λόγος that Pausanias has left incomplete. Completion here means extending without limit the range of things over which Eros presides: not only over the souls of humans, but also over the bodies of animals and things that grow in the earth—indeed, over just about all the things that are. Eryximachus says he has become aware of this vast range from and through medicine (ἰατρική)—which, he adds conspicuously, is his own τέχνη.[27]

Eryximachus takes over Pausanias's distinction between the two kinds of eros—however, he alters this distinction, and indeed transforms it, to fit his τέχνη. According to Eryximachus, one eros presides over the healthy state of bodies, while the other presides over the sickly state. It is καλός, he says, to gratify the one eros, but αἰσχρός (shameful) to gratify the other. Thus, the τέχνη of medicine is the knowledge (ἐπιστήμη) of the erotics of the body: one is skilled in medicine if one can discriminate between the eros that is καλός and the eros that is αἰσχρός. If, further, one can promote the acquisition of eros that is καλός and the removal of the other, then one would be a good craftsman (δημιουργός). This

---

27. The word τέχνη means primarily the craft or skill for making things.

is a matter of making things that are most opposed love one another—that is, it is a matter of instilling agreement or harmony among opposites. Eryximachus then generalizes this to cover virtually all τέχναι: gymnastics, farming, music, astronomy, and divination.

There are two matters that need to be considered at this point. First, Eryximachus's name is formed from two words: ἐρύκω, which means "to keep something in check," "to bring it under control," and μάχη, which means "battle" or "strife." Eryximachus is thus one who brings strife (of opposites) under control.[28] He exercises this control by his τέχνη, and others do so by their respective τέχναι. So, whereas Pausanias spoke of controlling eros by submitting it to law (νόμος), Eryximachus speaks of controlling it by τέχνη.[29]

Second, at the drinking party, there is a complex set of erotic relations. Eryximachus's proposal to banish Dionysus is, in accordance with his τέχνη, an attempt to shape the gathering into one that is erotically καλός by excluding the αἰσχρός in the form of Dionysus. However, there are two things that make us suspect that there may be something comic in such attempts to bring eros totally under the yoke of τέχνη. To begin with, Eryximachus's entire speech is set against a comic background—for while Eryximachus is speaking in his serious, authoritative, professional manner, Aristophanes is holding his breath until he is red in the face and, despite this, continuing to hiccup. Then he will be heard gargling away as Eryximachus continues to talk about the control that his τέχνη can exercise. And then—perhaps at that very moment when Eryximachus's speech reaches its high point and he speaks about harmony between gods and men—Aristophanes comes out with a huge sneeze. One sees here a commentary *in deed* on the technical λόγος of Eryximachus, and on the notion that eros might be wholly brought under the control of τέχνη.

Furthermore, by the time Eryximachus finishes, Aristophanes is over the hiccups and can speak—that is, he can give a commentary in λόγος. As he says, the hiccups "have stopped, to be sure; not, however, before sneezing had been applied to it. So I wonder at the orderly decency of the body desiring such noises and tickling as a sneeze is; for my hiccupping stopped right away as soon as I applied the sneeze to it" (*Symp.* 189a).

One suspects, then, that there is something *comedic* about the attempt to bring eros—and, more generally, the disorder that belongs to the body—completely under the control of τέχνη.

---

28. In the background of all of this is the Pythagorean theory of the body as composed of opposites, as well as Empedocles.

29. One sees, then, that the first three speeches treat eros in relation to μῦθος, νόμος, and τέχνη.

3. Aristophanes / Agathon (189a–197e)

When the proposal was first made to deliver beautiful speeches about Eros, Socrates said of Aristophanes that "all of his time is devoted to Dionysus and Aphrodite" (*Symp.* 177e). This suggests that, when he comes to speak about Eros (and so, by association, about Aphrodite), Aristophanes will reintroduce a Dionysian moment into the λόγος, and in this way begin to undo the banishment of Dionysus (and the disorder that he represents) that occurred at the outset of the party.[1] We have already seen that there is a comedic hint of this in Aristophanes's hiccupping episode, as well as in his remarks about "the orderly decency of the body" (*Symp.* 189a) requiring such noises as gargling and sneezing.

In this regard, it should be noted that Aristophanes's name means "the best bringer of light," or "the best lantern [φανός]." Given this name, one suspects that Aristophanes is the best at bringing things to light so that they can be seen, the best at making things manifest. Indeed, through the course of his speech, Aristophanes will bring to light the unruly, disruptive, Dionysian moment that the speeches of Pausanias and Eryximachus excluded in favor of control and order, and he will do so in the course of revealing the power (δύναμις) of eros (which neither of the two previous speakers acknowledged). This is one reason that Aristophanes begins his speech by saying that he "has in mind to speak otherwise" than Eryximachus and Pausanias did (*Symp.* 189c).

And yet, in speaking so as to bring things to light, Aristophanes the comic poet will do so *comically*. (This already became evident in the short exchange that he had with Eryximachus just before beginning his speech.) In general, comedy presents things that make us laugh—that is, things that are laughable (γέλοιος).[2] However, it is important to note that comedy in its Aristophanic form—and even more so in its Platonic form—is not simply a presentation of something laughable. Though there are numerous places in the Platonic dialogues where the discourse turns into a comedy—for example, the comedy of the city in the *Republic*,[3] and the linguistic (i.e., etymological) comedy of the *Cratylus*[4]—there is one passage in particular where the question of the nature of comedy is directly addressed:

---

1. [Editor's Note: See part 1, chap. 2 of the present volume.]
2. Forms of this word occur five times in this short passage just preceding Aristophanes's speech.
3. Cf. Sallis (1975), chap. 5, sec. 2d.
4. Ibid., chap. 4, sec. 4.

namely, in the *Philebus*. Socrates there raises the question about the laughable (τὸ γελοῖον) and says to Protarchus, "[The laughable] involves the opposite of the condition [πάθος] mentioned in the Delphic Oracle" (*Phil.* 48c). Protarchus identifies the inscription in question: "Know thyself." Socrates then identifies the opposite of this inscription: namely, *not* to know oneself at all—that is, self-ignorance. Thus, comedy in its Platonic guise presents something—namely, a person or a situation—that is laughable in that there is a lack of self-knowledge, a display of ignorance of self. One suspects, then, that in his speech that follows, Aristophanes will bring to light, in a laughable way, a certain ignorance of the self that belongs to a particular person, or indeed, to people as such.

However, Eryximachus, the serious physician, is intolerant and distrustful of laughable things. Thus, after Aristophanes makes his remark about the noises needed to restore the order of the body, Eryximachus says, "My good Aristophanes, look at what you are doing. You have made us laugh just as you were about to speak; and you compel me to guard over your own speech, lest you say something laughable—though you did have the chance to speak in peace" (*Symp.* 189a). Thus, Eryximachus is going to be the guardian, the watchman, watching over Aristophanes to be sure that he produces a serious λόγος rather than jokes and funny noises. Aristophanes's response to this is remarkable, and perfectly appropriate: he laughs! He then says, "Let what has been said be as if it were never spoken" (*Symp.* 189b). The point is that what has been said need not have been said, since his actions *show* sufficiently what it would say. Aristophanes goes on to say that he is not afraid to say laughable things, and he tells Eryximachus not to be his guard. Eryximachus then repeats his demand: "Speak so as to render an account [λόγον]" (*Symp.* 189b).[5]

Aristophanes's Speech (189c–193d)

Aristophanes begins his comedy by identifying the self-ignorance that will be displayed: "It seems to me that human beings have completely failed to perceive the power [δύναμις][6] of Eros" (*Symp.* 189c). If they had, he goes on to say, they would have erected sanctuaries and altars for him. He then says that the power of eros is such that it serves as the *physician* healing a great illness, later saying that it *heals* human nature (that is, the nature, the φύσις, that belongs to the human) (*Symp.* 191d). Thus, Aristophanes has begun his speech by displacing Eryximachus's claims, stating that it is eros, and not Eryximachus's τέχνη, that is the great physician, the great healer, and that what it heals has to do with the φύσις *of*—or,

---

5. This is a variation of the standard phrase λόγον διδόναι ("to give an account").
6. From δύναμαι, meaning "to be able," "capable," "strong enough (to do something)."

perhaps, *in*—the human being. (Moreover, φύσις is precisely what does not readily submit to τέχνη.)

Aristophanes then proceeds to tell the story of human nature and of this illness that eros has the power to heal. In their original state, according to Aristophanes, humans were double and globular, and in this way still resembled the sun, Earth, and moon from which they were descended. With their four legs and four arms, they could move rapidly, tumbling in a circle. They were fearfully strong and had great thoughts (τὰ φρονήματα μεγάλα), and as a result they set upon the gods—or, as Aristophanes says most tellingly, "they attempted to make an ascent into the sky [τὸ εἰς τὸν οὐρανὸν ἀνάβασιν ἐπιχειρεῖν ποιεῖν] so as to attack the gods" (*Symp.* 190b).

Aristophanes compares what he says here to what Homer says about Ephialtes and Otus. According to Homer, these were two sons fathered by Zeus with a mortal woman, Iphimedeia. They were the tallest and most beautiful (κάλλιστος) men ever born on Earth. While they were still very young, they bound Ares with chains and imprisoned him.[7] When they were only nine years old, they threatened to pile Mount Ossa upon Mount Olympus, and Mount Pelion upon Mount Ossa, so as to ascend to the sky and wage battle against the gods. Odysseus, who speaks with Iphimedeia in Hades, says that they would have succeeded had they not been killed by Apollo, though this latter point goes unsaid by Aristophanes.[8]

Confronted by these original humans, Zeus finally came up with a device (μηχανή) by which he could stop their licentiousness (or excess: ἀκολασία) without killing them off: namely, he cut each of them in two. Then each, desiring its other half, came together with another. Wanting nothing beyond this, they remained entangled with one another, and soon began to die off from neglect of their needs. Then Zeus turned their genitals around so that if a man and a woman were paired together in this way, there would at least be procreation, and in this manner the race could continue.

Aristophanes summarizes his speech: "So, it is really from such early times that human beings have had, inborn in themselves, eros for one another—Eros, the bringer-together of their ancient nature [τῆς ἀρχαίας φύσεως], who tries to make one out of two and to heal their human nature" (*Symp.* 191c–d). He then concludes by saying that "each of us, then, is a token of a human being [. . .]; and so each is always in search of his own token" (*Symp.* 191d). The word "token" translates the Greek σύμβολον, which refers to two pieces of a coin or other object that two contracting parties broke between them, each party preserving one part as indicative of the contract made. Eros, then, has the power to heal the wound that our ancient nature suffered as a result of its excess (ἀκολασία)—of

---

7. He was later rescued by Hermes. See Homer, *Il.*, 5: 385 ff.
8. See Homer, *Od.*, 11: 205 ff.

restoring, so far as possible, our lost wholeness and returning us to our ancient nature. As Aristophanes puts it, "Our race would be happy if we were to bring our eros to a consummate end, and each of us were to get his own favorite [i.e., beloved] on his return to his ancient nature" (*Symp.* 193c).

One can now see why Aristophanes's speech is comical—for, in the pursuit of one's other into which eros impels us, there is a lack of self-knowledge insofar as lovers pursue one another without any knowledge that they are seeking wholeness and seeking to be restored to their ancient natures. Moreover, as a force that drives us without our knowing even its aim, eros is not something that will submit to control by law of τέχνη. Rather, it is something inborn, something imposed upon us by our human condition, by our separation from that ancient nature in which we were like the gods. Thus, one who (like Eryximachus) believes that eros is controllable by τέχνη is himself comical—that is, he is so ignorant of this basic driving force in human φύσις that he thinks it can be controlled by mere τέχνη.

And yet, Aristophanes's speech is *not merely* a comedy of a usual sort. He indicates this at the end, where he requests twice that Eryximachus not "make a comedy out of his speech" (*Symp.* 193b–d). Between these two requests, he inserts a crucial statement indicating that he does not want his speech to be taken simply as referring to Pausanias and Agathon, nor to any *individuals*: "For whatever the case may be with them, I am referring to *all* men and women [λέγω δὲ οὖν ἔγωγε καθ' ἁπάντων καὶ ἀνδρῶν καὶ γυναικῶν]" (*Symp.* 193c). Whereas comedy of the usual sort is directed against individuals or particular groups or types, Aristophanes's speech is about *all* human beings, about human beings *as such*: in this respect, it is more akin to *tragedy* than to comedy. In fact, there is also an element of tragedy in *what* it says about human beings. The human condition is tragic, fragmented, separated from the wholeness and perfection of its ancient nature. Eros is the force that allows humans to move toward an overcoming of this condition: however, in the end, the very character of this movement only accentuates the tragic element that belongs to the human condition.

Moreover, if humans set out to restore their wholeness, to resume (without flaw) their ancient nature, this would be like a resumption of the original excess (ἀκολασία) itself. Such a resumption would lead only to further fragmentation, since (as Aristophanes's story reports) Zeus holds over humans the threat of splitting them again, so they would have to hop along on one leg (*Symp.* 190d). Indeed, even apart from Zeus's threat, any attempt by humans to restore their wholeness entirely is doomed to fail, for two lovers can never totally transcend their individualities. If in no other way, they remain individuals in the face of *death*. Aristophanes brings to light this tragic aspect in the otherwise laughable story about Hephaestus offering to fasten lovers together inseparably, "so that—through two—you would be one; and as long as you lived, you would both live together just as though you were one; and when you died, there again in Hades you would be dead together as one instead of two" (*Symp.* 192e). Yet, if they could somehow live as one, they surely could not die as one, sharing a common death. To reference a more recent philosopher in this regard: each person must die his own death.[9]

There is one other feature of Aristophanes's speech that needs to be considered. After Zeus had split humans in two, he instructed Apollo to turn the face and half-neck around to the side where the cut had been made, "so that in beholding his own cutting, the human being might be more orderly [κοσμιώτερος]" (*Symp.* 190e). Further, Apollo healed the wounds and tied off everything at the navel. However, he left a few wrinkles around the navel to remind humans of the trauma they had suffered. Hence, Apollo's service to human beings was to heal them *not* by restoring them to their ancient nature (as eros aims to do), but rather *in their present condition*. Furthermore, Apollo gave to humans a sign—a *bodily* sign (namely, the navel)—to warn them of the danger of excess. Thus, from Aristophanes's speech, there emerges the first configuration of the Dionysian and Apollonian. On the Dionysian side, humans are driven by the uncontrollable force of eros toward restoration of wholeness, toward recovery of their ancient—and excessive—nature. On the Apollonian side, humans are given a bodily sign that warns them of the danger of such excess and that tends to reconcile them to the human condition.

Although at this point Socrates remains completely silent, one cannot but wonder how he will engage this configuration, and how he will bring his own practice (i.e., philosophy) into relation with Dionysus and Apollo. We know from the *Apology*, of course, that he lives in *service* to Apollo, insofar as his philosophical practice has unfolded as a response to the god's saying delivered through the Delphic Oracle. And yet, he has also said, just before the speeches began, that his knowledge is of nothing but *erotics* (*Symp.* 177d–e).

* * *

When Aristophanes finishes his speech, he says to Eryximachus, "Don't make a comedy of it" (*Symp.* 193d). This statement could be read as an injunction to Eryximachus not to respond with any funny noises (such as Aristophanes had made during Eryximachus's speech) or with laughter. It could also be read as an injunction to Eryximachus—and perhaps to us—not to eliminate the tragic element that belongs to the speech, but rather to keep in mind that eros is a striving to return to the origin, to restore humans to their wholeness and perfection, even though it inevitably falls short of this.

---

9. [Editor's Note: See Heidegger (1977), sec. 47 ff.]

Yet, there is something missing in Aristophanes's speech: he does not say what this wholeness of perfection *is* toward which humans strive, except that they would be (comically) double what they are now. Thus, at the level of the question "What is the goal of human striving?," the Aristophanic tragedy reverts—even without Eryximachus's help—to comedy. Later, in the speech reported by Socrates, Diotima refers to this lack: "'And there is a certain account [λόγος],' she said, 'which says that those who seek their own halves are lovers. But my speech [λόγος] denies that eros is of a half or of a whole—unless, comrade, this happens to be good'" (*Symp.* 205d). Thus, is it highly appropriate that the transition following Aristophanes's speech is to the speech of Agathon (i.e., the "good"). This adds, at least in name, what was missing in Aristophanes's speech.

Eryximachus grants Aristophanes's request and says that he enjoyed the speech. He thus betrays the fact that he, though watchman over Aristophanes's speech, failed to see how thoroughly it countered his own speech by releasing eros from under the control of τέχνη. But then, referring to Agathon and Socrates, he remarks that, were they not experts in erotics, he would be afraid that they would be *at a loss for words* (ἀπορήσωσι λόγων) in the wake of Aristophanes's speech.[10] Yet, immediately at least, they are not at a loss for words, for both respond—Socrates by affirming what a tough spot he will be in when Agathon finishes, and Agathon by responding that Socrates is trying to bewitch and fluster him (*Symp.* 194a). Socrates counters by evoking the scene of Agathon on stage: "I saw your courage and greatness of mind in mounting [μεγαλοφροσύνην ἀναβαίνοντος] the platform with the actors and in facing so large an audience when you were about to display your own speeches, and I saw that you were in no way disturbed" (*Symp.* 194a–b).

In this statement, there are two words that anticipate the basic movement that Agathon's speech will carry out (as, in a sense, it repeats in deed his appearance in the theater). The first word is ἀναβαίνω, which means "to mount," "to go up," or "to ascend." As will be seen, Agathon's speech will enact a certain ascent, a certain ἀνάβασις (as have each of the other speeches in various ways). The second word of import is μεγαλοφροσύνη, translated above as "greatness of mind." However, this word is ambiguous, meaning "greatness of mind" or "high-mindedness," but also having the pejorative sense of "pride" or "haughtiness." As will be seen, precisely this ambiguity will be at issue in Agathon's speech: namely, whether the ascent is guided by a high-mindedness or is, rather, driven by a certain pride and haughtiness.

---

10. Form of ἀπορέω λόγων, meaning "to be at a loss for λόγοι," "to be without resources for speaking." From ἄπορος, "without passage," "impassable." The word ἀπορία refers to a difficulty, a lack of resources in the face of something, a lack of a πόρος ("path" or "passage") through.

One additional point must be made regarding this spectacle of Agathon that is evoked by Socrates's words. Socrates refers here to Agathon going up onto the platform (ἐπὶ τὸν ὀκρίβαντα) as his play was about to be performed. Ὀκρίβας was the name of the stage of the Odeum, a theater built by Pericles *next* to the theater of Dionysus. So, Agathon's tragedy, through performed at the festival dedicated to Dionysus, was not in fact performed *in* the theater of Dionysus. One might take this as indicating that, with Agathon, there is a certain separation or distance from Dionysus. One will indeed see that this is the case.[11]

* * *

Throughout the first four speeches, and in the intervals between them (which are progressively getting longer), Socrates has played a relatively minor role: indeed, he has remained completely silent. It is only after Aristophanes has finished his speech that Socrates finally speaks again, first of all to reaffirm what Eryximachus has just said about his being in ἀπορία. Then, after painting (with words) the scene of Agathon before the many, he launches into an interrogation of Agathon in pursuit of the following question: Would Agathon be ashamed of doing something shameful (αἰσχρός) before the few wise and before the many fools (including, as Socrates points out, some, like those present, who are not fools)? The question is complicated owing to the fact that it plays on a shift of meaning. The word αἰσχρός means "ugly," "disgraceful," "shameful"—in meaning, it is the very opposite of καλός ("beautiful," "noble"). The verb αἰσχύνω—"to make ugly," "to disgrace"—in the passive voice means "to be disgraced," "to be ashamed." So, the question Socrates asks Agathon is: Would you be ashamed (i.e., disgraced) of doing something shameful/ugly—that is, something not καλός—before the many? (What he did before the many was, of course, appear with the actors on a stage and present his λόγοι, his play.)

Just as Socrates has posed this question, Phaedrus interrupts, thereby interrupting the interruption that Socrates himself had made: "Dear Agathon, if you answer Socrates, it will not make any difference to him what effect this might have on our present arrangements" (*Symp.* 194d). Thus, Socrates's first real contribution since the speeches began is to call up the scene of the performance of Agathon's tragedy and to pose, in an only slightly veiled manner, the question of whether tragedy really presents something καλός. In doing so, Socrates has

---

11. We do not know much about Agathon. None of his tragedies are extant. From Aristotle, we know that he was responsible for making the chorus a mere diversion between acts, having no relation to the action (*Poetics*, 1456a20 ff.). If Nietzsche is right that the chorus is the Dionysian heart of tragedy (see *Birth of Tragedy*, chaps. 7–8), then clearly Agathon went a step beyond Euripides in driving Dionysus out of tragedy.

interrupted the succession of speeches, though only temporarily and without structurally altering it.

Agathon's Speech (194e–197e)

There are two features that stand out in the way that Agathon begins and then conducts his speech. First of all, and contrary to what the previous speakers did, he will first state what *sort* (ὁποῖος) Eros is and only then what gifts he bestows: "I want first to say how I must speak, and then to speak" (*Symp.* 194e). He then proceeds *to present* the god, *to portray* the god through his words—just as he had presented himself and the actors on the stage (and as Socrates had just re-presented), and just as his play itself had presented gods and men on stage. In other words, Agathon's speech is a theatrical production.

Second, in the way that Agathon begins his speech, there is the utmost attention given to *order*. Agathon first tells how he will speak and then speaks; he tells what sort the god is and then what gifts he bestows. Then he proceeds in the following perfectly orderly way:

> I. Of what sort eros is:
>
> Eros is happiest (εὐδαιμονέστατον) of gods, as he is the most beautiful (κάλλιστον) and the best (ἄριστον).
>
> > a. As the most beautiful, he is:
> > 1) youngest (νεώτατος)
> > 2) tender (ἁπαλός)
> > 3) supple (ὑγρός)
> >
> > b. As the best, he has virtue (ἀρετή):
> > 1) justice (δικαιοσύνη)
> > 2) moderation (σωφροσύνη)
> > 3) courage (ἀνδρεία)
> > 4) wisdom (σοφία)
>
> II. Gifts bestowed by Eros

As a perfectly ordered presentation of the god and his gifts, the speech is quite Apollonian in character—indeed, there are numerous points in the speech that serve to accentuate its bond to Apollo. To begin with, in speaking of Eros as the youngest, Agathon dissociates him from "events of old" about gods—that is, about "castrations and bindings of each other, and many other acts of violence" (*Symp.* 195c). He says, quite remarkably, that since Eros became "king of the gods," there is friendship and peace.[12] One could say, then, that there is a

---

12. Another thing that Aristotle tells us about Agathon is that he was the first to invent plots not based on familiar μῦθοι (*Poetics*, 1451b20), as he is doing here.

taming of eros underway in Agathon's speech: eros is made the advocate of peace and order without violence.

Furthermore, in speaking of Eros as supple in his look (ὑγρὸς τὸ εἶδος), Agathon associates him with beautiful appearance. He speaks further of the "harmony of his figure" (i.e., his elegant, graceful appearance), and says that his complexion is καλός because he lives amongst blooming flowers.[13] In speaking of Eros's justice, he says that "violence does not touch him, nor does he act with violence" (*Symp.* 196b), and this leads him to say that Eros is, of all things, exceptionally moderate. (Later he says that the god "banishes wildness" [*Symp.* 197d].) Thus, the violent, potentially disruptive, wild, unruly aspect of eros—that is, its bond to Dionysus—is excluded in favor of the beautiful, orderly, harmonious appearance characteristic of Apollo: just as, in the drinking party itself, Dionysus has been banished and an orderly progression of speeches has been established in his place.

And yet, even amid this Apollonian beauty, there is a hint, a trace, of Dionysus—as if repressed, persisting beneath the surface. This is perhaps most evident in Agathon's account of Eros as "tender." He refers to what Homer says about Ate (Ἄτη): "Tender are her feet, for she does not to the ground draw near, but lo! She walks on [or above] the heads of men" (*Symp.* 195d). The ostensible point is that, just as Ate does not walk on the hard ground and so has tender feet, so Eros walks only on (i.e., dwells in) what is softest in humans—namely, their character (ἦθος) and soul (ψυχή). However, these lines are in fact extracted from a context that alters their sense entirely. In this regard, one notes first that the word ἄτη means "distraction," "folly," "delusion," and "ruin." The goddess Ate is, according to Hesiod, daughter of strife and sister of lawlessness (*Theog.* 230). In Homer, she is the goddess who deludes humans and leads them to do ruinous acts, inducing within humans moral blindness such that good and ruinous acts cannot be distinguished. In the following passage from the *Iliad*, it is Agamemnon who is speaking, at a point where he and Achilles have reconciled: "Ate is the elder daughter of Zeus, the accursed who deludes all; tender are her feet, for she does not to the ground draw near, but lo! She walks on [or above] the heads of men, and leads them astray. She has entangled others before me. Yes, for once even Zeus was deluded" (*Il.* 19: 91 ff.). One could say, then, that Agathon has literally lifted this Apollonian portrait out of its otherwise Dionysian context. This is indicative of the fact that, beneath this extremely Apollonian portrait of eros, its Dionysian aspect remains—excluded for now (like heavy drinking and the flute girl), but waiting in the wings just offstage, capable of returning and breaking up the beautiful order of this Apollonian λόγος.

---

13. In the blossom, the living erotic fruition of a plant is gathered up into the form of ordered beauty.

Most, if not all, of Agathon's speech is an elaboration of his declaration that Eros is the most beautiful and the best (i.e., the most virtuous) of the gods. The first part of his speech is devoted to the beauty of Eros: he describes Eros as youngest, most tender, and most supple in his looks. He then proceeds (following the order he had laid out) to speak of the virtues of Eros. To begin with, he says, Eros is just (δίκαιος), owing to the fact that he has nothing to do with violence (βία) (*Symp.* 196c). Whoever serves Eros does so of his own accord, voluntarily (ἑκών), without any exercise of compulsion being imposed on him. Whatever is agreed upon voluntarily by two parties is declared just by "'the royal laws of the city'" (*Symp.* 196c).[14] Here we see precisely how Apollonian Agathon's speech is: it is as if love is a matter of voluntary choice, as if erotic desire were a matter of mutual agreement, and not something that comes over us and compels us.

Next, Agathon says that Eros is moderate (σωφροσύνη), claiming that moderation consists in dominating or ruling over (τὸ κρατεῖν) pleasures and desires (*Symp.* 196c). Since Eros is the strongest pleasure (i.e., desire), it dominates and rules over all others and thus is moderate. It is curious that moderation is here itself just a matter of desire—indeed, of the *strongest* desire—rather than of something *other* than desire, something *higher* than desire, that would rule over *all* desire. One wonders: Is there for Agathon anything higher than erotic desire? Is there anything that would limit it?

Agathon goes on to say that Eros is courageous or "manly" (ανδρείας), because "'not even Ares resists' Eros; for Ares does not possess Eros (for Aphrodite, as the story goes), but Eros Ares" (*Symp.* 196d). The ostensible point is simply that the mighty god of war, Ares, was overcome and conquered by love for Aphrodite. Since Eros conquered even him, who otherwise is the mightiest and most courageous god, Eros must be the most courageous of all. Here we note immediately the conflict with Agathon's earlier claim (with regard to justice) that erotic matters are a matter of voluntary choice, and not of being overcome, driven, or compelled as by necessity (*Symp.* 196c.). This issue is indicated also by Agathon's use of the cited phrase "not even Ares resists" Eros, which is from a mostly lost play by Sophocles. However, the actual passage reads: "not even Ares resists necessity [πρὸς τὴν ἀνάγκην]."[15] Agathon thus inserts Eros (Ἔρωτι) in place of necessity (ἀνάγκην).

In any case, what Ares did not resist was the love or erotic necessity that drew him to Aphrodite, "as the story goes." The story alluded to is told in Homer's *Odyssey* (8: 266 ff.). Beautiful Aphrodite was the wife of the lame, ugly blacksmith

---

14. The citation is identified by Aristotle as coming from an orator by the name of Alcidamas. See Rose (1985), 39.
15. Ibid.

god Hephaestus. According to the story, Aphrodite was having an ongoing affair with Ares right in the house of Hephaestus. The minstrel who tells the story sings of "how hidden in Hephaestus' house, they played at love together [. . .], dishonoring Hephaestus' bed" (*Od.* 8: 269). But it happened that the two were seen in their embrace by Helios, who then reported to Hephaestus what he had seen. Then Hephaestus forged a net of chain, light as a cobweb, and swung it from the rafters above the bed. Having prepared his snare, he feigned that he was going far off to Lemnos. As Hephaestus had intended, Ares saw him set out and so went immediately to the house, saying to Aphrodite: "Come and lie down, my darling, and be happy! Hephaestus is no longer here, but gone" (*Od.* 8: 291). The minstrel continues:

> As she, too, thought repose would be most welcome,
> the pair went in to bed—into a shower
> of clever chains, the netting of Hephaistos.
> So trussed they could not move apart, nor rise,
> at last they knew there could be no escape,
> they were to see the glorious cripple now—
> for Helios had spied for him, and told him;
> so he turned back this side of Lemnos Isle,
> sick at heart, making his way homeward.
> Now in the doorway of the room he stood
> while deadly rage took hold of him; his voice,
> hoarse and terrible, reached all the gods:
> "O Father Zeus, O gods in bliss forever,
> here is indecorous entertainment for you,
> Aphrodite, Zeus' daughter,
> caught in the act, cheating me, her cripple,
> with Ares—devastating Ares.
> Cleanlimbed beauty is her joy, not these
> bandylegs I came into the world with:
> no one to blame but the two gods who bred me!
> Come see this pair entwining here
> in my own bed! How hot it makes me burn!
> I think they may not care to lie much longer,
> pressing on one another, passionate lovers;
> they'll have enough of bed together soon.
> And yet the chain that bagged them holds them down
> till Father sends me back my wedding gifts—
> All that I poured out for his damned pigeon,
> so lovely, and so wanton." (*Od.* 8: 295–320)

In response to his shouts, the gods came and looked on at Ares and Aphrodite caught in the net of chains, and said:

> The tortoise tags the hare—
> Hephaistos catches Ares—and Ares outran the wind.
> The lame god's craft has pinned him. Now shall he
> pay what is due from gods taken in cuckoldry. (*Od.* 350–354)

One sees, then, that Ares is actually overcome twice: first by erotic desire for Aphrodite, but then a second time by the lame, ugly god Hephaestus. This says, in effect, that the course of beautiful, courageous Eros is arrested—that it is *interrupted*—and made into a laughable spectacle by the lowly, ugly, but crafty god. This outcome, implied but left unsaid in Agathon's speech, links up with the two previous speeches, for it is Hephaestus's τέχνη that allows him to gain control over the erotic situation, just as Eryximachus claimed to be able to do by means of his τέχνη (i.e., medicine). By this means, Hephaestus has coupled the couple together, conjoining them in the way desired by the two halves in search of one another in Aristophanes's story.

Granted that lowly, ugly Hephaestus—who could hardly be more unlike beautiful, shining Apollo (and is thus non-Apollonian)—interrupts the course of Eros, the question is whether he conquers eros in the end, disrupting it *entirely*. There is reason to think that he does not, for Hephaestus is finally compelled by mighty Poseidon to release the couple, receiving only a surety of payment. The couple then leaps away—Ares to Thrace, Aphrodite to Cyprus, very likely already planning their next meeting. Still more significantly, as the gods were looking on at the couple chained together in their embrace, Apollo said to Hermes:

> "Son of Zeus, beneficent Wayfinder,
> would you accept a coverlet of chain, if only
> you lay by Aphrodite's golden side?"
> To this the Wayfinder replied, shining:
> "Would I not, though, Apollo of distances!
> Wrap me in chains three times the weight of these,
> come goddesses and gods to see the fun;
> only let me lie beside the pale-golden one!"
> The gods gave way again to peals of laughter... (*Od.* 8: 357–365)

Following his discussion of courage, Agathon proceeds to speak about the wisdom (σοφία) of Eros, stating that "the god is a poet of such wisdom that he can makes poets of others too" (*Symp.* 196e). Here, and in what follows, there is a play on the double meaning of ποιητής, which means both "poet" and "maker."[16] He

---

16. The word is derived from ποιέω, which means "to make," "to produce," and "to bring about," but also "to compose," especially poetry and/or music. So, when Agathon says that Eros, as a *poet* (ποιητής), *makes* (ποιῆσαι) poets of others, both words are the same.

goes on to say that Eros is a good ποιητής (poet/maker) in every kind of making (ποίησις) of μουσική.¹⁷

Next, Agathon goes on to exploit the connection between Eros as poet and maker. Through so doing, Agathon in effect enacts an ascent, putting forth an elevating of Eros to the very highest place. This ascent occurs in several stages. First, it begins with what is by *nature*—that is, the making of animals, for it is through Eros's wisdom, according to Agathon, that animals come to be and grow. Next, there is what comes to be by *fabrication* rather than by nature—that is, the work of τέχνη. As the supreme maker, Eros is the one who teaches all those who make things by means of τέχνη. Yet, beyond this, Eros is the teacher not only of human artisans, but also of the gods who first invented the various τέχναι—that is, of Hephaestus, who was taught blacksmithing by Eros, and of Athena, who was taught weaving by the master maker.

But this ascent extends still higher, to higher τέχναι that do not just fabricate objects—namely, to archery, medicine, and divination (invented by Apollo with Eros as his teacher), and to music (invented by the Muses with Eros as their teacher). Finally, Eros is elevated even above Zeus, who is called the "captain of gods and human beings [κυβερνᾶν θεῶν τε καὶ ἀνθρώπων]" (*Symp.* 197b).¹⁸ Thus, by the ascent of Eros above all the gods and humans, all of their various affairs were arranged through eros (i.e., love) of beauty. As a result, beautiful and good things came to prevail over the necessity that had ruled before the advent of Eros.

When he begins to speak of the wisdom of Eros, Agathon says that he wants to "honor our τέχνη as Eryximachus did his" (*Symp.* 196d)—and so he identifies Eros as a ποιητής. Then, when he has finished, "all those present applauded vigorously, as the youth had spoken in a way as suited to himself as to the god" (*Symp.* 198a). In other words, the speech applies to Agathon himself as much as to the god Eros: it is a veiled self-evaluation, a eulogy in praise of his own youth, beauty, and virtue that blurs the distinction between himself and the god so that, at this event that is *his* celebration, he can praise himself without incurring the reproach that outright self-praise would bring.

Yet, in doing this, Agathon is not only elevating Eros to the very highest place—indeed, even to a place above "the captain of the gods," Zeus—but is also elevating *himself*. By enacting this ascent, he enacts what is already said in his name—that is, he places himself at the supreme height of the beautiful and the good. There can be little doubt but that the high-mindedness involved in this ascent, mentioned earlier by Socrates (*Symp.* 194a), is a matter of excessive pride—that is, of unrestrained ὕβρις.

---

17. Most generally, μουσική refers to any art over which the Muses preside. However, it primarily refers to poetry sung to music or accompanied by music (usually the cithara).
18. The appellation derives from the verb κυβερνάω, meaning "to steer."

4. Socrates (Diotima) (198a–212a)

After the applause that follows upon Agathon's speech, Socrates speaks, becoming the main speaker even before he begins his own speech (as he will soon do). He reiterates, now more strongly, that his situation is aporetic, especially in the wake of the wondrous way that Agathon has spoken. But then Socrates ironically modifies his praise and says that what was really wondrous about Agathon's speech was the last part—namely, the part where he broke into verse (in imitation of a passage from Homer's *Odyssey*)[1] and then finished with a flourish of empty rhetoric. Socrates says further that it reminded him of the sophist Gorgias, and then plays on the name Gorgias (as if it were "Gorgon"),[2] feigning fear that Agathon would send the head of Gorgias/Gorgon against his speeches and turn him to stone—that is, make him speechless.[3]

Socrates withdraws his earlier claim to be skilled in erotics and prepared to eulogize eros, now saying that that claim was based on his belief that the *truth* was to be told about it (*Symp.* 198d). However, he says that he is willing to speak only if he can tell the truth about eros in his own terms, since he is likely to be laughed at if he tries to speak in the manner that the others have (*Symp.* 199b). Yet, before he delivers his speech, Socrates engages Agathon in a series of questions—a manner of discourse that could not be more different from Agathon's rhetorical flourish.

Socrates proceeds slowly, step by step, to establish a conclusion. The discourse can be easily summarized in the following way:

Eros is eros (love) of beauty.
Eros is eros (love) of what one does not possess.
So, Eros does not possess beauty (i.e., Eros is not beautiful).
Since good things are beautiful, Eros is also not good.
Thus: Eros is neither beautiful nor good.

---

1. *Od.* 5: 388 ff.
2. The reference in question is to Book XI of Homer's *Odyssey*, where Odysseus is in Hades among the shades. Though he would like to meet still others who are there, such as Theseus, Odysseus quickly departs for fear that "Persephone might send upon me out of the house of Hades the head of the Gorgon, that terrible monster" (*Od.* 11:635).
3. In the Greek text of the *Symposium*, it can be seen that Agathon is indeed employing certain features characteristic of Gorgias, such as assonance (i.e., repetition of vowel or syllables), as at the very end: θέλγων πάντων θεῶν τε καὶ ἀνθρώπων νόημα (*Symp.* 197e). See Bury (1909), xxxvi.

In the wake of Socrates's discourse, Agathon concedes immediately: "I would not be able to speak against you [ἀντιλέγειν], Socrates" (*Symp.* 201c).[4] Yet, one wonders if Agathon truly grasps what Socrates has so easily and simply accomplished, having in effect interrupted the ascent of Eros to the lofty heights of the beautiful and good. Moreover, insofar as Agathon's elevation of Eros was also a self-elevation (to the extent that he portrayed Eros as an image of himself), Socrates's questioning amounts to an exposing of Agathon's self-ignorance. In this way, Socrates "makes a comedy of it" (see *Symp.* 193b–d) by rendering Agathon laughable in his self-ignorance. One could say, then, that the speech of the tragic poet Agathon turns out also to be comedic—a kind of comic tragedy—just as Aristophanes's comedic speech turned out to be tragic, a kind of tragic comedy.

Yet, the question remains: Has Socrates, in interrupting the ascent, disrupted it entirely? Or, rather, does interruption belong somehow to the ascent? Is such interruption capable of empowering the ascent in such a way that, unlike what happened in Agathon's speech, it does not end in an empty, rhetorical flourish?

Socrates's Speech (201d–212c)

Introduction (201d–e)

Following his exchange with Agathon, Socrates turns to the speech about eros that he once heard from a woman, Diotima of Mantineia. In a sense, then, Socrates gives no speech of his own, but only recounts the speech of another. Yet, it turns out that this speech was in fact a *dialogue* between a teacher (namely, Diotima) and a student (namely, Socrates himself). Thus, Socrates manages to substitute a dialogue in place of the kind of extended speeches that the others have given. Among other things, this strategy has the effect of extending even further the narrative structure belonging to the dialogue as a whole, for now it will be a matter of Apollodorus retelling to his unnamed companions the story he had recently told to Glaucon, which he had heard from Aristodemus, who was present at the drinking party and had heard Socrates recounting the speech of Diotima. The effect of this extension is to install even greater distance from the speech and from the Mysteries into which it offers some initiation.

As Socrates goes on to say, Diotima is from Mantineia, the major city in Arcadia in Western Peloponnesos.[5] From 420 BCE on, it was allied with Athens

---

4. The word ἀντιλέγειν here does not mean "contradiction" in the rigorous sense as later defined by Aristotle, but rather a *speaking against*.

5. Socrates says that Diotima delayed the onset of the plague for ten years (indicating that sacrifice is one of the things, in addition to erotics, in which she is wise). The reference here is to the plague that finally broke out in Athens around 427 BCE, weakening the city in the midst of war and claiming the life of its leader Pericles.

against Sparta, and was the scene of a major Spartan victory in 418 BCE. Reference to this city at the party in 416 BCE would have doubtlessly called the war to mind. Socrates's mention of Mantineia also marks the fact that Diotima is a foreigner—indeed, she is the only non-Athenian introduced within the *Symposium*. (Several times, Socrates will address her as "stranger" or "foreigner" (ὦ ξένη).) It is significant, as we will see, that the culminating speech of the dialogue is delivered by the voice of a foreigner—that is, of someone from beyond, or outside of, the Athenian polis.

There is something else that would seem to distinguish Diotima from the other characters: it seems that she is the only named character in any dialogue who does not correspond to a historical figure, but was rather invented by Plato. (There is no mention of her in any ancient text other than Plato's *Symposium*. Perhaps, too, the name itself is invented: it means "honored" or "esteemed" by the gods.) Yet, what distinguishes her even more strikingly is the fact that she is a *woman*. Socrates's claim to have been taught erotics by a woman is a direct affront to Pausanias, who praised homosexual love and demeaned love of women as low and common (*Symp.* 181b). Indeed, in a sense, it is an affront to the entire gathering, which consists only of men, most of whom are openly homosexual.[6] Contrary to nearly all that the context bespeaks, Socrates's introduction of a woman as having taught him erotics—the one thing about which he is knowledgeable—declares that an understanding of eros requires that the feminine be taken into account, and that feminine erotic wisdom be brought into play. As we will see, Diotima will introduce the feminine themes that have largely been missing so far: namely, the significance of pregnancy, giving birth, and nurturing. Also, at the mythological level, she will further emphasize the feminine by stressing the significance of Eros's mother and grandmother.

Diotima's speech will eventually incorporate elements of, or will comment upon, all of the other speeches, though in doing so it will also shift and transform them. As mentioned above, already with the very introduction of the woman Diotima, Pausanias's speech is criticized. There will also be mythical elements and even mention of some of the figures from Phaedrus's speech. Additionally, there will be an analysis of *making* (as in τέχνη) (*Symp.* 205b ff.), and hence implicit reference to Eryximachus's speech, as well as a conspicuous reference to Aristophanes's speech ("a certain speech according to which those who seek their own halves are lovers" [*Symp.* 205d]). As for Agathon, Socrates expressly agrees with him that one must first tell *who* (i.e., of what sort) Eros is and only then of his deeds by which he benefits humankind (*Symp.* 199c).

---

6. The party includes two overt homosexual pairs: Agathon/Pausanias, and Phaedrus/Eryximachus.

Furthermore, Socrates's exchange with Agathon, and specifically the conclusion, provides the starting point for Socrates's recounting of Diotima's speech: namely, the claim that Eros is neither beautiful nor good. Diotima rejects Socrates's surmise that, if eros is neither beautiful nor good, then it must be ugly and bad. She proceeds then to present eros as in between (μεταξύ) (*Symp.* 202a). She begins this presentation by giving an example of something in between: correct opinion or opining (ὀρθὴ δόξα), she says, is in between understanding (φρονήσεως) and lack of understanding (ἀμαθίας) (*Symp.* 202a).[7] As Diotima further explains, to opine correctly, without being able to give a λόγος, is not to know; however, neither is it simply ignorance, since it is correct about that of which there is opining.

It is important to note that this example is not just an example, but rather more of a *paradigm*, one which links up with, and is an inversion of, a pivotal passage from Plato's *Meno*. There, Meno—whose name means "I stay put"—poses a paradox: "But how will you look for something when you do not in the least know what it is? How on earth are you going to set up something you do not know as the object of your search? To put it another way: even if you come right up against it, how will you know that what you have found is the thing you did not know?" (*Meno*, 80d). Socrates then rephrases the paradox, filling it out somewhat. One cannot inquire about what one knows, owing to the fact that one already knows it and (thus) has no need to inquire. But neither can one inquire about what one does not know, since in that case one does not know what to inquire about. So, if there were only the extremes of knowledge and ignorance, there could be no inquiry, no learning—one would, like Meno, *just stay put*. But, then, the most direct response to the paradox (though not the one immediately pursued in the *Meno*) is the following: because things appear and look a certain way, one can have a correct view (i.e., an opinion) of them, and on that basis can go on to inquire further into them.[8]

The same theme comes up a bit later in the *Symposium* during Socrates's speech, when eros, as love of wisdom (and hence as philosophizing), is placed into this position between wisdom and ignorance. According to Socrates—or, rather, according to Diotima—gods do not philosophize: that is, they do not desire to become wise, owing to the fact that they are already so. At the same time, the ignorant do not philosophize, owing to the fact that they are unaware of their lack of wisdom. In other words, the difficulty with ignorance is that, unless it is tempered by correct opinion, it is also ignorance of ignorance. Thus, the philosophers are

---

7. It is crucial to recall here that opinion is not something merely subjective, but rather has implicit reference to *seeming*, to *appearing*. Ὀρθὴ δόξα would thus mean something like "having a (correct) view of something." [Editor's Note: See part 1, chap. 1 of the present volume.]

8. [Editor's Note: See Sallis (1975), 76 ff.]

those who are in between wisdom and ignorance. With this development of the paradigm of correct opinion as being situated between wisdom and ignorance, Diotima returns to the question of eros. Eros is neither beautiful nor good; however, this does not entail that it is ugly or bad (as Socrates himself supposes). Rather, eros is *neither* ugly nor bad. Thus, eros is in between beautiful and ugly and in between good and bad.[9]

Diotima proceeds to explain the in-between character of eros by denying what was assumed both at the beginning (in Phaedrus's speech) and just previously (in Agathon's speech)—namely, that Eros is a god. She says that all gods are happy by possessing the beautiful and the good. Eros, however, does not possess these, and hence is not a god. Yet, this does not mean that Eros is mortal: rather, Eros is "in-between mortal and immortal [μεταξὺ θνητοῦ καὶ ἀθανάτου]" (*Symp.* 202d). This, in turn, means that Eros is a daimon (δαίμων).[10] Socrates asks about the power (δύναμις) of a daimon, and Diotima explains:

> Interpreting and ferrying to gods things from human beings and to human beings things from gods: the requests and sacrifices of human beings, the orders and exchanges-for-sacrifices of gods; for it is in the middle of both and fills up the interval so that the whole itself has been bound together by it. Through this proceeds all divination and the art of the priests who deal with sacrifices, initiatory rituals, incantations, and every kind of soothsaying and magic. A god does not mingle with a human being; but through this occurs the whole intercourse and conversation of gods with human beings while they are awake and asleep. (*Symp.* 202e–203a)[11]

Diotima next tells of the birth of Eros. (This is in contrast to Phaedrus, who maintained that Eros, being the oldest of the gods, had no parents.) According to Diotima, when Aphrodite was born, the gods held a feast at which Poros ("Resource"), son of Metis, was present.[12] Penia ("Poverty") came begging, and hung

---

9. One notes that, at this point, beautiful and good are treated as perfectly parallel, as though both were in between in the same way. We will see later on that this is not so.

10. The term δαίμων tended to be applied to lesser divinities, yet also retained an older sense to a person's lot (i.e., what is allotted to him, as by fate). In Hesiod, it applies to the souls of heroes of the golden age who form a connecting link between gods and men, as is the case here (i.e., being in between mortals and immortals). The understanding of δαίμων as a "demon" (i.e., some evil spirit) was imposed later by Christianity.

11. Recall in this connection Socrates's account of his daimon in the *Apology* (beginning at 31c). It is a kind of voice (φωνή), something godly and daimonic, that holds him back from what he is thinking of doing, but never urges him forward. It is this voice that has, according to Socrates, kept him from engaging in politics. This account is Socrates's way of answering the charge that he does not acknowledge the gods recognized by the city, but other strange daimons. See Sallis (1975), 54 ff.

12. The word πόρος primarily means "a way through or over" something (e.g., a river), "a way of achieving something," and thus "resource" in a general sense. The name Μῆτις means "wisdom" or "skill." She was the wife of Zeus and mother of Athena, who was later swallowed by Zeus.

about near the door. Poros got drunk and fell asleep, and Penia, plotting to have a child by him, lay beside him and became pregnant with Eros (ἐκύησε τὸν Ἔρωτα) (*Symp.* 203c). Since he was conceived on Aphrodite's day of birth, Eros is the attendant of Aphrodite.

There are two points that need to be underscored. First, Eros was conceived at a banquet, and so at an event not wholly unlike the party presented in the *Symposium*. At the banquet, there was not yet wine, just as at the present party, there is (as yet) no heavy drinking. And yet, Poros managed to get drunk merely on nectar—and we will see that eventually most of those at the party will get drunk as well, despite the evening's earlier prohibition.[13] Second, Diotima takes this story, and the resulting account of Eros as sharing features of both parents, and brings it to bear on what was said earlier about Eros being in between mortal and immortal: "And his nature is neither immortal nor mortal; but at one time, sometimes on the same day [τῆς αὐτῆς ἡμέρας],[14] he flourishes and lives, whenever he has resources; and, at another time, sometimes he dies, but gets to live again through the nature of his father. And as that which is supplied to him is always gradually flowing out, Eros is never entirely without resources [ἀπορεῖ] nor wealthy, but is between wisdom and ignorance" (*Symp.* 203e).

Thus, Eros is not simply immortal (i.e., always unchangeably present) nor simply mortal (i.e., simply and continually dying away). Rather, Eros is a unity of death and rebirth—just as Dionysus was said to wither away and die with the coming of winter, only to be perpetually reborn in spring.

Here, an important connection comes to light: eros is profoundly related to *human temporality*. Specifically, eros involves the generation/production/bringing-forth by which the ceaseless passing away of time is continually overcome. Eros involves the bringing-forth of immortality in mortality, of permanence within

---

13. The scene here also makes one think of another banquet: namely, the divine banquet described in Socrates's second speech in the *Phaedrus* (246a ff.). Socrates pictures a grand procession of gods and daimons in their chariots as they ascend up to the divine banquet: "and behold, there in the heaven Zeus, mighty leader, drives his winged team: first of the host of gods and daimons, he proceeds, and the host follows after him, marshalled in eleven companies." The gods make the steep ascent up to "the summit of the arch that supports the heavens" (*Phaedr.* 247b). For the gods, this is easy, but for the other, mortal souls that follow, it is difficult. Then they "come forth and stand upon the back of the heavens and straightaway the revolving heaven carries them round and they look upon what is outside the heavens" (*Phaedr.* 247c). What they see there is *being itself* (οὐσία ὄντως οὖσα)—and beholding this is precisely their feast: to feast their eyes upon being itself. For the gods, the feast is accomplished and they return home, but mortal souls trample and tread on one another, their horses are lamed and the wings broken—and there is, at best, an imperfect vision of being. See Sallis (1975), 132 ff.

14. Eros lives and dies "on the same day"—the two moments (i.e., living and dying) belong together. However, as the formulation τοτὲ μὲν . . . τοτὲ δὲ makes clear, the two moments remain different in their togetherness.

flux. In other words, eros entails the bringing forth of *self-sameness* amidst the perpetual *self-differing* wrought by time.

Benefit of Eros (204c–205b)

At this point, Diotima has explained of what sort Eros is: Eros is in between mortal and immortal and wisdom and ignorance. Thus, as the love of wisdom, Eros is a philosopher. Proceeding in the proper order, Socrates then asks her: What *use* is eros for human beings? She responds by referring to eros as love of beautiful and good things, specifically, the love of *acquiring* them. The question is, then: What is the benefit of acquiring beautiful and good things? Socrates cannot say what the benefit is of acquiring beautiful things, but does say what the benefit of acquiring *good* things is: namely, that one will be *happy* (εὐδαίμων).[15] This, says Diotima, is a final (i.e., ultimate) answer—for one does not want to be happy for the sake of anything further. Thus, eros is beneficial insofar as it is directed toward acquiring what is good, and thereby attaining happiness.

ποίησις (205b–207a)

The account of eros as the unity or togetherness of production (i.e., bringing-forth) and flowing away (i.e., dying) makes it clear that eros extends beyond what is usually called "love." This is even more evident from Diotima's description of eros as the love of (having) good things and so of being happy. This, she says, is common (κοινόν) to *all* humans.[16]

In order to indicate how the name of a whole can come to be used for only a part (i.e., only a certain kind), Diotima takes the example of ποίησις: making, production, bringing-forth. But this is not simply an example, since, as she will stress, eros involves a production or bringing-forth (ποίησις). All those who practice a τέχνη are in fact makers (ποιητής). Indeed, ποίησις is the cause whenever something passes from nonbeing to being. Yet, one kind of making—namely, one concerned with music and meter—is separated off from the others, and it alone is called ποίησις (i.e., poetry). Moreover, its practitioners alone are called ποιητής (poets).

The situation is likewise with eros. Eros is the whole desire (ἐπιθυμία) of good things and of being happy (εὐδαίμων). But this desire may be pursued in many ways—for example, in money-making (i.e., acquiring good things), gymnastics (i.e., acquiring a good body), or philosophy (i.e., acquiring a good soul). Yet, those who pursue it in one particular way—and only they—are called by the name of the whole: namely, "lovers" (ἐραστής/ἐρασταί).

---

15. Literally, "with a good daimon."
16. With this claim, one sees a certain universalizing moment that allies with the universalizing move made by Eryximachus (though not as extensive).

The question is this: What does one do in pursuing eros *as such*, and not just in the partial, specific sense? Granted that eros is desire of the good—namely, that it be one's own always, by the possession of which one is made happy—what is the character of the deed (τὸ ἔργον) by which one pursues this? What is an erotic deed *as such*? Diotima's answer is decisive: "Their deed is bringing to birth [τόκος] in beauty both in terms of the body and in terms of the soul" (*Symp.* 206b).[17]

Diotima adds an extended clarification before eventually repeating, in almost the same words, her description of the erotic deed: "It [eros] is of engendering and of bringing to birth in the beautiful [τῆς γεννήσεως καὶ τοῦ τόκου ἐν τῷ καλῷ]" (*Symp.* 206e). Here, when she repeats the description, she uses not only the word τόκος ("bringing to birth") but also γέννησις ("producing," in the specific sense of producing offspring, either by begetting or bearing). But she could also have used the word ποίησις, though it is more general (being the name of the whole), for the two words τόκος and γέννησις both denote a producing, a bringing-forth. So, eros is a kind of ποίησις—and it was for this reason that Diotima introduced ποίησις as an example.

The clarification is inserted between the initial description and its repetition: "'All human beings, Socrates,' she said, 'are pregnant [κυοῦσιν] both in terms of the body and in terms of the soul, and whenever they are at a certain age, their nature [φύσις] desires to bring to birth [τίκτειν]; but it is incapable of bringing to birth in ugliness, but only in beauty'" (*Symp.* 206c).

This says that all humans—both men and women—are *pregnant*, in body and in soul. At a certain age, their *nature* desires to bring (something) to birth.[18] What Diotima says here has a strange implication that is quite contrary to what one would expect: namely, that when erotic desire awakens, humans are *already* pregnant. In other words, pregnancy *precedes* erotic desire rather than resulting from the fulfillment of that desire. It is not as though someone comes near a beautiful person, has erotic desire aroused, and then through its fulfillment becomes pregnant. Rather, one is *already* pregnant, comes near a beautiful person (or perhaps something else beautiful), and then brings something to birth. This is explicit in what Diotima goes on to say: "It is for these reasons that whenever the pregnant draws near to beauty, it becomes glad and in its rejoicing dissolves and then gives birth and produces offspring" (*Symp.* 206d).

---

17. The word τόκος ("bringing to birth," or simply "childbirth") derives from the verb τίκτω, meaning "to bring into the world," "to bring forth (as a mother)," "to beget (as a father)." It is said by Diotima that the deed is a bringing to birth ἐν καλῷ: in beauty, in the beautiful, in something beautiful. The word ἐν can also mean "on," "near," or "with (i.e., "by means of")."

18. One wonders: Does this mean simply that all human beings desire by nature? Or, is it that the nature in them desires? (This would be different than saying simply that "they desire.")

Now, the larger implication is that the erotic deed is not identified with the sexual act, with the fulfillment of sexual desire, but rather consists primarily in *bringing to birth*: "The being together of man and woman is a bringing to birth [τόκος]" (*Symp.* 206c). In other words, their being-together (συνουσία) is not primarily the sexual act, but rather their production of offspring. Here we see how decisive the feminine is to Diotima's account of eros: the erotic deed, the deed in which erotic desire is fulfilled, consists in bringing to birth. Though the man must have begotten the child, it is the woman who bears and gives birth to the child. In the speech of Diotima, then—the only speech in the text given by a woman—the erotic deed is centered in what is most directly carried out by the woman.[19]

Three further points must be noted. First, Diotima says that "eros is not, Socrates, of the beautiful, as you believe" (*Symp.* 206e). Contrary to what Socrates had supposed, then, eros is not love of the beautiful in the sense of a desire to possess the beautiful. The *only* thing that eros desires to possess is the good (so as to be happy), but *not* the beautiful. The erotic relation to the beautiful is thus not one of possession or desire to possess, but is quite different: eros brings to birth in/on/at/near/by means of the beautiful (ἐν καλῷ). Here, then, there is a divergence between beautiful and good, at least insofar as eros relates to them.

Second, Diotima says that "beauty is the Μοῖρα and Eileithyia for birth" (*Symp.* 206d). Eileithyia was the daughter of Hera, and was tasked with helping women in childbirth. (Because of this connection to childbirth, she is sometimes identified or associated with Artemis.)

Μοῖρα means "fate," and refers specifically to the Fates (Μοῖραι), who delimited the life of humans.[20] So, beauty is the Eileithyia of birth, in that birth is assisted by beauty and occurs ἐν καλῷ. But how is beauty the μοῖρα for birth? What does beauty have to do with μοῖρα, with the delimitation of the life of humans?

Third, Diotima says that "this thing, pregnancy and bringing to birth, is divine, and it is immortal in the animal that is mortal" (*Symp.* 206c). As we saw earlier, the deed of eros is a bringing-forth of immortality within mortality. (This is seen in the basic structure of temporality.) However, Diotima will go on to show that this erotic structure goes far beyond this. At this point, she simply adds that, since eros is of the good's *always* being one's own, it is also a desire for immortality. Yet, already it is clear that eros is not just an empty longing for

---

19. That the erotic deed is primarily the act of bringing to birth is foreshadowed in the story of Eros's conception, where the emphasis is not at all on the sexual act. Poros is passed out drunk and seems not even to have been aware of what happened; and when Diotima describes the result, she says simply, "Penia conceived [or became pregnant with: ἐκύησε] Eros" (*Symp.* 203c).

20. There were three such Fates: Clotho, the spinner, who spun the thread of life; Lachesis, the disposer of lots, who assigned to each person his destiny; and Atropos, who cut the thread at death.

immortality, but is rather a production, a bringing-forth, of immortality within the mortal being.

Immortality (207a–209e)

Socrates next marks a break—or, at the very least, a transition: "All of these things she used to teach me whenever she made her speeches about erotics" (*Symp.* 207a). He continues, saying that she once asked him about the cause (αἴτιον) of eros. She then explained that the cause is that "mortal nature [φύσις] seeks as far as possible to be forever and immortal" (*Symp.* 207d). She then appeals to a series of five attestations of this seeking (and production) of immortality.

First, Diotima refers to how uncanny the disposition of beasts is with regard to the production and nurture of offspring, how they are intent on intercourse with one another, and how they will fight, starve, and die for the sake of their offspring. As she goes on to say, "Mortal nature is capable of immortality only in this way, the way of generation [τῇ γενέσει], that it is always leaving behind another that is young to replace the old" (*Symp.* 207d). So, in bringing forth offspring, each is reborn in another and, in this respect, lives on.

Second, there is an attestation within the individual of such production of immortality within mortality, for the entire body (e.g., hair, flesh, bones, blood) is continually suffering loss, passing away, and yet is continually being replaced, becoming young, so that the individual lives on. This is true also for what pertains to the soul, for character, opinions, desires, and so on are continually passing away, yet also always coming to be. This is true also of knowledge (ἐπιστήμη), which we forget and which has to be restored by fresh memory. Concluding this point, Diotima says, "For in this way every mortal thing is preserved, not by being absolutely the same forever, as the divine is, but by the fact that that which is departing and growing old leaves behind another young thing that is as it was" (*Symp.* 208a).[21]

Third, the love of honor (φιλοτιμία) and the uncanny disposition it brings about also attest to erotic production for the sake of immortality. She mentions the two examples that Phaedrus previously cited as instances of people who were willing to die for someone they loved—namely, Alcestis (who died for Admetus) and Achilles (who died for Patroclus). She also adds another example: namely, Codrus, a legendary king of Athens who lived in the eleventh century BCE.[22] During Codrus's reign, the Dorians invaded Attica, and had heard from the Delphic oracle that they would be victorious if Codrus's life was spared. However, an

---

21. One notes that much of what Diotima refers to here, especially erotic production in/of the body, is *not* something that a person *does* as a conscious, deliberate act, but is rather carried out by the *nature* within the person. Here one sees clearly the bond of eros to φύσις.

22. [Editor's Note: Regarding Codrus, see Lycurgus, *Against Leocrates*, secs. 84–87.]

informer told the Athenians about the oracle, and Codrus went out in woodcutter's clothing and invited death by quarreling with Dorian warriors, and so with his death saved Athens. Now, it is important to observe that, whereas Phaedrus took such characters to have died for loved ones, Diotima says that their deaths were *erotic*—that is, they died for the sake of "an immortal remembering of their virtue"—which, attesting to this, she says "we now retain" (*Symp.* 208d). It is also important to note the manner in which the example of Codrus underlines Diotima's divergence from Phaedrus, for Codrus did not die for loved ones, but rather in order to live on in the memory of his countrymen.

Fourth, the procreation of children brings about a certain immortality. As Diotima says: "Now, there are those who are pregnant in terms of their bodies, and they turn to women and are erotic in this way" (*Symp.* 208e). One also notes again here the priority of pregnancy at play in Diotima's speech.

Fifth, and finally, "there are others who are pregnant in terms of the soul" (*Symp.* 208e), who are "pregnant with those things that it is appropriate for the soul to be pregnant with and to bring to birth" (*Symp.* 209a). What are these things that they bring to birth? She answers: "prudence and the rest of virtue [φρόνησίν τε καὶ τὴν ἄλλην ἀρετήν]" (ibid.). She then adds that the greatest and most beautiful part of prudence is the arrangement and ordering of cities and households (οἴκησις), and the name for this is moderation and justice.[23]

Continuing, Diotima says that these are the things that poets and inventive makers produce, of which they are producers (ποιηταί). Thus, she brings eros, at this level, into relation with ποίησις in two senses: first, in the *making* (that is, the arranging and ordering) of cities and dwellings, regarding which she mentions the "fathers" of Sparta and Athens (i.e., Lycurgus and Solon), and second, in *poetry*, regarding which she refers to Homer and Hesiod and to the immortal offspring they have left behind, which have also given them immortal fame.

These, then, are the Lesser Mysteries of eros, into which Diotima has sought to initiate Socrates. Before attempting with Socrates to pass through the initiation that Diotima will offer into the Highest Mysteries, there is one other point that must be considered. When erotic memory brings back knowledge that has been forgotten—thus bringing it again to birth, to rebirth—it brings it back as *the same*. This belongs to the very sense of bringing-back: namely, that what is brought back is the same knowledge that had disappeared into oblivion. Diotima speaks of how "study [μελέτη], instilling a fresh memory again to replace the departing one, preserves the knowledge, so that it seems [δοκεῖν] to be the same" (*Symp.* 208a). She goes on to say that "in this way, every mortal saves itself [σῴζεται]; not by being absolutely [παντάπασιν] the same always, as the divine

---

23. One sees here how the relation of eros to virtue has been reconfigured: whereas Agathon simply attributed virtues to eros, Diotima regards virtues as brought forth by eros.

is" (*Symp.* 208a-b), but rather by producing offspring and in general producing immortality within mortality. We see here, then, that the operation of eros, its bringing-forth (ποίησις) of immortality within mortality, is a production of sameness of/with self. Mortals cannot be entirely and always selfsame, as the gods can, but through eros they can, in this measure and within these limits, be selfsame.

The Highest Mysteries (209e–212a)

Diotima expresses uncertainty as to whether Socrates will be able to be initiated into the Highest Mysteries, but she encourages him to follow if he is able. She indicates that she will speak about moving correctly along a certain course. This course, as she initially lays it out, will have five stages.

At the first stage, the one who is to traverse this course must begin with eros of one beautiful body—that is, he advances to the first stage of the course by going to a single beautiful body. Already Diotima has indicated that, in loving such a beauty—that is, in going to this beautiful body—it is not a matter of possessing it: rather, it is a matter of bringing something to birth in/near/with it. What is it, precisely, that is brought to birth? Diotima tells us, "He must love one body and there generate beautiful speeches" (*Symp.* 210a). What is brought to birth, then, is neither children, bodily tissue, memories, nor even the capacity to arrange cities and dwellings, but rather beautiful λόγοι. Here we see why she spoke of the *Highest* Mysteries: this course lies entirely beyond those kinds of erotic deeds that she had described previously. She says now that the earlier erotics are a means for these on which she is now launching.

However, regarding this first stage, one can ask the following question. Diotima has said that "he must love one body and *there* [ἐνταῦθα] generate beautiful speeches." But what, or where, is the *there*? Are the beautiful speeches generated *in* the beautiful body, or in the one who goes *near* the beautiful body? Or, perhaps, in the space between them, by one being *with* the other? There is an ambiguity belonging to ἐνταῦθα here that makes this question difficult to resolve.

At the second stage, Diotima says that he must realize that the beauty in one body is related to (ἀδελφόν)[24] that in another body, "and if he must pursue the beauty in its look, it is great folly not to believe that the beauty of all bodies is one and the same" (*Symp.* 210b). Thus, at the second stage, he becomes lover of all beautiful bodies. One should note here especially the phrase τὸ ἐπ'εἴδει καλόν, which we translate here as "the beauty in its look." Diotima's point is that, in its look, the beauty of one body is no different from that of another: all have the same

---

24. Literally, "the brother of."

look—all, with regard to their being beautiful, look the same, however different they may be in other regards. And so, at this second stage, he attends to the look that all beautiful bodies have in *common*.[25]

At the third stage, he comes to believe that the beauty in souls is more honorable than in the body. Here, too, he attends to the beauty in its look—or to beauty as its look, as a look. Yet, here the look is less identified with sensible presence: rather, it is what shines forth through sensible presence, as the beauty of a soul can shine through in a smile or some other gesture.

What is brought to birth in relation to such beauty? Again, speeches (λόγοι), in this case such as to make the beloved better. Here, Socrates—playing ventriloquist for Diotima—alludes to the discussion of pederasty (especially in Pausanias's speech), though now the aspect of gratification (and hence of an exchange economy between lover and beloved) has dropped out entirely.

At the fourth stage, he comes to behold the beautiful in pursuits and laws (τὸ ἐν τοῖς ἐπιτηδεύμασι καὶ τοῖς νόμοις καλόν).[26] Diotima says that he "sees [ἰδεῖν] that all [or each of] these is akin [συγγενές] to itself" (*Symp.* 210c). As was the case above, what is decisive here is *sameness*, that it is one and the same beautiful look that shines through practices, customs, and laws.

At the fifth and final stage, he goes on to knowledges, to the beauty that shines through knowledge. As Diotima says (*Symp.* 210d), "with a permanent turn to the vast open sea of the beautiful, [he will] behold it and give birth—in ungrudging [or bounteous] philosophy—to many beautiful and magnificent speeches [λόγους] and thoughts" (*Symp.* 210d). Thus, at the first, third, and fifth stages, Diotima says explicitly that what is brought forth is beautiful λόγος, and we can suppose that this is the case across the entire course.

As the erotic person advances along this course, the beauty that he beholds becomes ever more selfsame, as it becomes more and more remote from the sheer, ceaseless passage (i.e., the passing away, flow, and flux) of φύσις. Through proximity to this ever more selfsame beauty, the erotic person is drawn to bring forth ever more selfsameness (i.e., immortality) within his mortal being, subject to the continual dying away and separation from himself. This is accomplished

---

25. Such common looks are designated by the word εἶδος, which comes from the *obsolete* present tense verb εἴδω, which means "to see." An εἶδος is the look that presents itself when one looks at something, when one attends to the way it looks. This word and the near-synonym ἰδέα come down to us as "form" or "idea." Plato is supposed to have held something like a theory of forms or ideas. More nonsense has been written about this than about almost any other topic in Greek philosophy. Seldom has it even been considered that the very concept of *theory* (and of *concept*) relies upon, and indeed presupposes, what was said about the εἴδη in the Platonic dialogues.

26. The word ἐπιτήδευμα means "pursuits," but also "custom" and "practice." When Socrates describes his practice of questioning people (in his service to Apollo), he uses this word (*Ap.* 28b).

preeminently by bringing beautiful λόγοι to birth. For λόγος, above all, serves to gather up into selfsameness what otherwise would simply flow away.[27]

Following her account of these five stages, Diotima marks a break, saying to Socrates—and also perhaps to the reader—"Try to pay as close attention as you can" (*Symp.* 210e). Now she speaks of an advance even beyond the previous stages, an advance toward the τέλος of erotics. At, or in proximity to, this τέλος, one "suddenly beholds something wonderfully beautiful in its nature" (*Symp.* 210e).

There are two things to note here. First, the word "suddenly," which translates ἐξαίφνης—which also means "in/for a moment," "momentarily," and "instantaneously"—is important. In Plato's *Parmenides*, there is a discussion about the connection between rest and motion that bears upon this word. The question being considered is this: If something at rest is set in motion, when does the change from rest to motion occur? Change cannot occur when it is at rest (for then it cannot also be in motion). Yet, the change cannot occur once it is already in motion. Regarding this, Parmenides says, "[. . .] when being at rest it changes to motion, it must itself be in no time at all [. . .] There is no time in which anything can be at once neither in motion nor at rest" (*Parm.* 156c). Continuing, he asks, "Then when does it change? For it does not change when it is at rest or when it is in motion or when it is in time" (*Parm.* 156c). There is, then, this strange thing (τὸ ἄτοπον) in which it would be when it changes—namely, τὸ ἐξαίφνης, the instant or moment. In light of this, one can say that, in the *Symposium*, the beholding that occurs at (or near) the τέλος of erotics occurs *instantaneously* (like the change from rest to motion). There is no sustained view of what is seen, but only an instantaneous glimpse.

Nonetheless, what is glimpsed is wonderfully beautiful (θαυμαστὸν . . . καλόν). This means that, in being beheld—even if only instantaneously—it nevertheless evokes wonder, and hence is evocative of philosophy.[28] Yet, what is it that is glimpsed at this final stage? According to Diotima, it is "always being [ἀεὶ ὄν]" (*Symp.* 211a): it is thus neither coming to be nor perishing, neither increasing nor passing away. One could say, then, that it is pure immortality. The immortality that erotic mortals install within their mortal frame is *like* this, but is mixed with coming-to-be, perishing, etc.—that is, it is impure.

The second point to consider is Diotima's comment that what is beheld— again, if only instantaneously—is "not beautiful in one respect and ugly in another" (*Symp.* 211a). In other words, it is entirely the same as itself, and is unmixed

---

27. This occurs even in a single word: the word "tree," for example, gathers up into selfsame unity all individual trees, gathers them into the look that they all have in common, and posits that look as something beyond the mere passing away of the individual trees. Thus, the verb λέγειν means "to say," "to tell," "to declare," *and* "to lay in order," "to arrange," "to gather."

28. [Editor's Note: See *Theat.*, 155d.]

with anything else. Diotima goes on to claim that it is also not somewhere in something else (e.g., in an animal, in earth, in heaven): rather, it is itself alone by itself with itself (αὐτὸ καθ᾽αὑτὸ μεθ᾽αὑτοῦ) (*Symp.* 211b). Moreover, it is, as she says, μονοειδές: it has a simple, unique look.

Diotima continues her speech. However, in what follows, a certain, important turn occurs of which one must remain mindful. As Diotima says, "So whenever anyone begins to behold [καθορᾶν] that beauty as he goes up [or ascends: ἀπανιὼν] from these things through the correct practice of pederasty, he must come close to touching [or "grasping" or "apprehending": ἅπτοιτο] the perfect end [τοῦ τέλους]" (*Symp.* 211b). Again, there are two points to consider here. First, one should note that Diotima changes the directionality of the progression, turning the course upward and making it vertical—it is now a matter of *going up*, of *ascending* (ἐπανείμι). Yet, the word ἐπανείμι can also mean "to go back," "to return"; and, in this statement, Diotima does, in a sense, go back, returning momentarily to the theme of pederasty, though now in a corrected form. This reference serves to indicate how far the present discourse has advanced beyond those with which the drinking party began. Second, it should be observed that it is stated that the one who ascends so as to begin to behold that beauty only comes *close* (σχεδόν) to touching the τέλος (which presumably is this beauty itself). But why does one only come *close* to the τέλος? Why does one only *almost* reach the height at which the ascent would end?

Diotima now combines her account of the various stages and her account of the final stage (in which one comes close to touching the τέλος), reiterating—now as an ascent—the entire movement of proceeding correctly to erotics:

> beginning from these beautiful things here, always to ascend for the sake [ἕνεκα][29] of that beauty, using these beautiful things as steps [ὥσπερ ἐπαναβασμοῖς]:[30] from one to two, and from two to all beautiful bodies; and from beautiful bodies to beautiful pursuits [ἐπιτηδεύματα]; and from pursuits to beautiful learnings [μαθήματα]; and from learnings to end at that learning which is the learning of nothing else that the beautiful itself; and at last to know what is beauty itself [αὐτὸ . . . ὃ ἔστι καλόν].[31] (*Symp.* 211c)

As he goes on narrating Diotima's words of praise for this place where one would behold the beautiful, Socrates inserts two interruptions: first, Diotima's words "my dear Socrates" (which have occurred several times), and then his own words,

---

29. The word ἕνεκα can also mean "by means of." This would mean that the beautiful, as the τέλος, is what enables the ascent, presumably by evoking wonder.

30. The word ἐπαναβασμός refers to steps on a staircase, *not* on a ladder as is sometimes supposed.

31. One could also translate this as "that very thing which the beautiful is," "the beautiful which is itself (or itself is)."

spoken as his own and thus withdrawn from the ventriloquy in which he has been engaged—"the Mantinean stranger [ξένη] said. . . ." But these interruptions *of* the narrative only serve to hint at the interruption that has just occurred *within* the narrative—for in her reiteration of the stages, reconfigured vertically as steps up which one would ascend, Diotima entirely omits one stage: namely, that of the *soul*. This is especially remarkable owing to the fact that the soul is not only something whose beauty is beheld at a stage (namely, the middle stage, in her first enumeration), but that it is precisely the soul that would make the ascent, and that would be initiated into the Highest Mysteries. Thus, in telling of the ascent, Diotima also enacts a forgetting of the soul—and so the ascent of the erotic mortal turns out to be a way of self-forgetfulness! Such forgetfulness is clear when, almost at the end of her speech, Diotima portrays the erotic mortal as giving birth to true virtue so that "it is within him to become beloved of the gods [θεοφιλεῖ], and if any other among humans is immortal, he is too" (*Symp.* 212a).

At the end of Diotima's speech, it becomes all the more evident that a forgetfulness of self, and an obliviousness to the limits of our mortal nature, is broached in the ascent: "'What then,' she said, 'do we believe happens to one, if he gets to see [ἰδεῖν] the beautiful itself, pure, clean [καθαρόν], unmixed, and not infected with human flesh, colors, or a lot of other mortal foolishness, and can behold [κατιδεῖν] [i.e., not merely *glimpse*] the divine beautiful itself as a single look?'" (*Symp.* 211e). It is important to note that, in this passage, Diotima speaks of *seeing* the beautiful, but now conspicuously omits the word ἐξαίφνης ("momentarily"). Now it is a matter not of a momentary glimpse—so momentary that it would not even occur in time—but rather of a *seeing*, a *beholding* (κατεῖδον), to which the beautiful would be present. She also says that such a person beholds the beautiful "pure" and "clean." "Clean" translates καθαρόν, which can also mean "perfect" or "complete." Thus, the one now said to behold the beautiful does so perfectly, completely, and not just momentarily, as in a brief glance. Moreover, in the final part of the sentence quoted above, Diotima uses the word κατιδεῖν. This word can mean, simply, "to behold"; however, more literally it means "to look down" upon something, as from above. Diotima's use of the word suggests playfully, even facetiously, that such a person who beholds the beautiful even soars *above* it and looks down upon it. Therefore, as she now describes it, the ascent would culminate in a beholding of the beautiful itself—that is, in a vision of the pure, complete beautiful itself, totally absolved from all connection with all that pertains to mortality: a vision of the beautiful that would be set utterly above the realm of human flesh and human mortality.

Diotima continues with two further sentences about this vision. But, like the sentence we just examined, both of these sentences are *questions*, not assertions. Diotima first asks: Do you suppose (οἴομαι) "that life would prove to be a sorry sort of thing when a human being gazes in the direction of the beautiful and beholds it [. . .] and is together with it [συνόντος αὐτῷ]" (*Symp.* 212a)? Then, she asks, "Or don't you consider that only here [ἐνταῦθα], in seeing in the way the beautiful is seeable, will he get to engender not phantom images of virtue— because he does not lay hold of a phantom—but true, because he lays hold of the true; and that once he has given birth to and cherished true virtue, it lies within him to become dear to god [θεοφιλεῖ] and, if it is possible for any human being, to become immortal as well?" (*Symp.* 212a).

And yet—this *place*, this *here* (ἐνταῦθα), where the mortal is together with the beautiful itself and so has it present before his vision, and where he becomes the beloved of god (i.e., where his erotic engagement is with a god) and becomes virtually immortal—this place is *not* the place of mortals. It is a place that exceeds the μοῖρα of humans—and the ascent to it, which Diotima marks finally with three questions marks, is excessive: it is forgetful of our mortal nature.

5. Alcibiades (212b–223d)

According to Aristodemus's report (as narrated by Apollodorus), when Socrates had finished narrating Diotima's speech and had offered it up to Phaedrus, Aristophanes tried to say something in response to Socrates's having mentioned his speech. However, before he could do so, there was an interruption—namely, a loud hammering on the courtyard door, along with the sound of the flute girl. Just then, they heard the voice of Alcibiades in the courtyard, who was excessively drunk and was shouting loudly, asking about the whereabouts of Agathon. Then he was led in by his attendants, one of whom was the flute girl, at which point he was thickly crowned with ivy and violets and had bands of ribbon on his head, such as were customarily worn as a token of victory (as in the drama contest that Agathon had won). He then announced that he had come to crown Agathon with this wreath.

The arrival of Alcibiades is, dramatically speaking, the most significant moment in the *Symposium*. At the end of Diotima's speech, the erotic philosopher has ascended up to the heights where he would be engaged with the gods and has become virtually immortal, as he came to achieve an unbroken vision of the pure beautiful itself. Then, suddenly, there is the immediate interruption of such a vision and a concomitant descent to the level of loud commotion, the flute girl, and the drunken Alcibiades.

In this register, one recalls that the party began with the decision not to indulge in heavy drinking, a decision that entailed the dismissal of the flute girl (*Symp.* 176e). These provisions amounted to a banishing of Dionysus and of the ambivalence represented by him as god of wine—that is, the ambivalence of joy and ecstasy coupled with wild frenzy and disorder. With such a banishing, the drinking party was recast in the direction (or the image) of Apollo.[1]

Apollo's epithet "Phoebus" linked him to light and sun, and hence to *truth*. (It is thus significant that Diotima comes to speak of truth at the culminating point in her speech (*Symp.* 212a).) Apollo was also associated with *order*—and, except for the interruption caused by Aristophanes's hiccups, the speeches at the party have proceeded in a prescribed order, watched over by the father of the λόγος, Phaedrus.[2] But now, disorder has erupted, and the wild sound of the

---

1. One recalls, too, that the entire account is being narrated by Apollodorus, "Apollo's gift," as he and Glaucon are going up to the city.
2. Apollo, father of Asclepius, was also associated with medicine, and, indeed, it has turned out that eros seems virtually capable of healing the malady of all maladies—namely, mortality.

flute is heard. There in the doorway stands Alcibiades, very drunk and wearing a wreath of ivy and violets—just like Dionysus, supported by his attending satyrs and sileni. Indeed, at this dramatic moment, Alcibiades is the very embodiment of Dionysus, and his arrival at Agathon's house is equivalent to Dionysus's return from banishment, like the inevitable return of the repressed.

It is crucially important to attend both to the speech and also to the deeds that occur once Alcibiades enters and takes a place among those present at the party. Even before he enters, Alcibiades/Dionysus lays claim to the *truth*: "Will you laugh at me because I am drunk? But all the same, even if you do laugh, I know well that I am telling the truth [ὅτι ἀληθῆ λέγω]" (*Symp.* 213a). His rhetoric here draws implicitly on the proverbial saying οἶνος καὶ ἀλήθεια, "wine and truth" (to which he will soon refer explicitly [*Symp.* 217e]). But, most importantly, this claim to tell the truth is, in effect—without his having heard Socrates's narration—a challenge to the τέλος of Diotima's speech, to her claim (or, rather, her question) about laying hold of the true: namely, that it is accomplished by one who ascends to the pure vision of beauty itself.

When Alcibiades first entered, he did not see Socrates, although Socrates had made room for him (παραχωρῆσαι) so that he could sit between him and Agathon. The word παραχωρῆσαι is related to the word χώρα, and means to move aside so as to give place, and thereby to open a space (χώρα). This simple deed of making room for Alcibiades enacts an opening of a space for Dionysus within, or beside, the Apollonian, a space where the negativity, the limits, and the μοῖρα of mortal life can be recalled and allowed to return.

When Alcibiades sees Socrates, he leaps up and exclaims "Heracles!" Just a bit later, he explains the remark: Socrates "conquers all human beings in speeches" (*Symp.* 213e), just as the hero Heracles conquers all human beings—and not *only* human beings—in combat. In light of Alcibiades's remark and his elucidation of it, one recalls that it was Heracles who went down to Hades to bring Alcestis back to life. One might ask: Does Socrates, despite the utterly ascensional character of Diotima's speech, also have the capacity *to go down, to descend* among the shades, the *images*?

At this point, Alcibiades displays (or at least feigns) jealously, in the face of which Socrates admits his love for Alcibiades, insisting also that it is a troublesome love. Alcibiades takes some of the ribbons he has brought with him and crowns Socrates, just as he had also crowned Agathon. Here it is important to recall what Agathon said to Socrates back near the very beginning of the text, just after Socrates arrived at his house: "You are outrageous [ὑβριστής], Socrates," Agathon said. "A little later you and I will go to court about our wisdom, with Dionysus as judge" (*Symp.* 175e). It is now later, and Dionysus has indeed arrived.[3]

---

3. One should recall what was said in previous chapters about Alcibiades. (See part 1, chap. 1.) At the time of the drinking party (416 BCE), Alcibiades was at the height of his fame and power. He

As would be expected of this surrogate Dionysus, Alcibiades orders everyone to imbibe, appointing himself as leader of the drinking. He asks Agathon to have someone fetch him a large drinking cup. But just then, he spies a wine cooler (with a capacity of eight κοτύλαι at a half-pint each—thus, a total of four pints), and so he just has the slave boy bring it to him. Alcibiades proceeds to drink it down, and then ask that it be filled for Socrates, observing that no matter how much wine Socrates drinks, he can never get drunk. His remark suggests that Socrates is attracted or drawn to the Dionysian (just as he is attracted to Alcibiades), that he is drawn back from the excess (or the purity) of the Apollonian, *but* that he has a certain immunity to the negative side of the Dionysian.

Observing that they are all sober, Alcibiades orders them to drink and sets about doing so himself. But Eryximachus objects to their merely drinking, and proposes that, since the others have already spoken, Alcibiades should now speak in praise of Socrates. Alcibiades agrees, and then for the second time since his arrival, he lays claim to the truth: "I shall tell the truth" (*Symp.* 214e). He then says that he intends to tell of Socrates's strangeness (ἀτοπίαν), and even instructs Socrates to interrupt him if he says anything untrue. Remarkably, Socrates will *not* interrupt Alcibiades a single time during the course of his speech; and when responding to Alcibiades after the conclusion of his speech, Socrates does not say that anything in it is untrue. Rather, he comments only on *why* (that is, with what motives) Alcibiades has given this speech, and on the *way* Alcibiades has concealed his intention. Thus, looking ahead, it would seem that Socrates regards what Alcibiades says about him as true.

Alcibiades proposes to praise Socrates through images (εἰκών), adding that "the image will be for the sake of the truth" (*Symp.* 215a). What then follows—almost to the end of the text—is a very remarkable series of images of Socrates.

Alcibiades's Speech (215a–222b)

Alcibiades immediately launches into his speech, during which he presents five images of Socrates. Because the images are presented in praise of Socrates, they

---

came, on both sides, from families that were among the richest and most powerful in Athens. He was relatively young (thirty-five), quite handsome, and deeply involved in Athenian politics, especially in the affairs of the Peloponnesian War. In the same year as the drinking party, he instigated the brutal Athenian attack on the island of Melos. At this time, plans were also underway for the invasion of Sicily, which he (together with Nicias) would lead the following year (415 BCE). (This huge military expedition proved to be utterly disastrous for Athens.) Just before the fleet sailed, there was the mutilation of the herms and profanation of the Mysteries. Alcibiades was thought, probably correctly, to be involved in both. When he was recalled to Athens to stand trial, he escaped to Sparta and betrayed Athens. It is important to observe that Socrates's relation to, and influence on, Alcibiades was what most of all was behind the charge brought against him at his trial: namely, the charge of corrupting young men. Athenians saw Alcibiades as a brilliant, prominent young man who had shown great promise of becoming a leader of his city, but who had been corrupted by the influence of Socrates.

are images in and through which the virtues or excellences (ἀρετή) of Socrates are displayed and made manifest. However, they are also images of Socrates as *erotic*, either explicitly so, or implicitly by virtue of the highly erotic context. Hence, through these images, eros itself will also be presented in the form (or the guise) it takes in the erotic Socrates. Thus, Alcibiades's praise of Socrates will turn out also to praise eros, and in this respect it will turn out to be like all of the preceding speeches.

Moreover, these five images are, as Alcibiades has said, for the sake of the truth. This means that they will present Socrates as he truly is—that is, as he shows himself, as he is manifest, when he is unconcealedly present. And yet, it will turn out that Socrates does *not* simply show himself, is not simply manifest, in complete unconcealment, but rather harbors something veiled within himself, keeping it so concealed that perhaps even his beloved Alcibiades can get only a glimpse of it. Thus, the truth of Socrates will turn out to be something other than pure, unconcealed presence.

First Image

Alcibiades begins by comparing Socrates to the sileni. This refers to two different mythical creatures, both of whom were ugly and animal-like in their features. Silenus was a jovial fat old man with horse ears who was a companion of Dionysus's and who helped him make—and drink—wine. Because he was frequently too drunk to walk, Silenus typically rode on a donkey; and it was rumored that, if he were to be caught, he would reveal his wisdom to whoever had caught him. The seleni, for their part, were mythical creatures who were part man and part horse. They walked on two legs but had horses' hooves instead of feet, as well as horses' tails and ears. On sixth-century vases, the sileni are shown pursuing nymphs through the woods.

Alcibiades connects these old mythical figures to the present—in fact, to the *double* present (i.e., that of the drinking party and of Apollodorus's narration)—in referring not to the seleni themselves, but rather to the sculpted images of them found in the shops of herm sculptures. The reference to herms will no doubt, years later when Apollodorus narrates the story, call up memory of Alcibiades's role in the mutilation of the herms, and the consequences thereof. Alcibiades says also that these figures are carrying flutes (αὐλός) with them, thereby further emphasizing their relation to Dionysus. Most importantly, Alcibiades says that, if these statues are opened up, they prove to have images of gods within them.

This image is (an image) of an image (namely, the sculpted figures), which contains within it images (of gods): a nest of images, then. Moreover, it is an image that links Socrates to Dionysus. Whatever virtues Socrates will be shown to have, imaged by the images of gods within, they will be shaped by the connection to Dionysus. This connection will be enacted dramatically—indeed, the enactment is already underway—in the concrete relation of Socrates to Alcibiades and to the progressively more Dionysian scene that the drinking party becomes.

This connection to the Dionysian indicates that the truth of eros, as presented in praise of Socrates—indeed, as embodied in Socrates—is quite different from the austere Apollonian eros presented, but left in question, at the end of Diotima's speech. Whereas the Apollonian eros would elevate the lover beyond mortal flesh, up into company with the gods, Socratic eros retains its connection to the shaggy, lustful, partly animal forms represented by Silenus and the sileni.

Second Image

Alcibiades compares Socrates to the satyr Marsyas. Satyrs were grotesque creatures, mainly of human form but with some bestial parts, usually the legs of a goat. They were attendants of Dionysus who, as such, were associated with the fertility of wild nature and were represented as lustful and as fond of revelry.[4] Marsyas was a satyr who played the flute (αὐλός) so enchantingly that he dared to challenge Apollo to a musical contest—a competition that Apollo, being a god, of course won (by playing his lyre). After his victory, Apollo punished Marsyas for challenging him by flaying him alive. Alcibiades draws the comparison—or, rather, one aspect of it—in the following way: "Now, that you are like them [the sileni and Marsyas] at least in looks [εἶδος], Socrates, surely not even you would dispute" (*Symp.* 215b). The reference is, of course, to Socrates's ugliness, shared with these hideous creatures. However, the reference is also perhaps to a certain trace of their animal-like features, a certain connection to nature, that remains operative within Socrates.

According to Alcibiades, Socrates also resembles Marsyas in another respect. Alcibiades refers to the flute songs of Olympus, which (he says) were taught to Olympus by Marsyas and which, when heard, induced a state of possession. Olympus was associated in legend with Marsyas, but he was in fact a celebrated musician from around 700 BCE who was credited with having brought the flute, and thus flute music, to Greece, and also with having invented a system of harmony.[5]

Alcibiades then draws the further comparison: "And you differ from him [Marsyas/Olympus] only in that you do the same thing with bare speeches [λόγοις] without instruments" (*Symp.* 215c). Alcibiades says that when he hears Socrates speak, he is thunderstruck and possessed, and that his heart jumps far more than the Corybantes.[6] Alcibiades also says that Socrates's words are capable of making

---

4. They were not always distinguished from sileni, and sometimes Silenus was considered a satyr.

5. [Editor's Note: See Plutarch, *De Musica*, 11.]

6. Corybantes were devotees of Cybele, a Phrygian goddess. They worshiped her with cries and shouts, and clashing cymbals and drums.

even him (of all people) feel shame. This is presumably why Alcibiades also charges Socrates with being hubristic, which in this context means "insulting," "insolent," and also "overbearing"—perhaps even a bit "untamed." This is the same charge that Agathon leveled against Socrates at the beginning of the party (*Symp.* 175e). At that point, Agathon said that they would later go to court with Dionysus as judge. Now that Dionysus has arrived (in the guise of Alcibiades), this has indeed happened—and Alcibiades/Dionysus has upheld Agathon's accusation.

Three brief points regarding this image should be noted. First, this image, along with the first, portrays Socrates as ugly on the outside but bounteous in what he harbors within himself and in what he can bring to birth from within. What he brings to birth are beautiful (and powerful) speeches. What he harbors within are like images of gods. Second, following the comparison with Marsyas, Alcibiades returns to the figure of the sileni, saying that, though Socrates wraps himself in the guise of ignorance (i.e., of knowing nothing), when he is opened up (like the selenic figures) he proves to be full of *moderation* (σωφροσύνη). This image of Silenus, as revealing his wisdom when captured, suggests that Socrates also harbors within himself a certain Dionysian *wisdom*. Third, Marsyas's challenging of Apollo could be taken allegorically as representing the venture of the erotic mortal (at the end of Diotima's speech) to ascend to the heights of the gods. As Marsyas was defeated and punished, so the erotic mortal is fated to fall from the heights—that is, to suffer a κατάβασις.

Third Image

The third image is conveyed by the account Alcibiades gives of the erotic affair between himself and Socrates. Having seen—or perhaps only *glimpsed*—something of the images within Socrates, Alcibiades decided that, by gratifying Socrates, he could perhaps come to hear all of what Socrates knew. To this end, he sent the attendant away so as to be alone with Socrates. At this point, Alcibiades momentarily interrupts the narrative in order to say, "For the whole truth must be told to you, but pay attention, and if I lie, Socrates, try to refute me" (*Symp.* 217b). But, remarkably, Socrates remains silent.

Alcibiades continues the narration, recounting that he was alone with Socrates and conversed with him, but that, at the end of the day, Socrates simply took his leave. Then Alcibiades got Socrates to join him in stripping down and wrestling, but still made no headway. Then he had Socrates join him at supper "simply as a lover plots against a beloved" (*Symp.* 217c); but, after dinner, Socrates simply went away. Then, the next time they met, Alcibiades kept on conversing far into the night and persuaded Socrates to stay.

Again—though this time less abruptly—Alcibiades interrupts his narrative, saying that he would not go on were it not that "wine—with boys and without boys—is truthful," and that it would be unjust to keep hidden Socrates's "magnificent overweening deed [ἔργον ὑπερήφανον]" (*Symp.* 217e).[7] Then, speaking of what it's like to be bitten by Socrates's philosophical speeches (as though by a viper), he addresses all of those present, calling them by pluralized forms of their names: "You all have shared in the philosophic madness [τῆς φιλοσόφου μανίας] and Bacchic frenzy [i.e., Dionysian revelry]" (*Symp.* 218b). Then, finally, he goes on to finish the account, telling of how he slept with Socrates without anything more having happened than if he had slept with his own father or brother. In the very midst of this, he inserts, "And not even in this, Socrates, will you say that I lie" (*Symp.* 219c). Here, as before, Socrates remains silent.

The image of Socrates that is framed by this narrative presents him in a way similar to the first two images, but now more specifically geared toward the individual Socrates and toward his erotic character. His moderation is displayed in the fact that, even though (as Alcibiades says) Socrates is inclined toward (or affected by: διάκειμαι) the beauties and stays around them, he does not yield to Alcibiades's enticements. Furthermore, Alcibiades attests to the wisdom that lies within Socrates, beneath his guise of ignorance. Alcibiades takes all those present to have experienced the power of the philosophical λόγοι to which Socrates gives birth, their power to induce philosophical madness and Bacchic frenzy—in other words, their Dionysian power.

Fourth Image

Before Alcibiades presents the fourth image, he speaks directly of Socrates's virtues. He maintains that he admires Socrates's moderation and courage, as well as his nature (φύσις)—or, perhaps, the nature within Socrates. He also mentions Socrates's prudence (φρόνησις) and his endurance (καρτερία), and that he was more invulnerable to money than Ajax was to iron (σίδηρος).[8] Then, Alcibiades presents the narrative in which the image of Socrates is set out. Alcibiades tells of the time when he and Socrates were together in the army in Potidaea.[9] Alcibiades speaks of how Socrates endured the hardships of the campaign, and how even in harsh winter he wore his normal garments and went without shoes. He speaks also of the time that Socrates saved him in combat.

---

7. The word ὑπερήφανος, in a negative sense, means "overweening" or "arrogant." In a positive sense, it can mean "magnificent" or "noble."
8. Ajax, the great Greek warrior, was invulnerable primarily because of his shield, which in Sophocles's *Ajax* is described as "this sevenfold, oxhide, thick unbreakable shield" (Soph., *Ajax*, 575).
9. As mentioned previously, this was one of the first trouble spots that led to the Peloponnesian War. Potidaea had belonged to the Athenian alliance, but in 432 BCE, after difficulties with the Athenians went unresolved, Potidaea, assisted by two thousand soldiers from the Spartan alliance, revolted. Nevertheless, Athens defeated the force and lay siege to Potidaea.

In this image of Socrates in the military campaign, then, it is especially the virtues of courage and endurance that are displayed. Indeed, his endurance—his steadfastness, his being gathered to himself—is displayed not only by these various aforementioned deeds, but also by the incident in which, having received a thought, Socrates stood considering it from one dawn to the next—as he did also, for a shorter time, on the way to Agathon's house for the evening's festivities.

Fifth Image

Alcibiades adds yet another image of Socrates on a military campaign. In this case, it is the battle of Delium in 424 BCE, when the Athenians were soundly defeated by the Thebans. The image is of Socrates as the Athenian army was retreating in flight. Alcibiades borrows a phrase from Aristophanes's *Clouds* to describe Socrates's demeanor during the retreat: "stalking like a pelican, his eyes darting from side to side" (*Cl.* 362). Here it is Socrates's shrewdness (or good sense: ἔμφρων), as well as his courage and endurance, that are displayed.

* * *

When Alcibiades finishes his speech, there is laughter, owing to the manner in which he seems to be still so erotically attached to Socrates. There then commences a lovers' quarrel between Alcibiades, Socrates, and Agathon that is enacted in the form of a dispute over who is to sit next to whom. Agathon suspects that Alcibiades lay down between him and Socrates in order to keep them apart from one another:

Agathon – Alcibiades – Socrates

Socrates, however, tells Agathon to come lie beside him, which would result in the following configuration:

Alcibiades – Socrates – Agathon

In the face of this request, Alcibiades insists that Agathon lie between him and Socrates:

Alcibiades – Agathon – Socrates

To this, Socrates says, "No, since you [Alcibiades] praised me, I must praise the one to my right" (*Symp.* 222e), thus implying that Agathon should come lie beside him. Being unable to resist the thought of Socrates praising him, Agathon begins to move toward Socrates in order to lie beside him. However, just as he is getting up, a large crowd of revelers enters the room, and everybody is compelled to drink large quantities of wine. Utter commotion and disorder thus ensue.

As Aristodemus reports it, he himself fell asleep around this time. When he stirred, only three were still awake: Agathon, Aristophanes, and Socrates. Socrates was compelling them to agree "that the same man should know how to make comedy and tragedy, [and] that he who is by art [τέχνῃ] a tragic poet is also a comic poet" (*Symp.* 223d). The premises from which this conclusion follows were not remembered by Aristodemus, and indeed they need not have been, for what Socrates is saying was demonstrated (i.e., *enacted*) in the speeches by the two poets—namely, by the tragic comedy of Aristophanes and the comic tragedy of Agathon. Once he had put the two poets to bed, Socrates left, followed by trusty Aristodemus.

In the end, Socrates had endured the collapse—that is, the *descent*—of the party into a Bacchanalia. And though he silently affirmed the images Alcibiades presented of him, images that link him to the Dionysian, he also displayed virtues (such as moderation and endurance) that provide him with resistance to the destructive side of the Dionysian. This resistance is indicated by the fact that no matter how much wine Socrates drinks, he does not get drunk.

After Socrates left Agathon's, he went to the Lyceum, a garden with covered walkways next to the temple of Apollo Lyceus (from which it gets its name). Here he passed his day in his usual manner: philosophizing. Having endured the Dionysian—retaining, like the sileni and satyrs, this bond to it—Socrates resumed philosophizing at a place not within, *but next to*, the temple of Apollo.

PART II.
PLATO'S *STATESMAN*

Lecture course presented at Boston College, Chestnut Hill, Massachusetts
Fall 2014

1. Introduction

Among the Platonic dialogues, there are only three that have titles referring to the political realm: the *Statesman*, the *Republic*, and the *Laws*. These three dialogues constitute the primary locus of Plato's political thought, though it is of course not solely in them that Plato's political thought is enacted. "Political thought" here means *philosophical* thought about the political realm. Such thought cannot be separated from philosophical thought *as such*—that is, from philosophical thought about being, about the nature of humans, about nature as such, etc. Even in these "political" dialogues, there is much that does not bear directly on the political realm;[1] moreover, there is much in other dialogues that bears directly or indirectly on the political thought enacted in these three dialogues.

In what follows, we will focus primarily on the *Statesman*.[2] On the one hand, it is the dialogue that, perhaps with the exception of the *Laws*, is most persistently oriented toward the political realm. On the other hand, it is informed by other modes of thought by virtue of its explicit connection to certain other dialogues. We will at times need to consider these other dialogues, including the *Republic* and the *Laws*, as they bear upon the *Statesman* and serve to supplement our understanding of it.

The title "Statesman" translates the Greek word πολιτικός. Whether the word "statesman" is a good translation of the word πολιτικός—that is, whether it says adequately what is said in this Greek word—is very much open to question. The word πολιτικός derives from the word πόλις, and is primarily an adjective that designates the character of belonging to a πόλις or to its administration. On this basis, it is then used as a noun to designate one who belongs in the most decisive way to the πόλις, one who administers or governs the πόλις—in other words, what we today would call, in its positive aspect, a "statesman" or, with pejorative connotations, a "politician." Clearly, then, whatever πολιτικός means depends upon what the Greeks understood by the word πόλις.

What, then, is a πόλις? One might translate this word as "state"—and yet, among the ancient Greeks, in so-called Greek "political life," there is nothing corresponding to the state in the modern sense. (Ancient Athens was not a state

---

1. Consider, for example, the middle books of the *Republic*.
2. The translation consulted and sometimes quoted is Benardete (1986). However, many translated passages are the author's own. [Editor's Note: For an additional analysis of the *Statesman*, see Sallis (2017), 1–14.]

in the sense that, say, modern France is a state.) One might try to compensate for this difference by translating πόλις as "city" or "city-state," but this, too, is inadequate, for the πόλις of Athens was not a city in the way that Paris or New York are cities. What is it, then, that is said in this *fateful* word πόλις? It is fateful in that it comes to name, for all of subsequent Western thought, what is accordingly called "politics" and the "political," and in so doing comes to name the very phenomenon itself in all of its complexity. As soon as one speaks of "politics" and "the political," one has already appropriated the word πόλις and its legacy: that is, one has already let what one understands as the political be determined by what is said in and through this fateful word.

But what, precisely, is said in this word? What did the Greeks hear in it? How is it that a certain way in which humans can be together is named by this word? And what experience of human community is expressed by it? These questions cannot be immediately and directly answered, nor is it clear that they can be fully answered at all. It is sufficient here to mention only one dimension that belongs essentially to the πόλις and distinguishes it from the cities and states of the modern age: namely, the manner in which the πόλις is not solely or simply a *human* community. Rather, the πόλις is a community to which the gods, in their own way, also belong. For example, Athens was regarded as having been founded by the goddess Athena, and in the Parthenon she was given a place where she could be present in the πόλις. The same was true in Ephesus, which was centered around the temple of Artemis.[3] The Greek temple, unlike the churches in Christianity, was not really a place for humans, especially for those other than the priests. Rather, it was a place where the god (or goddess) could have a place in, yet apart from, the πόλις—for example, elevated above it, as with the Acropolis. It is instructive in this regard to consider the contrast between a Greek temple and a Gothic cathedral. A Gothic cathedral has an upward directionality, both inside and especially outside: it points beyond the πόλις to something that is utterly distinct—namely, the figure of the divine (though in the third person, that is, as the Holy Spirit, it can descend).[4] A Greek temple does not have such upward directionality at all. It is a closed space consisting of inner walls inside of columns. The sculpted figure of the goddess (e.g., Athena) is not just a representation, but rather makes visible the presence of the goddess within the temple. In this way, gods, too, are *in* the πόλις: they belong to it, as do human beings. And yet, because the gods belong to the πόλις differently than human beings do, even the word "community" (κοινωνία) is not really an adequate translation of the word πόλις.

---

3. It was here that Heraclitus came to dedicate his book *On Nature* to the goddess. See Diogenes Laertius, *Lives of Eminent Philosophers*, Book IX, chap. 1.

4. See Sallis (1994), especially chap. 3.

Insofar as the full sense of the word πόλις remains undetermined, so does the full sense of the word πολιτικός, as the latter derives its essential character from the former. The translation of πολιτικός as "statesman," though employed in what follows, is used tentatively, and in a somewhat makeshift way. As it turns out, much of the *Statesman* is oriented precisely toward determining the sense of the πολιτικός, and indeed even toward determining how such determination of the πολιτικός must proceed.

One other point regarding the title must be mentioned. The word πολιτικός is related to πολιτεία, which means the constitution of a πόλις, in the sense of its makeup, its composition, and its structure. Only secondarily does the word πολιτεία refer to a written document that codifies the constitution of a πόλις. The word πολιτεία was translated by Cicero as *res publica*, from which we derive our English word "republic." It is also the Greek title of the Platonic dialogue that we conventionally (though somewhat misleadingly) refer to as the *Republic*.[5] Thus, the mere titles πολιτικός (*Statesman*) and πολιτεία (*Republic*) already suggest a deep affinity between the two dialogues.

We turn now to the author of this dialogue that we tentatively, and in a makeshift way, refer to as "the *Statesman*." To say the least, Plato is an unusual kind of author. There is something odd about his authorship, especially in comparison with other authors in the history of philosophy. In the *Statesman*—as, indeed, in all of the dialogues attributed to Plato—Plato never speaks in his own name. The dialogues are akin to what the Greeks called ὁ μῖμος (mimes), which were dramatic pieces set in the context of everyday life (in contrast to the tragedies). Since they are dramas, what is said is always attributed to someone. In the case of the *Statesman*, what is said is attributed to Socrates, Theodorus, the Eleatic Stranger, etc. However, there are no speeches attributed to Plato himself: in this dialogue, as in all of the dialogues, Plato never says a word. Of course, many people are prone to using the phrase "Plato says . . ."; however, as soon as one says this, one has become careless and has failed to attend to the character of the Platonic dialogues. Because the author Plato attributes no speeches to himself, one could say that he maintains a certain *reserve* of the writer, a reserve that imitates the reserve belonging to writing as such—namely, the manner in which, through the very act of writing, the author becomes decisively absent. In this way, one could say that Plato practices a kind of *graphic ventriloquy* in his texts.

How, then, are the Platonic dialogues to be read?[6] Needless to say, one cannot, prior to reading the dialogues, set down a method that would prescribe how to read them. Rather, one learns to read the dialogues primarily by reading them. Still, it is important to have some provisional hermeneutical orientation, if only

---

5. [Editor's Note: See Sallis (1975), 312 ff.]
6. [Editor's Note: See Sallis (1975), 1–5.]

in order to avoid closing off certain aspects or dimensions of the dialogues. Plato's dialogues are perhaps the most carefully composed and finely crafted texts that Western philosophy has produced. In any given dialogue, every word counts and must be weighed carefully and as it functions within the dialogue as a whole. Often, what seem to be the most casual remarks can turn out to have enormous significance. As just one example of this, consider the very first words of the *Republic*: "I went down yesterday to Piraeus . . ." (*Rep.* 327a).[7] Each part of this seemingly simple beginning is important, and bears upon the dialogue as a whole. The very first word is crucial in this regard: "I went down [κατέβην]." *Going down* (i.e., descending) is what the souls of the dead do: they descend down to Hades. (This word κατέβην is exactly the same word that is used in Homer's *Odyssey* when Odysseus tells Penelope of the day when "I went down [κατέβην] to Hades to inquire about the return of myself and my friends" [*Od.* xxiii, 250].) It turns out that the *Republic* has much to do with going down (as into a cave) and with going up (as in ascending into the light and turning one's vision upward and toward the source).[8] The *Republic* ends with the story of Er's descent into the underworld and his return to the world of the living—that is, it ends with the exhortation to keep to the upward way.[9] The word "yesterday" (χθές) in the opening line is also significant, as it indicates that Socrates (as the narrator) is telling about events in which he took part on the previous day and from which he can only have just returned. The mentioning of Piraeus, too, bears special meaning. Piraeus was the principal harbor of Athens, connected to the city by the Long Walls: as such, it was both in and outside of Athens proper. It was a place where native Athenians mingled with foreignness and came into contact with strange sights and strange ideas. (Socrates goes on to say that he wanted to see a festival in honor of a somewhat foreign goddess, Bendis, a goddess of the underworld). This example makes it clear that, when one reads Plato, one must do so slowly and carefully, so as to weigh the significance of every word.

In reading the dialogues, one must also be attentive to the fact that they have a multitextured character, insofar as one finds in the dialogues various kinds of speeches and discourses, a variety and diversity that belongs to their very character as texts, to their very textuality. In particular, the dialogues do not consist solely of assertoric and interrogative discourses, let alone *arguments*, the latter of which is a post-Platonic invention that is rarely appropriate for characterizing what happens in a dialogue.[10] Beyond these forms of discourse, and perhaps

---

7. [Editor's Note: For an extensive treatment of Plato's *Republic*, see Sallis (1975), chap. 5.]

8. [Editor's Note: See *Republic*, Books VI and VII.]

9. [Editor's Note: See *Republic*, 614b ff.]

10. One should avoid projecting later concepts back upon earlier texts that provided the very basis for logic, but do not themselves yet move within the sphere of logic (as formulated by Aristotle). [Editor's Note: See Sallis (2012), 26 ff.]

most strikingly, many dialogues contain stories of the sort that one would readily call *mythical*.[11] Indeed, such a mythical story forms a prominent part of the *Statesman*. Following the initial attempt to arrive at a definition of the statesman, the Stranger proposes that they must begin again, that they must break off their previous attempt and proceed from a different beginning. He says explicitly that what they have to insert at this point in the discussion is a "great myth" (μεγάλος μῦθος) (*Stat.* 268d).[12] He also says that what they will thus be doing will be like *play* (παιδιά). This points to another feature that is often found in Platonic dialogues: namely, their *playfulness*, as well as their character as plays, as dramas.[13]

Finally, a word should be said regarding the dramatic form of the dialogues. This is not a form that just happens to be imposed on a philosophical content, nor a form that is merely contingent and from which the content could simply be extracted. Rather, the form and the content belong together essentially. As Schleiermacher puts it, in the Platonic dialogues, "form and content are inseparable and every sentence is to be rightly understood only in its place and in the connections and delimitations that Plato has assigned to it" (Schleiermacher 1836, 71). This entails that one must take into account not only *what* is said in the dialogues, but also *how* it is said (i.e., in what kind of speech), as well as *by whom* and at what *place* and *time*. In a dialogue, all of these various moments have an appropriateness to one another and to the whole of the dialogue.

* * *

Following these general considerations, we turn now to the opening line of the *Statesman*, which serves to situate the *Statesman* within a broader context of Platonic dialogues. It is Socrates who is speaking: "I owe you a lot of gratitude, Theodorus, for my acquaintance with Theaetetus and with the Stranger as well" (*Stat.* 257a). This acquaintance, for which Socrates expresses his gratitude, was obtained in other conversations that occurred prior to the *Statesman*—in fact, in two conversations that are linked in dramatic time to the *Statesman*. As the introductory section of the *Statesman* continues, Socrates mentions that he has just now been listening to Theaetetus answering. This and other indications make it clear that the conversation of the *Statesman* is a direct continuation of that of the *Sophist*. The one with whom Theaetetus conversed in the *Sophist* was

---

11. The word μῦθος originally just meant "speech" in a broad sense, and was thus in no way opposed to λόγος, as comes to be the case later on. The word μῦθος was used especially for speech in which one told a tale or story; it later came to refer to a poetic or legendary story in particular, in distinction to a historical account (ἱστορία).

12. [Editor's Note: The Stranger's myth is discussed at length in part 2, chap. 5 of this volume.]

13. See, for example, the *Sixth Letter* (whose authenticity is disputed), where there is a reference to the "playfulness that is the sister of seriousness" (*Epist.* VI, 323d).

the Stranger, and so in that conversation, Socrates became acquainted with the Stranger, as well as with Theaetetus.

And yet, Socrates had already, though only the day before, become acquainted with Theaetetus. He mentions in the introductory section of the *Statesman* that he himself had a conversation "yesterday" with Theaetetus; and at the very beginning of the *Sophist*, Theodorus says, "According to our yesterday's agreement, Socrates, we have come" (*Soph.* 216a). That agreement is the one expressed at the very end of the *Theaetetus*: "But in the morning, Theodorus, let us meet here again" (*Theaet.* 210d). Thus, it is in the conversation in the *Theaetetus* that Socrates has the discussion with Theaetetus to which he refers at the beginning of the *Statesman*. There is therefore a sequence that takes place over two days, and it is this sequence to which the first line of the *Statesman* refers:

First day: *Theaetetus*
Second day: *Sophist, Statesman*

We will see soon enough that there is a linking together of these three dialogues not only dramatically, but also thematically (though their thematic connection is more complex and serves to raise several difficult, fundamental questions). In any case, these three dialogues are more explicitly linked than any others within the Platonic corpus; as a result, they are sometimes called "Plato's Trilogy."[14] Clearly, our inquiry into the *Statesman* will thus require some detours back through the *Theaetetus* and the *Sophist*, both of which precede it in dramatic time.[15] It is in the interconnection between the three dialogues that we will see how mathematical and ontological thought come into play in the political thought of the *Statesman*.

There are also other, less explicit dramatic links that nonetheless are highly significant for the *Statesman*. At the end of the *Theaetetus*, just before Socrates proposes that they meet again the following day, he says, "Now, however, I must go to the portico of the king to answer to the indictment that Meletus has drawn up against me" (*Theaet.* 210d).[16] The *Euthyphro* begins with Euthyphro asking Socrates, "What strange thing has happened, Socrates, that you have left your usual haunts in the Lyceum and are now spending your time at the portico of the King Archon?"

---

14. See Klein (1977).
15. [Editor's Note: For additional treatments of the *Theaetetus*, see Sallis (2015); see also Sallis (2005). For additional treatments of the *Sophist*, see Sallis (1975), chap. 6, and Sallis (2014).]
16. Athenian legal process required that a prosecutor first issue an indictment and that he and the defendant then appear before the appropriate magistrate for a hearing. Here the charge was read, and questions were put to the defendant by the magistrate; prosecutor and defendant could also question each other. When the hearing was over, a date for the trial would be set. Since Meletus's charge against Socrates was impiety, the hearing was before the King Archon (βασιλεύς), who dealt with all matters pertaining to religion.

(*Euthyph.* 2a). The conversation in the *Euthyphro* thus takes place as Socrates awaits the hearing, and so right after the *Theaetetus*:

$$\left.\begin{array}{l} \textit{Theaetetus} \\ \textit{Euthyphro} \end{array}\right\} 1^{st} \text{ day}$$

$$\left.\begin{array}{l} \textit{Sophist} \\ \textit{Statesman} \end{array}\right\} 2^{nd} \text{ day}$$

One finds another such connection in the *Cratylus*.[17] In the relevant passage, Socrates has set about testing the fitness of names by spinning out etymologies that are supposed to show that the names of things are fitting to those things. Specifically, he has just been testing the names of the gods, and in a very comical manner. What makes it especially comical is that such testing would require, and indeed presuppose, knowledge of the gods, whereas Socrates races on as if there were no such requirement.[18] On the other hand, such knowledge—specifically, knowledge of what is pleasing to the gods—is precisely what Euthyphro (foolishly) claims to have. Thus, the thematic connection is already established when Socrates, granting that his speech is "inspired," says to his interlocutor Hermogenes, "Yes, Hermogenes, and I am convinced that the inspiration came to me from Euthyphro the Prospaltian, for I was with him and listening to him a long time early this morning" (*Crat.* 396d). From this, it is clear that the conversation to which Socrates refers is that of the *Euthyphro*. Thus:

$$\left.\begin{array}{l} \textit{Theaetetus} \\ \textit{Euthyphro} \\ \textit{Cratylus} \end{array}\right\} 1^{st} \text{ day}$$

$$\left.\begin{array}{l} \textit{Sophist} \\ \textit{Statesman} \end{array}\right\} 2^{nd} \text{ day}$$

But then, a short time after the dramatic date of the *Theaetetus* and *Euthyphro* (when Socrates appeared before the King Archon), the trial of Socrates took place, as presented in the *Apology*. From this, one finds another, very different trilogy:

Apology – a short time later
Crito – twenty-eight or twenty-nine days later
Phaedo – thirty days after the *Apology*

---

17. [Editor's Note: For an extended treatment of the *Cratylus*, see Sallis (1975), chap. 6.]
18. As is discussed in part 2, chap. 3, Platonic comedy involves abstracting from something essential, a kind of forgetfulness of it. [Editor's Note: See also part 1, chap. 3 in this volume.]

From all of this, the significance is clear: the *Statesman* (and the dialogues most closely linked to it, the *Theaetetus* and the *Sophist*) belongs to the sequence of dialogues leading up to the trial and death of Socrates. Since it was the Athenian πόλις that condemned and finally executed Socrates, it is little wonder that this sequence of dialogues includes one devoted to the πολιτικός. As we inquire into the *Statesman*, we will do well to keep in mind that when this conversation takes place, Socrates has already had the hearing before the King Archon. It has thus already been decided that Socrates will be tried, and very probably the date of the trial has already been set.

* * *

As seen above, in the first sentence of the text Socrates expresses his indebtedness to Theodorus for his acquaintance with Theaetetus and the Stranger. Who are these characters with whom Socrates is interacting? In answering this question, we will need to circulate between the *Theaetetus*, the *Sophist*, and the *Statesman* for a moment, weaving a kind of web between them.

a) Theodorus

Theodorus (born around 460 BCE) is present throughout the entire conversation that begins in the *Theaetetus* and continues into the next day with the *Sophist* and the *Statesman*. In the third sentence of the *Statesman*, Socrates describes Theodorus as "the mightiest in calculation and geometry [περὶ λογισμοὺς καὶ τὰ γεωμετρικὰ κρατίστου]" (*Stat.* 257a). At the beginning of the main conversation in the *Theaetetus*, Socrates's first words are (as in the *Statesman*) addressed to Theodorus (*Theaet.* 143d). He there identifies Theodorus as being from Cyrene.[19]

Theodorus was originally a pupil of Protagoras's, and by 399 BCE, he was teaching in Athens. This is referred to in the *Theaetetus*, where Socrates is criticizing Protagoras's maxim that "man is measure of all things." Socrates shows that, if one grants the truth of this maxim, one can just as easily say that "pig is the measure of all things," or "dog-faced baboon" is such a measure. At this point, Theodorus jumps into the conversation, replacing Theaetetus in the conversation (as if to defend Protagoras), and after a bit more criticism remarks that Socrates is running down his friend too much (*Theaet.* 171c).

Theodorus eventually gave up philosophy for mathematics and related things. In the *Theaetetus*, Socrates says that Theodorus is an astronomer, a calculator,[20] a musician, and a highly educated man—literally, "a man with much παιδεία" (*Theaet.* 145a). (He is said to be especially adept with diagrams.) Just after that, Theaetetus

---

19. Cyrene was a prominent πόλις in Libya, and was a very prosperous Greek colony founded around 630 BCE that, during the mid-fifth century, introduced various democratic reforms.
20. I.e., one skilled in calculation (λογιστικός).

mentions that Theodorus had been showing him some things regarding roots and squares, and specifically regarding incommensurable roots (*Theaet.* 147d).[21]

b) Theaetetus

When Socrates speaks to Theodorus at the beginning of the conversation in the *Theaetetus*, he asks him about the young men of Athens who are pursuing geometry "or any other sort of philosophy" (*Theaet.* 143d). Socrates says he is eager to know which of them are outstanding and likely to gain a reputation. In response, Theodorus begins to speak of a young man who (he says) is Socrates's fellow citizen. Theodorus remarks that this young man is not beautiful (καλός), saying even that he looks like Socrates (with his snub nose and protruding eyes) (*Theaet.* 143e). Thus, this young man, whom Theodorus eventually identifies as Theaetetus, is a kind of *double* of Socrates: he looks like Socrates, resembling him in appearance. This double of Socrates refers a little later (*Theaet.* 147c–d) to another double of Socrates, a companion of his who is also named Socrates. This companion of Theaetetus's is called Socrates's ὁμώνυμος (*Theaet.* 147d), his homonymous double—that is, his double not in appearance, but rather in λόγος or ὄνομα. This other Socrates and Theaetetus had been talking about the problems of roots and squares to which Theodorus had introduced them.[22]

These two doubles of Socrates—that is, this double of doubles—are referred to in the introductory conversation in the *Statesman*: "And furthermore, Stranger, both have a kind of kinship with me from somewhere or other. One, you all say, appears similar to me in accordance with the nature [φύσις] of his face, and the other is called by the same name as me, and this name makes for a kind of family relation" (*Stat.* 257d). So, the two doubles, Theaetetus and young Socrates, are doubles in these two distinct respects: in nature (φύσις) as it shows itself, and in name (i.e., in the order of λόγος).

We return for the moment to Theodorus's introduction of Theaetetus in the *Theaetetus*. Regarding the young mathematician, Theodorus says that he has "never met a young man with a nature so wondrously fine [οὐδένα πω ᾐσθόμην οὕτω θαυμαστῶς εὖ πεφυκότα]" (*Theaet.* 144a). Thus, the first words of praise regarding Theaetetus invoke *wonder* (θαυμαστός): his nature is so fine as to be wondrous, to be something at which to wonder. This foreshadows the affiliation of Theaetetus

---

21. For example: a square containing three or five square feet is incommensurable with the unit—i.e., $\sqrt{3}$ and $\sqrt{5}$ are what we call "irrational numbers," and cannot be expressed as fractions (ratios).

22. Theaetetus is famous in the history of mathematics, and anticipated Euclid in various ways. He is known for having developed a theory of incommensurables, as well as for having discovered how to construct the five regular solids (i.e., the tetrahedron, the cube, the octahedron, the dodecahedron, and the icosahedron), to circumscribe spheres around them, and to determine the relation between spheres and solids.

with wonder that will culminate at the point where wonder is disclosed as the ἀρχή of philosophy (*Theaet.* 155d). Theodorus continues his praise, saying that Theaetetus is one who learns easily (εὐμαθής). Then Theodorus concludes with a "wonderful" remark, saying that this young man advances toward learning and investigation "like a stream [ῥεῦμα] of olive oil flowing without a sound, so that one wonders [θαυμάσαι] that he accomplishes all this at his age" (*Theaet.* 144b).

At this point, Theaetetus and several companions appear. Theodorus notes that they have been oiling themselves in the outer course and are now approaching. This suggests that the scene of the conversation is a gymnasium, where the young men have been exercising (see *Stat.* 257c). As they approach, Theodorus says regarding Theaetetus that "he is the one in the middle" (*Theaet.* 144b), thus implying that there are at least two more accompanying him. Presumably, one of these is (young) Socrates; the other goes unnamed and never speaks, and is never referred to except (indirectly) here. On the other hand, there could have been still more—perhaps even a whole crowd of vigorous, oily young men.

At the end of the *Theaetetus*, the participants agree to meet "here" (δεῦρο) again tomorrow. "Here" means, presumably, either at or next to the gymnasium, which is thus the site also of the *Sophist* and the *Statesman*. One might think that this is a curious site for the intense philosophical conversation that begins in the *Theaetetus* and continues to the end of the *Statesman*. After all, a gymnasium is a place for the care of the *body*, whereas one might think that philosophy has to do primarily with the care of the soul. And yet, even if it were possible for discussions of knowledge (*Theaetetus*) and of being and nonbeing (*Sophist*) to proceed without reference to the body, clearly this is not the case with the discussion of the political (*Statesman*). A primary function of the πόλις is to provide a site for the practice of the various crafts (τέχναι), and these have their purpose, above all, in supplying food, shelter, and clothing—that is, in addressing the needs of the body.

We have now obtained some indications regarding two of the principle characters of the trilogy: namely, Theodorus and Theaetetus. Both are present throughout all three conversations, and both speak extensively in the *Theaetetus*, where they respond to Socrates's questions. (Theodorus speaks in defense of Protagoras, though he says that he is "unused to conversation of this sort" [*Theaet.* 146b].) In the *Sophist* and the *Statesman*, Theodorus speaks only at the beginning, and thereafter becomes a silent auditor, as does (old) Socrates. In the *Sophist*, Theaetetus continues as respondent, responding to the Stranger (rather than to Socrates). In the *Statesman*, Theaetetus is replaced by (young) Socrates, who plays the role of the respondent to the Stranger. Regarding this (young) Socrates, we learn very little compared to Theaetetus. We know only that he is a young man, companion to Theaetetus, who has been at the gymnasium with him. We learn also that he has some expertise in mathematics, since, along with Theaetetus, he has been instructed by Theodorus regarding roots and squares.

c) The Stranger

The proper name of this character is never mentioned, but is withheld throughout the long conversations depicted in the *Sophist* and the *Statesman*. Rather than being called by a proper name, as are all of the other characters (even those who share a name—i.e., Socrates), he is referred to only by the general designation that Theodorus uses in introducing him at the very beginning of the *Sophist*: he is simply, throughout the entirety of both the *Sophist* and the *Statesman*, called "stranger" (ξένος).[23]

Despite going unnamed, the Stranger becomes the main speaker in the *Sophist* and the *Statesman*. If we consider these dialogues in relation to the *Theaetetus* (and most other dialogues), we can say that, in the *Sophist* and the *Statesman*, the Stranger replaces, and displaces, (old) Socrates. Indeed, in both dialogues, (old) Socrates is reduced to almost complete silence, for beyond the opening passages, he merely listens in silence as the Stranger instructs him and the others regarding the sophist and the statesman, setting out what each one is.

At the beginning of the *Sophist*, Theodorus says the following about the Stranger: "In accordance with yesterday's agreement [i.e., at the end of the *Theaetetus*], Socrates, we ourselves have come in due order; and we bring along this man, a sort of stranger, who by birth is from Elea, a comrade of the circle of Parmenides and Zeno, and a man very much a philosopher" (*Soph.* 216a). Hereby the Stranger is associated with Parmenides, and more generally with the Eleatic school. Especially significant for what follows is the fact that this school advocates the oneness of all things (i.e., one being).

(Old) Socrates's first real question in the *Sophist*, though addressed to Theodorus, is in fact directed at the Stranger. Socrates mentions three figures: the sophist, the statesman, and the philosopher. He then asks the following in reference to the Eleatics: "Were they accustomed to hold all these one or two, or, just as their names are three, to divide their genera into three as well and attach a name to each individually?" (*Soph.* 217a). Theodorus then urges the Stranger to speak, and the Stranger responds by saying that "in just this way, Theodorus [. . .] they believed them three. It's no small and easy work, however, to distinguish with clarity whatever they severally are" (*Soph.* 217b).[24] In the *Sophist*, they speak at length about the sophist; then, at the beginning of the *Statesman*, there is an explicit reference to the other two that are still to be determined (*Stat.* 257a). To

---

23. In Homer, ξένος means "the guest," in distinction to the host; then, by extension, it refers more generally to any stranger who, as such, is entitled to the rights of hospitality. The word ξένος is also used for a foreign friend (with whom one had a treaty) and even just for a foreigner as such (i.e., a βάρβαρος).

24. Note the implicit opposition to Parmenides here, who advocates the *one*, whereas the Stranger advocates for *three*, and even attributes this to the Eleatics.

Socrates's opening expression of gratitude, Theodorus replies, "But soon you'll owe triple this, Socrates, when they [i.e., Theaetetus and the Stranger] produce for you both the statesman and the philosopher" (*Stat.* 257a). In the *Statesman*, they go on to treat the statesman, and the dialogue concludes with a certain determination of the statesman.

At the beginning of the *Statesman*, the Stranger insists that they must continue until they have finished with all three, at which point (old) Socrates, referring to (young) Socrates, says to the Stranger, "Let him answer me at a later time, but now you" (*Stat.* 258a). These hints seem to suggest that there was to be a subsequent conversation in which the philosopher would be defined, just as the sophist was defined in the *Sophist* and the statesman in the *Statesman*. And yet, there is no sequel dialogue, no dialogue entitled the *Philosopher*, nor is there any mention of such a dialogue in any ancient source.

What is one to make of this? Did Plato simply fail to complete this series of dialogues? Did he plan to write, but never in fact write, a dialogue called the *Philosopher*, which surely would have been the most important of all? Or is the series complete as it stands? Does one indeed find somewhere the seemingly missing discourse on the philosopher? This question is not easy to decide, and is perhaps even, in the end, undecidable. But at least two hypotheses can be proposed. First, at the beginning of the *Sophist*, Socrates remarks that philosophers sometimes appear disguised as statesmen and sometimes as sophists (*Soph.* 216d). This can be taken to suggest that the philosopher comes to be determined somehow in the course of determining the sophist or the statesman. This would suggest further that, in the determination of the philosopher, the differentiation from the sophist and the statesman would be essential.

In any case, the philosopher does in fact turn up in place of the sophist in one of the divisions carried out in the first part of the *Sophist*. In these divisions, the Stranger begins with τέχνη and then divides this (into "productive" and "acquisitive") and then repeatedly redivides.[25] There are at least six such processes of division aimed at "capturing" the sophist. But the outcome of the sixth division—namely, "cross-questioning" (ἔλεγχος)—sounds more like a description of (old) Socrates: "They question a man about the things about which he thinks he is saying something when he is really saying nothing" (*Soph.* 230b). In this connection, the *Theaetetus* too could be seen to play a role, even granted that it alone does not suffice, for, indeed, right at the center of the *Theaetetus* (172c–177c), there is an extended discourse on the philosopher. This is the place where, among other things, (old) Socrates relates the famous story about Thales falling into a well because he was looking upward at the stars, and about how he was laughed at by a Thracian servant girl (*Theaet.* 174a).

---

25. See Sallis (1975), 470–471.

The second hypothesis regarding the missing dialogue the *Philosopher* is linked to the patterning of speakers:

Theaetetus: (old) Socrates – Theaetetus
Sophist: Theaetetus – Stranger
Statesman: Stranger – (young) Socrates

Following up especially on Socrates's remark (at the beginning of the *Statesman*) regarding (young) Socrates—"let him answer me at a later time . . ." (*Stat.* 258a)—one might suppose that, in the discourse on the philosopher (wherever it occurs), there would be a conversation between (young) Socrates and (old) Socrates. But this might also suggest, more playfully, that the discussion of the philosopher occurs when Socrates speaks about—or even in some sense *to*—himself. Klein suggests in this regard that the *Apology*, where Socrates speaks at length regarding his philosophical activity, takes the place of the missing dialogue the *Philosopher*.[26] One could perhaps say this also—perhaps even more appropriately—of the *Phaedo*, where one finds (old) Socrates speaking of how he began his philosophical investigations as a young man with inquiries into φύσις (*Phaed.* 96a ff.). The *Phaedo* would thus be a case of the old Socrates, on his last day of life, speaking about—or perhaps *to*—a young Socrates. In this case, the dramatic link we found between the two trilogies would gain added significance.

---

26. See Klein (1977).

2. Initial Divisions (257a–259d)

THE QUESTION ANIMATING the *Statesman* is one of number.[1] It is also a question of the number *one*—if indeed *one* is a number. It is a question of how many, of how many distinct *ones*: Just as there are three names—"sophist," "statesman," "philosopher"—are there also three kinds (γένη) such that each individual name can be attached to each individual kind? One can see the mathematics, the counting, operative in the question as Socrates poses it at the beginning of the *Sophist*. Referring to those in the Stranger's πόλις of Elea, Socrates asks the following: "Were they accustomed to hold all these as one, or two, or, just as their names are three, to divide their kinds into three as well and attach a name to each kind [γένος] individually?" (*Soph.* 217a). The expression translated as "individually" is καθ'ἕν: literally, "one by one." Here, then, it is a question of (the) one. This is not surprising, considering that the Stranger is associated with the Eleatics, for whom the all is one (i.e., one being). And yet, the Stranger answers, in his very first speech of the dialogue (and so of the entire conversation on the second day, which continues in the *Statesman*), "They believed them three" (*Soph.* 217b).

To his answer regarding Socrates's question about the three, the Stranger adds, "It is no small and easy deed, however, to determine [διορίσαθαι] clearly what each is" (*Soph.* 217b). The word translated as "to determine" is a form of διορίζω, which means "to divide by limits," "to draw a boundary," and hence also "to distinguish," "to delimit," "to define," "to determine." The root word is ὅρος, meaning "boundary," "limit," or "border." The word itself tells how the Greeks understood definitions and delimitations. To define or determine something, so as to be able to say what it *is*, means to draw its boundary, to establish and mark the limit(s) that delimit(s) it. One could say, in this regard, that to define something is to determine it *from* its limit: it is to mark the limits that delimit it with regard to other things, the limits that separate it from other things.

Here, then, we can see why, in order to determine what a statesman is, the Stranger sets out a series of divisions. In these divisions, it is a matter of marking the limit that separates (or delimits) one kind of thing from another kind of thing.

---

1. This should hardly be surprising, considering that three of the characters in the *Sophist* and the *Statesman* are mathematicians: Theodorus, Theaetetus, and (young) Socrates. We will see gradually that mathematics, and the relation between mathematics and philosophy, is a primary factor in structuring the framework of this dialogue.

However, this is not all that is involved in the divisions. Before he begins the divisions (in the *Sophist*), the Stranger says very precisely what they involve. He declares that they will begin with the sophist, "seeking and making manifest in speech [ἐμφανίζοντι λόγῳ] what he is" (*Soph.* 218b–c).[2] The Stranger explains further, speaking to Theaetetus: "As of now, you and I have only the name [τοὔνομα][3] in common about him, but we might perhaps have by ourselves in private the thing that we call by the name" (*Soph.* 218c). At the outset, then, they would have only the name in common, whereas they might have very different conceptions regarding what the name names. He continues, "And one must always, in regard to anything, have gained together an agreement [συνωμολογῆσθαι][4] about the matter itself [τὸ πρᾶγμα αὐτό] through speech [διὰ λόγων] rather than only about the names apart from the speech" (*Soph.* 218c).[5] Thus, the interlocutors begin with the mere name of the matter, and then proceed to develop a λόγος in which they come to say the same about the matter itself (e.g., about the *what* of a sophist or a statesman).

Yet, what happens in this movement from the mere name to saying the same about the matter itself? The λόγος makes manifest what the matter itself is, bringing it to light. Here, we begin to see how the Greeks understood language (λόγος). To be sure, they no doubt recognized the common features of language: namely, that it serves for communication, and that it involves the production of vocal sounds or the inscription of written signs. Yet, what is most fundamental in language for the Greeks is neither communication, nor phonation, nor inscription, but rather the power to make manifest, to bring things to light in such a way that they shine forth to us. This is attested to by the double meaning of the word λέγειν, which means "to say" or "to speak," but also "to lay out" and "to gather" in the sense of drawing things together and setting them out in their articulations. In order to understand this connection, a simple example will suffice. Imagine that one were to gesture toward a distant object and utter the name "mountain." In this moment, one would possess the name, and as a result have a kind of global, unarticulated view of the thing itself. Suppose then one were to say, "The mountainside is green, yet strewn with boulders." Now one would have said something about the thing, about what and how it is, and would thereby have gone beyond the mere word, the mere name. By doing so, one would have focused on the mountainside itself, and through the saying have let the character of the mountainside *as* green and *as* strewn with boulders stand out and become manifest. Of course, it was green and strewn with boulders all along,

---

2. The word translated as "making manifest" is a form of ἐμφανίζω, which means "show forth," "make evident," or "make manifest." It bears a semantic and etymological connection to φαίνω, "to bring to light."

3. This is a variant of ὄνομα.

4. Literally, "to come to say together the same."

5. The contrast is between ὄνομα (*mere* name) and λόγος (a speech in which something is said).

even prior to the articulation of those qualities: however, these features remained submerged and unarticulated until the λόγος made them manifest.

This example is much simpler than what is at issue in the *Sophist* and the *Statesman*—for what is to be made manifest within these dialogues is not a particular visible thing, but rather a *kind* (γένος). In a sense, one cannot see a kind at all. One can see *this* particular sophist (e.g., Protagoras) or *that* particular statesman (e.g., Solon), but one does not ever see the sophist *as such* or the statesman *as such*. On the other hand, when one sees a sophist, one can recognize him as a sophist only because one already has somehow in view what a sophist as such is. So, in some sense, one must have a vision of the kind—but everything here depends upon what the sense of this sense is. In any case, it is clear that, in the matter of kinds, making them manifest by way of λόγος will prove much more complex. An index of this complexity is given by the extended chains of divisions that the Stranger undertakes in his search for the sophist and the statesman.

We return now to the opening scene of the *Statesman*, and specifically to the contention that breaks out and is played out almost at the beginning. The *Statesman* begins with Socrates expressing his gratitude to Theodorus for his acquaintance with Theaetetus and the Stranger. Theodorus replies by saying that "soon you will owe triple this, Socrates, when they produce for you both the statesman and the philosopher" (*Stat.* 257a). Socrates scoffs at what Theodorus—"the mightiest in calculation and geometry"—has said. Then he explains why: "Because you set down each of the men as of equal worth, though in honor [τιμῇ] they stand further apart from one another than according to the proportions of your art" (*Stat.* 257b). Theodorus realizes that Socrates has gotten the best of him, and so swears by the god Ammon:[6] "By our god Ammon, Socrates, that's a good and just point, or rather your rebuke of my mistake in calculation was a credit to your memory" (ibid.). Theodorus then playfully promises, "And I will get you for it at a later time" (ibid.).

On the surface, this interchange seems relatively straightforward. By simply counting up the debt owed by Socrates—now one, but later three—Theodorus treats the sophist, the statesman, and the philosopher as being of equal worth. Socrates insists, on the other hand, that in *honor* (τιμή) they are not equal. The word τιμή can mean simply "worth" (even "price" or "cost"), but here it clearly has the sense of the honor in which a person is held, the esteem or respect afforded to him. Socrates suggests that the three kinds stand so far apart in honor that Theodorus's τέχνη—that is, mathematics and, specifically, proportions—could not express this difference. Theodorus, swearing, grants that he was wrong, and that he has made a "mistake in calculation."

---

6. Ammon was a Libyan analogue to Zeus. One recalls, in this connection, that Theodorus is from Cyrene (in Libya).

However, there is more going on here than is apparent on the surface. Notice that Theodorus says he made a mistake in "calculation" (λογισμός). What calculation, exactly? The calculation of Socrates's debt. How did he arrive at such a calculation? By counting off the three kinds: the sophist, the statesman, and the philosopher—so, one, two, three. Yet, from what Socrates says, it would seem that his mistake was to think he could calculate *at all* in the case of such kinds, to think that he could just count off each one (and each *as* one), as in one, two, three. Notice also that Theodorus, in responding to Socrates's rebuke, refers specifically to Socrates's *memory*: "your rebuke of my mistake in calculation is a credit to your memory" (*Stat.* 257b). Theodorus is not just referring to the fact that Socrates remembers his numbers and knows how to count. Rather, he is referring to the fact that Socrates remembers something he has heard about what *can* be counted, about what is countable—something, in fact, that he has just heard in the conversation that immediately precedes the *Statesman*, for indeed, there is a great deal in the *Sophist* that bears directly upon the question of the countability of kinds.

* * *

In order to understand the broader context of what is going on here, one must consider the role of counting (ἀριθμέω) in Greek mathematics. Ἀριθμέω means, more precisely, "to count out," "to count off," a number of *things*. The word that is uttered last in counting off a number of things is the number (ἀριθμός) of the things. Thus, a number refers to a definite number of definite things. In other words, for the Greeks, number is not an abstract concept that stands over against things (as is the case in modern mathematics), nor is it something to be submitted to operations carried out quite apart from things. One sees this articulated clearly by Aristotle: "and a number, whatever it may be, is always of something [τινῶν ἐστιν], for example, of parts of fire, or of parts of earth, or of units [μοναδικός]" (*Metaph.* 1092b). As a result of this understanding of number, *one* is not a number, for only what can be counted (i.e., a number of things) is a number. Thus, the smallest number is *two*.

On the other hand, the things being counted do not have to be sensibly present things. Especially in the Platonic dialogues, a level of theoretical arithmetic is worked out in which number becomes a number of pure units (the "units," or "monads," to which Aristotle refers)—or, said in a more Platonic way, *pure ones*. But in such a case, a number would refer to a number of pure *ones*, and so still to a number of *things*. Now, these *pure ones* to which the number would refer are identical. Indeed, they could not be counted otherwise, just as one cannot count apples and oranges except insofar as they are the same—that is, insofar as they are both fruit. Furthermore, these *ones* (determined by the reference to counting) are not divisible. What we today regard as fractions are treated by the Greeks as ratios.[7]

But what about the countability of kinds? We have seen that kinds also are *ones*: that is, each is what it is, is one with itself, is selfsame. For example, a particular thing that is at rest may also be in motion—say, a stationary sphere spinning on its axis. But rest *as such*—that is, the *genus* or *kind* of "rest"—cannot be motion or in motion. Rest, in staying the same as itself, is not motion, but is rather other than motion. Insofar as kinds—for example, sophist, statesman, philosopher—are *ones*, they are like that with which arithmetic and calculation deal. To this extent, it is understandable that Theodorus makes the mistake of counting them as one, two, three.

Yet, why precisely is this a mistake? It is a mistake because of what was shown about kinds in the immediately preceding conversation that takes place in the *Sophist*—and it is this demonstration that Theodorus compliments Socrates for remembering. What the *Sophist* shows is that kinds (i.e., ontological *ones*) are not simply countable, owing to the fact that they are not just uniform units, not just simply and solely *ones*. In other words, their relationality is nonarithmetical, and it is only by abstracting from this relationality that they can be considered—or, indeed, mistaken as—countable.

But why are the kinds not simply *ones*, in such a way that *this* kind is one, *that* kind is one, and together they are two? Because, as the Stranger's analysis in the *Sophist* shows, there must be relations (i.e., community) between kinds, relations that go beyond, and are quite different from, the purely external relations between identical arithmetical ones. For example, the Stranger shows that rest is not motion. But this means that rest is *other* than (or *different* from) motion. Yet, if rest is other than motion, this means that rest partakes of otherness with respect to motion: that is, it has a relation also to otherness (or difference) (*Soph.* 250a ff.). With arithmetical *ones*, by contrast, this one is not that one—rather, the ones are distinct, as they must be in order to be countable. With countable *ones*, then, one cannot say that this *one* is other than (or different from) that *one*—for all *ones* are, as mere *ones*, identical. In a larger context, this shows how philosophy, as ontology or dialectic, is akin to mathematics, for both have to do with *ones*. But it also shows how they are different, for in arithmetic, the *ones* lack precisely those relations between kinds that are the primary concern of philosophy.

In this register, we again note Socrates's remark, made at the beginning of the *Sophist*, that the philosopher sometimes appears disguised as the statesman and sometimes as the sophist (*Soph.* 216c). Such disguise, where one kind appears as another kind, would not be possible if the kinds were pure, distinct, unmixed

---

7. Thus, ½ is not a number, but is rather the ratio 1:2. See Klein (1968).

ones. Rather, in the very phenomenon of disguised appearing, there is a mixing between kinds that goes beyond all mere arithmetical relations.

* * *

The task that the Stranger and (young) Socrates take on is to determine what a statesman is—that is, to mark the boundary or limits that delimit what a statesman is, to delineate the limits that separate such a figure from other things. The marking of these limits is what is undertaken in the divisions. But this is not all that is involved. It is also a matter of beginning with the name and then proceeding so as to make manifest through speech what it is—that is, to make manifest this kind (γένος) that is called by the name "statesman." It is the speech (λόγος)—specifically, at least in the first part of the *Statesman*, the speech in which the divisions are carried out—that allows (or effects) this making manifest. In the background of the divisions in the *Statesman* are the complex divisions one finds in the *Sophist* aimed at determining what a sophist is. There, the interlocuters again and again make a fresh start, so that there are at least six different series of divisions.[8]

There is also a brief discussion of division in the *Phaedrus* (265e-266b) that bears upon the discussion underway in the *Statesman*. Here, it suffices to mention three relevant points. First, Socrates tells Phaedrus that he is a *lover* (ἐραστής) of these divisions, which are for the sake of speaking and thinking (*Pheadr.* 266b). Thus, there is somehow an *erotic* element at play in the divisions; and this is somehow connected to that for the sake of which the divisions are undertaken—namely, *speaking*, which is directed toward making something manifest, and *thinking*, in the sense of coming to apprehend what something is. Second, Socrates describes this method as one of dividing "where the natural joints [ἄρθρα ᾗ πέφυκεν] are, and not trying to hack off parts like a clumsy butcher" (*Phaedr.* 265e). In the *Statesman*, too, the Stranger refers to a "natural joint [διαφυήν]" at the point where they are about to set about dividing cognitive (gnostic) knowledge (*Stat.* 259d).[9] Third, and finally, Socrates says that he calls one who can carry out such divisions by the name "dialectician" (διαλεκτικός). Thus, this method of division is nothing other than the method of dialectic (διαλεκτική) (*Phaedr.* 266c).

Back in the *Statesman*, the Stranger has proposed to search for the statesman, with (young) Socrates as his respondent. The Stranger observes that this will require that they take the knowledges apart—that is, that they divide knowledge into its proper parts. He further notes, however, that the sectioning will

---

8. See Sallis (1975), 170 ff.
9. The word translated as "science" is ἐπιστήμη, meaning "knowledge." The word translated as "cognitive" or "gnostic science" is γνωστικός (from γνῶσις), meaning "discipline of knowledge."

be different. He then adds something absolutely crucial that was not mentioned earlier. He speaks of the statesman's path (ἀτραπόν), the path leading straight to the statesman: "We have to find it and, once we've separated and removed it from anything else, stamp a single look on it" (*Stat.* 258c). He then goes on to speak of putting the seal of a single other species upon all the other turnoffs. Thus, at each juncture where a division is made, it is imperative not only to divide properly (whatever this may require), but also to put a seal (ἐπισφραγίζω) or mark (ἐπισημαίνω)[10] on each of the two parts divided (i.e., the one on the straight path to the statesman and the one on the turnoff). Of crucial importance here are the two words that the Stranger uses to identify this seal, mark, or sign that is applied (so as to seal off): namely, ἰδέα and εἶδος (in fact, ἓν εἶδος).[11] These two words have a fateful history: they have themselves become seals that have, perhaps more than any others, sealed off the Platonic texts. These are the words that get translated as "idea" and "form," respectively, and so give rise to all sorts of gossip about the so-called "Platonic theory of forms." Rather than entertaining such gossip here, let us keep to what the Greek words say, and translate them as "look," as the look that something presents to one's vision when one looks at it.[12] Perhaps in this way we can begin to translate Plato back into Greek.

Even before the little discourse on sealing, the Stranger has already established the starting point—namely, the *kind* from which the divisions will proceed. Referring back to the sophist (sought in the earlier conversation that takes place in the *Sophist*), the Stranger says that the statesman (πολιτικός), too, must be set down as one of the knowers. They must therefore divide knowledge "just as when we were examining the sophist" (*Stat.* 258b). To be sure, back in the *Sophist*, when the Stranger first started the search for the sophist, they did not actually place him among the knowers. In fact, Theaetetus says there explicitly that the sophist is *not* wise, that he is in fact far from being wise, even though the name (σοφιστής) suggests that he is wise (σοφός). What the Stranger and Theaetetus there agree to assume (τίθημι) is that the sophist must have some kind of τέχνη (*Soph.* 221d).

Still earlier in the *Sophist*, as they are about to begin the search for the angler (which is given as an example of division), the same assumption is made: the angler is assumed to be a τεχνίτης, one who has or practices a τέχνη. In this context, the Stranger divides τέχνη itself into two kinds:

---

10. The word ἐπισημαίνω ("mark") contains the word σῆμα, meaning "sign," and so suggests a link to speech (λόγος).
11. The two words ἰδέα and εἶδος have the same root—εἴδω, meaning "to see."
12. Take, for example, the "look" of a dog. Whatever is a dog has the look of a dog, such that we will say, "This animal looks like a dog." In other words, the dog has the kind of look that what we call "dogs" have. Thus, there is a connection between *look* (ἰδέα, εἶδος) and *kind* (γένος).

i) Production (ποίησις): bringing into being something that previously was not, producing it (ποιεῖν). This includes farming and the treatment of mortal bodies (presumably animal husbandry) and that which has to do with things that are put together (σύνθετον), fabricated or molded (πλαστῶν), as well as imitation (μιμητική). These are all grouped under the name ποιητική (*Soph.* 219b).
ii) Acquisition (κτῆσις). With this it is not a matter of working or fabricating (δεμιουργέω), but rather of coercing by deeds or speeches things that have already been produced. This includes learning (i.e., acquiring knowledge) and moneymaking, as well as fighting and hunting. These are all grouped under the name κτητική (*Soph.* 219c).

In the *Statesman*, however, the initial kind is ἐπιστήμη (knowledge) rather than τέχνη, and it is this that is to be further divided. And yet, the Stranger says that they will divide knowledge just as when they were examining the sophist. And, in fact, the very moment the Stranger begins the division, he speaks of arithmetic and "some other τέχναι akin to it" (*Stat.* 258d). The question thus becomes: Which is it, ἐπιστήμη or τέχνη? Or, perhaps the better question is: What is the relation between these?

In order to answer these questions, one must look more closely at what the Greeks understood by τέχνη. Τέχνη refers to any art or craft, any way of making something or of gaining something already made. Obviously, the practice of the various τέχναι is the primary activity of people in the πόλις, and is the way by which they provide for their various needs. Clearly, then, ruling the city (as the statesman is to do) will have a great deal to do with τέχνη. The problem of the statesman is never far removed from that of τέχνη; it is thus essential to look more closely at what τέχνη is.

Τέχνη is linked to making (ποίησις), and its sense is determined by this link. By τέχνη, one either makes something that previously was not, or one acquires something that has already been produced. The decisive contrast here is between things that are produced, and are thus *by* τέχνη, and things that are not produced but are rather *by nature* (φύσις). Farming and care of domesticated animals is a kind of τέχνη grafted onto nature—their production uses materials given by nature. But this is only marginally the case with things that are put together (i.e., fabricated or molded). Here, the τεχνίτης merely uses material from nature but fabricates (molds) the material into something quite different from anything that occurs by nature. For example, there are trees and hence wood in nature, such as would be used in making a bed, but there are no beds in nature.[13] This is even more the case with imitation (μιμητική), for though a painting may imitate nature, there occurs in nature nothing like a painting.

---

13. [Editor's Note: See Aristotle, *Physics*, 193a10.]

Now, for the Greeks, it is fabrication that most fully and purely constitutes τέχνη. Other sorts of τέχνη (e.g., farming) graft themselves onto nature or add the element of imitation (e.g., painting). The acquisitive τέχναι have a kind of secondary status, then: they presuppose production and a certain familiarity with the things produced. This centrality of production (i.e., "pure" production) to the very sense of τέχνη is such that τέχνη and production (ποίησις) are sometimes virtually identified.[14] Thus, if one wants to know what τέχνη is, one needs to consider ποίησις: pure production, fabrication, putting together, molding.

When a τεχνίτης makes something, she has in mind in advance what she is going to make. For example, the potter has in mind ("in the mind's eye") the size and shape of the vase she will make. And then, with this in view, the potter makes the actual vase. Now, let us articulate the same process, but now in terms of an ancient Greek understanding. In advance, the potter has in view the *look* of the vase to be made. She then makes a vase that has the same look, that looks like this look. In this making, the look, already seen beforehand, plays a determinative role. As the vase is molded, its look has to be constantly compared with the paradigmatic look. It is also by comparison with the paradigmatic look that it can be determined when the production process is complete and the vase is finished—namely, when it looks like the paradigmatic vase. Now, substitute the above instances of the word "look" with the Greek word εἶδος. Then one can say that, before the production and throughout it—indeed, right up to its very end—there must be a vision of the εἶδος on the part of the τεχνίτης. But having a vision of the εἶδος of a certain sort of vase means *knowing* what such a vase looks like. Hence, what constitutes the central moment in the structure of ποίησις—and hence, by extension, of τέχνη—is knowledge (ἐπιστήμη).

Thus, to take τέχνη as the starting point of the divisions is similar to taking ἐπιστήμη as the starting point, since knowledge is the central moment in τέχνη. The question that the divisions made by the Stranger and (young) Socrates is supposed to answer is: What kind of knowledge (or τέχνη) is πολιτική, if indeed it is a knowledge or τέχνη?

* * *

Having referred back to the *Sophist*, and having proposed to begin with "knowledge," the Stranger abruptly says that the division will not be along the same lines. He proceeds then to divide knowledge (or the τέχναι) into two kinds—but *not* the same two kinds as in the *Sophist* (i.e., "productive" and "acquisitive"). Rather, he divides it into the following two kinds:

---

14. See, for example, the *Symposium*: "The works of all τέχναι are productions [ποιήσεις] and their artisans [δημιουργοί] are all producers [ποιηταί]" (*Symp.* 205c).

i) Arithmetic ("and some other τέχναι akin to it" (*Stat.* 258d)). These are stripped bare of actions (τῶν πράξεών) and furnish only cognition (γνῶναι).
ii) Carpentry and all manufacturing. These "possess their knowledge [τὴν ἐπιστήμην] as if it naturally inheres in their actions, and they bring to completion along with their actions the bodies that come to be through them and were not before" (*Stat.* 258e).

Thus, the Stranger proposes to divide all knowledge (ἐπιστήμη) in such a manner, calling one side "practical" (πρακτικήν) and the other "only cognitive" (μόνον γνωστικήν).

What is going on here? And how is it that the division of the very same genus (namely, knowledge) in the *Statesman* can be so different from that in the *Sophist* (i.e., "productive"/"acquisitive")? There are two clues that help answer these questions. First, the word initially used to describe the second kind (i.e., "practical") is "manufacturing" (χειρουργία).[15] But this means practice of any τέχνη in general, not of some specific kind of τέχνη. Second, the Stranger says of practical arts not that they involve *no knowledge* whatsoever, but rather that their knowledge "inheres in their actions." Thus, it is not just that there are two kinds of τέχνη, either simply coordinate—like carpentry and shoemaking—or one secondary to the others, as acquisitive τέχναι are secondary to productive τέχναι. Rather, the division is between τέχνη *as such*, which is "practical," and mere cognition taken independently of its being directive for a production.[16] In a sense, what the Stranger is setting apart from τέχνη, which in the usual sense is always practical, is purely theoretical knowledge, a knowing that merely sees (θεωρέω) without serving as the directive for any production. Such knowing merely sees the εἶδος (or pure unit) without making anything that looks like that εἶδος—indeed, without making anything at all.

The Stranger does not say immediately to which of the two kinds the statesman belongs. Instead, he abruptly brings into consideration several others alongside the statesman: namely, king, slave master, and household manager. He then asks whether these types are *one*, or whether their τέχναι are different. He then gives the following example. If someone in a private station is competent to advise a public physician, wouldn't we have to address him by the name of the same art—that is, wouldn't we call him by the name "physician"? And likewise, if a private person is competent to advise the king of a land (χώρα), mustn't we say that he has the knowledge proper to rulers—namely, royal knowledge (βασιλική)?

---

15. Literally, "handiwork."
16. For example, counting would be an integral, directive cognition in a certain τέχνη say, carpentry. But it can also occur alone, outside all practice of τέχνη, in arithmetic, and especially in pure arithmetic (that is, in the counting of pure units).

Also, the slave master and the household manager, if they rule competently, have the knowledge of ruling (i.e., the royal science), even though they rule only slaves or women and children instead of the entire land. The Stranger then says, "The figure [σχῆμα] of a large household or, in turn, the bulk [ὄγκος] of a small city—the pair of them won't at all differ in point of rule, will they?" (*Stat.* 259b).

It is important to note here the mathematical language being employed: namely, figure (σχῆμα) and bulk (or mass) (ὄγκος). One recalls in this register that (young) Socrates, along with Theodorus and Theaetetus, are all mathematicians. One recalls also that the only example the Stranger gave of the cognitive τέχνη was arithmetic. Finally, one recalls the mathematical contention that broke out at the very outset of the dialogue. There is, then, every reason to suspect that mathematics remains at issue here, and that, in particular, the Stranger's counting of all these kinds (i.e., private person, slave master, household manager, king, statesman) as *one*—that is, as identical *ones*—is problematic.

One could say that what happens here, in an arithmetical guise, is a kind of *abstracting* from what is properly distinctive about πολιτική, an eroding of the difference between it and the ways of being in charge or giving directions in other, very different contexts in which human beings are ordered. In other words, the Stranger leads (young) Socrates—and one can only imagine what (old) Socrates would be thinking as he is silently listening to all of this—into an obliviousness to the difference between public and private, citizen and slave, and political and economic, so that it seems to the Stranger that there really is no difference between the private advisor, the slave master, the household manager, the king, and the statesman. In a word, they all seem to be *one*: they are all identical *ones* which, if he wanted to, (young) Socrates could count off as simply as if he were counting one, two, three. Moreover, each of these is assimilated not only to one another, and so to arithmetical units, but also to arithmetic itself, as if they were some of the τέχναι akin to arithmetic, for the Stranger assigns them to the cognitive (γνωστική) τέχναι rather than to the practical τέχναι. It is as if being the master of slaves or the manager of a household were a purely theoretical science!

Needless to say, a *comedy* is being prepared—indeed, what one could call an *arithmetical* or *mathematical* comedy: and as this comedy runs its course, the statesman will come to find himself in even stranger company than the slave master and the household manager.

3. The Mathematical Comedy of Animals (259e–268e)

IN THE PLATONIC dialogues, there is a great deal of comedy. To give just two brief but instructive examples, consider first Books IV and V of Plato's *Republic*, where the possibility is broached that women might serve as guardians alongside men (*Rep.* 451c ff.). In this proposal, the difference between men and women is disregarded—and, more generally, the workings of ἔρως ("desire") are left out of account. In other words, there is an *abstraction* away from these elements, a kind of performative ignorance about them: the interlocutors proceed with a forgetfulness of certain key elements that bear upon their analysis.¹ In this regard, consider also the *Cratylus*, where the participants undertake to determine the fittingness of names to that which they name, and do so while disregarding the fact that this would require that they have knowledge of the things named.² Here, too, there is an abstracting away from, and a disregarding of, something essential, something that in the final analysis cannot be abstracted away from or disregarded. With the abstraction in place, the dialogue then plays out the comedy to the point where that which has been disregarded shows itself.³

With these examples in mind, we turn back to the *Statesman*. As seen in the previous chapter, the task undertaken by the Stranger and (young) Socrates is to determine the kind that is called "statesman" by marking its limits or boundaries. In such a determination, one begins with the mere name and unfolds a λόγος in such a way as to make the kind to which the name refers manifest. In the initial part of the *Statesman*, this λόγος takes the form of a series of divisions. In these divisions, there are two things that are imperative. First, it is necessary to divide where the natural joints are; and second, along the straight path leading to the statesman, it is necessary at each juncture to put a seal both on the straight way and on the turnoffs. This seal will take the form of a word designating a kind.

Operating under these imperatives, the Stranger begins by dividing knowledge (or τέχνη). (We saw previously that knowledge is the central moment in production [ποίησις], which is the primary form of τέχνη.) The Stranger divides

---

1. [Editor's Note: See Sallis (1975), 377 ff.]
2. [Editor's Note: See Sallis (1975), 185 ff.]
3. [Editor's Note: For more on the character of Platonic comedy, see Sallis (2008), chap. 7.]

knowledge (or τέχνη) into those kinds like arithmetic that are stripped bare of action and furnish only knowledge, and those kinds in which knowledge inheres in their action (for example, carpentry). Taken straightforwardly, the Stranger is simply dividing knowledge (or τέχνη) into the merely cognitive and the practical. But, in fact, the division is between τέχνη as such, which is practical, and mere cognitive knowledge taken independently of its being directive for production (i.e., purely theoretical knowledge that merely beholds the *look* without making anything that looks like the look).

As they set out to divide the kind named "cognitive," the Stranger asks whether or not there is a natural joint (διαφυήν) to be found in it. Such an expression echoes what is said in the *Phaedrus* about dividing at the natural joints, and not hacking away at things like a clumsy butcher (*Phaedr.* 265e). Yet, one may well wonder about this expression. Its sense is clear enough if what is being divided is an animal carcass.[4] However, the sense of the expression is much less clear when it is a matter of dividing *kinds*. In particular, how does nature (φύσις) relate to kinds such that there can be *natural* joints?

In order to locate the joint, the Stranger mentions "logistics" (λογιστική). Logistics has to do with numbers, and so we see again how thoroughly the discourse is being governed by arithmetic. Yet, what exactly is logistics? For the Greeks, there are two forms of knowledge dealing with numbers: arithmetic (ἀριθμητική) and logistics (λογιστική). The exact character of the distinction between these is a subject of dispute,[5] but a simple way of formulating it is as follows: arithmetic has to do with correct counting, while logistics is the knowledge of the relations between numbers that makes calculation possible. So, in calling it simply "logistics," the implication is not that it is *applied* arithmetic, for it is just as theoretical as arithmetic proper (that is, it is purely cognitive, as the Stranger explicitly says).

Now, in order to recognize the relations between numbers, one must properly discriminate between them; and this—namely, to discriminate (κρῖναι)—is precisely the task (ἔργον) that the Stranger attributes to logistics. The Stranger then contrasts this with the work of the master builder. The master builder, too, must discriminate, presumably because he must calculate, like one who practices logistics. However, unlike one who practices logistics, the master builder is not finished once he has discriminated, but must further give orders to the workmen regarding what they are to produce and how they are to produce it. Thus, there is a difference between discrimination (κρίσις) and injunction (or commanding: ἐπίταξις). This is, then, the division proposed for cognitive knowledge:

---

4. Indeed, this is what the word διαφυή, and the reference to the butcher, suggest. Insofar as this is the case, animals are already implicitly involved in the scene, long before they actually show up in it, as they will shortly.

5. Cf. Klein (1968).

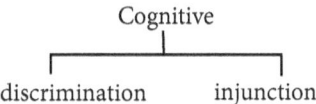

The king—and presumably also the statesman—is to be assigned to the side of "injunction."

There are two points that must be considered here. First, the master builder can give proper injunctions only on the basis of having properly discriminated. In other words, it is the discrimination that constitutes his theoretical or purely cognitive knowledge. However, it seems that giving orders is not a matter of theoretical knowledge at all but, at most, of practical knowledge. If this is so, the consequences will be serious—or, rather, *comical*, for it is "discrimination" that is left aside as being a byway, and "injunction" that is further divided in the search for the statesman. One suspects, then, that from this point on, purely cognitive knowledge has been omitted from the constitution of the statesman.

Second, something else is left out: namely, the very activity in which they are presently engaged (i.e., *division*), for the word translated as "discriminate" is κρίνω, whose primary meaning is "to separate," "to divide," "to set apart." Thus, the Stranger and (young) Socrates here pass by the very thing they are doing, consigning it to a byway. They thereby enact a bit of self-delusion, a kind of self-forgetfulness—that is, they enact a comedy. This is reinforced by their statement that as long as they are unanimous, they can dismiss the opinions of everyone else. None are more self-confident than those who are forgetful of themselves!

In order to divide further, the Stranger introduces a proportion (ἀναλογία). (One sees here again that mathematics is governing the discourse.) The proportion is as follows:

τέχνη of retailers (those who sell goods made by others) :: kingly kind	:	τέχνη of self-sellers (those who sell goods they make) kind of heralds

The point of the proportion is that, just as retailers sell something already sold to them (enjoining others to buy them), so heralds enjoin on others injunctions already enjoined to them. Thus, the division is as follows:

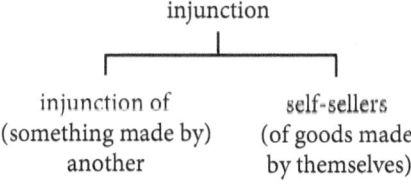

The Stranger begins to expand one side of the division. Along with heralds, he says, there are interpreters (of dreams), criers (such as town criers), and soothsayers. Then he observes that neither this nor the self-injunctive kind have a name, and further suggests that they simply put the king under the self-injunctive kind and disregard the others.

There are three points to observe regarding this division. First, this disregard for the name of the byway kind is curious, for earlier the Stranger said that a seal should be put on each byway as well as on the straight way (*Stat.* 258c). More generally, the fact that both subkinds here lack names could make one suspect that what is cut—or, perhaps, clumsily hacked—is not a natural joint. Second, this introduction of the herald and others akin to him is curious, especially if we look back and note that this is a subkind of purely cognitive knowledge. After all, a herald simply repeats what he is told to repeat, and need not have any knowledge whatsoever, let alone purely cognitive knowledge. This calls attention to the digression of the divisions, the wandering away from anything having to do with knowledge (even though they are on an allegedly straight path). Third, there is a peculiar confusion in the statement of the proportion. The proportion should be:

Retailer : self-seller :: herald : king

However, it is stated as

Retailer : self-seller :: king : herald.

Such a formulation suggests that the king—or, at the very least, the king that they are going to find through their divisions—is perhaps a kind of retailer, that he thus does not originate the thoughts that get promulgated by the herald, but rather passes along thoughts that have been passed along to him. Such a result is hardly surprising, considering that the king has been placed on the side of "injunction" rather than on the side of "discrimination."

Next, the Stranger divides "self-injunction" by distinguishing between two kinds of things with respect to which injunction may be issued. These two kinds are in fact *the* two kinds into which all things that come to be can be divided— namely, the soulless and the ensouled.[6] The Stranger then says that the search must continue in the direction of the self-injunctive kind that deals with that which is ensouled: namely, animals. From this point on, then, animals arrive explicitly on the scene, though they have been implicitly present for some time now.

Next, the general kind "animals" is divided into "single-animal nurture" and "herd-nurture." In order to determine which is the straight way, the Stranger draws a ludicrous comparison, suggesting that the statesman has more of a

---

6. That which is ensouled (i.e., that which has ψυχή) is a living being or animal (ζῷον).

resemblance to a horse feeder and cattle feeder than to an ox driver and horse groom.[7] Thus, in this comedy—what one could now call not just a mathematical or arithmetical comedy, but also a comedy of *animals*—the statesman, who was to have ruled by means of theoretical knowledge, has been reduced to one who feeds his herd of subjects, either literally or with the opinions that they eagerly consume. In his first contribution to the divisions, (young) Socrates readily draws this conclusion by dividing "herd-nurture" into "nurture of human beings [ἄνθρωπος]" and "nurture of beasts [θηρίον]."

One matter should be noted. When the Stranger asks about the name of one of the kinds—namely, whether this is "common nurture" or "herd-nurture"—(young) Socrates replies, "Whichever it turns out to be in the speech [λόγος]" (*Stat.* 261e). To this, the Stranger says the following: "Beautiful, Socrates! And if you guard against taking names seriously, you show up richer in thoughtfulness [φρονήσεως] as you approach old age" (*Stat.* 261e). This extends a point made by the Stranger at the outset of the *Sophist*. It was said there that one begins with a mere name and then unfolds a λόγος through which what the name names becomes manifest (*Soph.* 218c). What is now being added is that the manifest-making λόγος reflects back upon names, confirming or disconfirming the appropriateness of certain names.

In response to (young) Socrates's suggestion, the Stranger tells him that he has been too eager and has made an error that they need to avoid subsequently: "Let's not remove a single and small proper part over against many and great parts, and let's not do it apart from looks [εἴδους] either, but let the part [τὸ μέρος] have at the same time a look [εἶδος]" (*Stat.* 262a-b). Thus, the parts divided off should have "looks"—that is, each part should be a distinctly looking kind. The Stranger adds that it is better to cut through the middle, since one is then more likely to "encounter looks [ἰδέαις]" (*Stat.* 262b). Here, then, the Stranger begins to explain what the phrase "natural joint" can mean when it is a matter of dividing a kind rather than hacking up the carcass of an animal. One could say that the natural joint is the limit, or the boundary, that separates (and thus joins) two distinct looks, two distinctly looking kinds.

---

7. Here, already the conception of the statesman as a shepherd or cowherd tending his flock of humans—a very traditional Greek view—begins to come into play. This conception is introduced in the polemics between Socrates and Thrasymachus in Book I of Plato's *Republic*. In response to Socrates's conclusion that a ruler, insofar as he is a ruler, considers not his own advantage but rather that of his subjects, Thrasymachus, mocking Socrates, replies that shepherds and cowherds do not consider the good of the sheep or cows, but only that of the master and of themselves (*Rep.* 342a). A bit later, as the discussion shifts, Socrates returns to the theme. Referring to the "true shepherd," he says, "The shepherd's τέχνη surely cares for nothing but providing the best for what it has been set over" (*Rep.* 343c). So it is, he concludes, for "every kind of rule," which "considers what is best for nothing other than for what is ruled" (*Rep.* 345d). This is the case, he implies, for "rulers in the cities."

(Young) Socrates does not understand this explanation; however, the Stranger merely replies by saying that "in the present circumstances, it is impossible to make this manifest without falling short" (*Stat.* 262c). In other words, it is impossible for the Stranger to enter into a manifest-making discourse on looks (εἴδους). Instead, the Stranger illustrates the point with some examples of what should and should not be done. They should not, he says, divide humankind (as the Greeks do) into Greeks and barbarians, labeling all sorts of different kinds with the single name "barbarian." Additionally, they should not divide number into two kinds by separating ten thousand from all other numbers. Rather, they should divide numbers into odd and even, and humankind into male and female.

Despite the Stranger's examples, (young) Socrates wants to know how one can recognize a kind (γένος) in distinction from a mere part (μέρος). But the Stranger says that this question would make them stray even further. He insists that they turn back, and yet adds a hypothetical note: "Don't ever get the impression that you've heard it from me as a vividly established distinction" (*Stat.* 263b). To this, the Stranger adds only that whatever is an εἶδος is necessarily also a part (τὸ μέρος), but that there is no such necessity that a part be an εἶδος.

The Stranger points out that (young) Socrates's error resulted from failing to recognize this difference between a look and a part, and that he removed only a part (i.e., "humans"). One would expect the Stranger then to say that this part is not an εἶδος. However, he does not say this—that is, he does not explicitly deny that "humankind" is an eidetic kind. Rather, what he says is that (young) Socrates made the mistake of lumping together the remainder after the part was removed—as though it were one kind—and that he did this because he was *misled by the name*. In other words, because there is a single name "beast," (young) Socrates assumed there is a single, corresponding kind. Then the Stranger draws a comical comparison, saying that it is just as if cranes were to set up cranes as one kind in opposition to all the other animals (including humans). In such a scenario, cranes would simply lump humans together with other animals, disregarding the differences between the two. Although this comment is meant in jest, such disregarding of the difference between human and other animals has already been in play throughout the divisions, most notably when the king appeared to be nothing but one who feeds his herd (*Stat.* 261d). In fact, such disregarding of this difference—such mixing of human and animal—will become more prominent as the comedy continues. The fact that the Stranger focuses on this difference and criticizes (young) Socrates for drawing the distinction so abruptly does not mean that the distinction is to be dissolved, but rather that it is a distinction that is very difficult to establish. Indeed, the failure to establish it is what, most of all, drives the comedy from this point on.

The Stranger then points out that they have made a further mistake—namely, they have divided too rapidly and so have left a gap in the divisions. Significantly, this mistake occurred in dividing "animal-kind." Instead of going directly from "nurture of animals" to "herd-nurture" (as opposed to "single-animal nurture"), they should first have divided "animals" into "tame" and "wild," for only tame animals, which can be domesticated, can be nurtured (either singly or in herds).

Two corrections have thus been made by the Stranger: first, the final division between "beasts" and "humans" is retracted, and second, the missing division between "wild" and "tame" is inserted. With these corrections made, the Stranger proposes that they begin again by dividing "herd-nurture." He prefaces the division by referring to some foreign scenes that (young) Socrates has not seen: namely, domestication of fish on the Nile or in the lakes of the great king, and the Thessalian plains where there are feeding ponds of geese and cranes. Now, ostensibly these references are meant to justify the introduction of "aquatic-nurture" as a kind. But what they also suggest is that dialectic is not so formalistic as it might seem, and that a certain range of experience might be needed in order to divide well. In any case, the Stranger goes on to divide "dry-nurture" into "feathered" and "pedestrial."

At this point, something unexpected happens: the Stranger says that, from this point on, there are two possible ways leading to the statesman. More precisely, what he says is that "our speech [λόγος] appears to catch sight of a pair of two extended roads" (*Stat.* 265a). In other words, the λόγος underway makes manifest two throughways to the statesman. One can thus conclude that the way leading, by way of division, to a particular kind is not unique: rather, there can be more than one way to hack up a kind into subkinds. Moreover, one can see that the λόγος that is unfolding not only constitutes one way, but can also serve to light up the way so that we can see ahead to it. (Young) Socrates says that he wants to go both ways—each in turn, that is, since it is not possible to go both ways at once.

On the long way, the intention is to cut more down the middle; yet, even the first stretch of this way is curious. As we have seen, they have just divided "pedestrial" animals from "feathered" animals. Now they divide thusly:

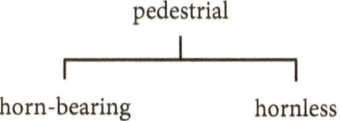

The Stranger calls this a *natural* division—that is, a division *by nature*. However, it is in fact nothing of the sort. Rather, it is purely formal, purely *logical*, in character, along the lines of "A or not-A." Then the Stranger says, "And it is evident to us besides that the king, at least, grazes some kind of herd docked of horns" (*Stat.* 265d). The king is thus conceived to be the shepherd of a herd of hornless animals. Such a designation reveals how the human is being herein determined: namely, as an animal without feathers and without horns. In other words, the human is being determined in terms of the animal traits or parts it does *not* have. Thus, by abstracting from what is genuinely human and what really distinguishes the human from animals, we are left with the comical scene of a king grazing a herd of animals that have lost their feathers and horns:

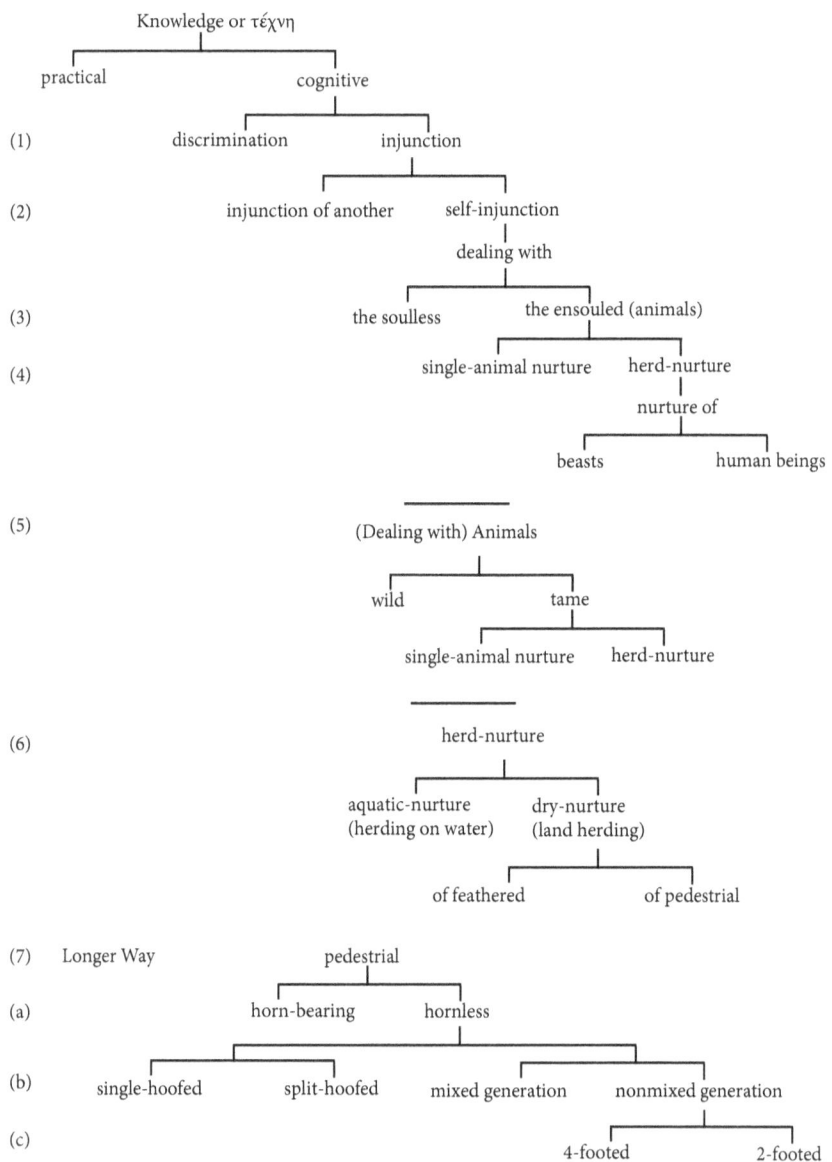

We have now followed the series of divisions almost to its end. The series began with knowledge or τέχνη; then, through the reiterated division (between the throughway and the turnoffs), it is supposed to arrive at the delimitation of the statesman, to the point where the λόγος, laid out as the series of divisions, makes manifest the kind that is named by the name "statesman." In formal terms, the λόγος that is laid out takes the form of a straight path leading to the statesman. And yet, as it is actually carried out, it takes the form—most remarkably—of a *mathematical comedy of animals*. To fully understand this, we must first consider how it is mathematical, then how it is concerned with animals, and finally how it is played out as a comedy.

Mathematics

There are four ways in which the λόγος of the *Statesman* is mathematical. First, it treats different things (e.g., private advisor, slave master, household manager, king) as if they were the same: in other words, it treats them as identical *ones*, just as we, in arithmetic, treat the things counted as identical *ones*. This manner of treatment is made explicit near the end of the divisions, just before the Stranger finishes off with the shorter way. There, the Stranger says that "a pursuit of speeches of this sort no more cared for the august [σεμνοτέρου] than for what was not" (*Stat*. 266d). In other words, all were treated as the same, as identical *ones* that could be counted together. It was precisely such treatment that was evident in Theodorus's remark at the very outset of the *Statesman*, and which (old) Socrates severely criticized (*Stat*. 257a).

Second, the Stranger appeals several times to mathematics in order to illustrate or effect certain steps in the divisions. In the very first division, he divides knowledge into "practical" (i.e., τέχνη in its full structure) and "cognitive" (i.e., purely theoretical). The sole example that he gives of the cognitive kind is "arithmetic and some other τέχναι akin to it" (*Stat*. 258d). Then, in the second division, he characterizes "discrimination" in distinction to "injunction" by referring to "logistics," which involves discriminating among numbers. In other words, the mathematical discipline of logistics serves as a decisive clue for discriminating between "discrimination" and "injunction."[8]

Third, in the third step in the divisions, the distinction between two forms of injunction (i.e., "injunctions of another" and "self-injunction") is carried out by means of a proportion (in the mathematical sense). Yet, the proportion mixes up the terms, so that the king turns out to be a retailer of opinions. It is quite remarkable that this mix-up occurs, since at least three of those present are mathematicians. Even more remarkable is that this bad mathematics goes unmentioned, and presumably unnoticed. One could say that, while mathematics guides much of the discourse, it can

---

8. "Discrimination" here equates to κρίνω, meaning "to separate," "to divide," "to put apart," but also "to decide" (as in a contest or dispute), "to expound," or "to explain."

also, as here, lead it astray—for it is this very transition from "injunction" to its two kinds that diverts the entire series away from "cognition" (as discrimination)—even though it is, formally speaking, "cognition" that is being divided.

Fourth, just after the Stranger has distinguished between the longer and shorter ways to the statesman, he comes eventually to the penultimate division—namely, of "nonmixed generation" into "four-footed" and "two-footed." But, instead of simply saying "four-footed" and "two-footed," the Stranger takes a very roundabout geometrical path. As he puts it, the division of "nonmixed generation" is to be made by the diameter and the diameter of the diameter:[9]

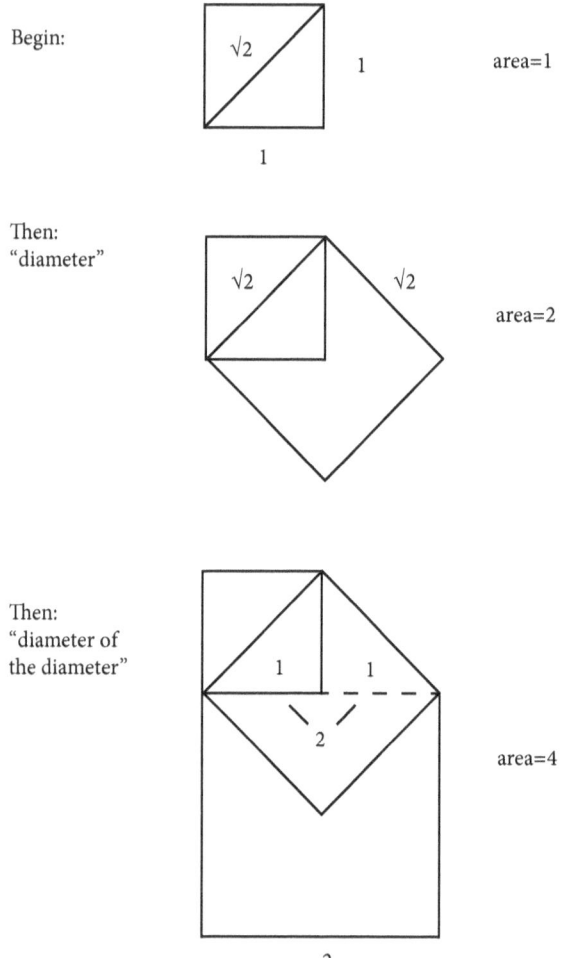

---

9. Diameter here refers to the diagonal of a square.

This is a roundabout geometrical way of saying "two and four," and so distinguishing between "two-footed" and "four-footed."

There is a linguistic play here on the Greek phrase δυνάμει δίπους, which literally means "the power of two feet" (i.e., the capacity of a two-footed animal). This phrase also means the power of two—that is, the *root* of two—in a mathematical sense: $\sqrt{2}$ (in modern mathematical symbology). So, the Stranger begins with $\sqrt{2}$, which is incommensurable, and through the construction ends up with four, which is commensurable. But this is precisely the kind of mathematical problem with which Theaetetus and (young) Socrates, in connection with Theodorus, were involved in at the beginning of the *Theaetetus* (*Theaet.* 147c ff.). This is why the Stranger introduces this entire discussion by saying that they will divide "by the very means it is quite just for Theaetetus and you to distribute by, since the pair of you are involved in geometry" (*Stat.* 266a).

These, then, are the ways in which mathematics remains determinative of the discourse—and, indeed, the comedy—underway. We turn now to the role that animals play in the unfolding λόγος.

Animals

There are various ways in which the λόγος and its divisions entail animals. To begin with, the division is supposed to be at the natural joints—as in chopping especially the carcass of an animal—and not just hacking away like a clumsy butcher. The problem is this: How does λόγος, like an animal carcass, have natural joints? What are the natural joints, precisely? The Stranger indicates that the natural joints distinguished in λόγος are the boundaries or limits that distinguish (i.e., set apart) one *kind* or *look* from another. The parts that are chopped off by the butchery of λόγος should be distinctly looking kinds, and not mere parts.

Animals arrive explicitly on the scene when the Stranger divides "self-injunction" into dealings with "the soulless" and with "the ensouled." Because "animals" lie on the straight part and "the soulless" is a turnoff, animals remain on the scene from this point on. Several types of animal put on their distinctive performance. Most conspicuously, there is the story of the cranes. As the Greeks distinguish between "Greeks" and "barbarians," and (young) Socrates between "beasts" and "humans," so the cranes would distinguish between cranes and all other animals (including humans).[10] There are also the foreign animal scenes pictured by the Stranger: "the domestication of fish on the Nile and the lakes of the great king" (*Stat.* 264c). What the Stranger says stresses the foreignness of these scenes, their distance from the current (human) discussion.[11] The foreignness,

---

10. Here, there is also an allusion to the theater, for the word γέρανος can refer both to the bird and to the kind of cranes used in the theater to lift heavy objects or scenery.

11. The Stranger says to (young) Socrates, "I know that you have never met up with these" (*Stat.* 264c).

remoteness, and distance of these animals from the current human discussion brings out by contrast the failure of the divisions to distinguish properly the difference between humans and animals.

In addition to the cranes and foreign fish, there are several other kinds of animals that put in an appearance. On the longer way, the Stranger comes to the point where "hornless" is to be divided. Yet, something strange then happens. Instead of proposing a single pair into which "hornless" is to be divided, the Stranger mentions two different pairs, and then goes with one pair with no apparent justification. Here the way, which should be straight, seems to become split and multiple. The Stranger mentions, in this regard, "split-hoofed" animals—for example, horses, cows, sheep—and "single-hoofed" animals, which encompasses many others, including humans. Yet, one might ask: Do humans, like many animals, have hooves?

Then the Stranger also mentions "mixed generation" and "nonmixed generation." He gives the example of horses and donkeys as mixed generation—that is, as generation in which kinds are mixed. Such mixture produces mules, which are sterile, and which cannot generate at all and thus fall outside of these two kinds, violating and disrupting the divisions. Now, the mixing of kinds is of course precisely what the Stranger and (young) Socrates ought *not* to be doing: rather, they should be *separating* the various kinds. And yet, there is much to suggest that they are mixing precisely the human and the merely animal, so that the king becomes a shepherd of a herd of featherless, hornless animals.

Immediately after this compounded division, the Stranger remarks that the genus of dogs "does not deserve to be counted among herd nurslings" (*Stat.* 266a). (The word "to count" [καταριθμεῖν] indicates that arithmetic continues to govern the discourse.) But why are dogs not worth counting? To understand this, one must trace back from "nonmixed generation" through "hornless," "pedestrial," and "dry-nature" to the divisions between "single animal nurture"/"herd nurture" and "wild"/"tame." Then it becomes evident why dogs must be excluded, for there are dogs that are wild and roam in herds or packs, as well as domesticated dogs that are tame and are nurtured singly by their master. Thus, dogs fall on both sides of these divisions, and in doing so disrupt the course of them, contaminating their purity. One wonders, too, what (old) Socrates, listening quietly, might think about the dismissal of dogs. Not only does he refer to dogs as an important example in the *Republic*,[12] but there is also the matter of his characteristic swear, "by the dog."[13]

As they near the end of the longer way, the Stranger speaks in a way that now completely collapses the difference between the human and the animal: "Our

---

12. [Editor's Note: See *Rep.* 335b, 376a, and 416a.]
13. [Editor's Note: See *Apol.* 22a; *Crat.* 411b; *Charm.* 172e; *Hipp. Maj.* 287e and 288b; *Gorg.* 461a, 466c, and 482b; *Phaedo* 98e; and *Rep.* 400e and 592a.]

human genus has simultaneously got the same lot as—and run the course to a tie with—the noblest and most accommodating genus of the things which are" (*Stat.* 266c). This ironic remark refers, of all things, to *pigs*.[14] The reference is even clearer in the Stranger's next remark: "Isn't it likely that the slowest things arrive last [ὕστατα]?" (*Stat.* 266c). Here there is a play on words: the word ὕστατα, meaning "last," suggests the word ὗς, which means "pig." And so, as the Stranger goes on to say, "The king comes to light as still more laughable in running along with his herd [i.e., of pigs]" (*Stat.* 266c–d). Here, the comedic character of the entire discourse becomes most evident.

Comedy

There are five ways in which the λόγος underway within the *Statesman* plays out as a comedy. First, there is a digression operative within the divisions themselves, a wandering away from anything having to do with *knowledge*. We see this especially near the beginning, when the Stranger and (young) Socrates follow the side of "injunction," leaving aside "discrimination"—that is, leaving aside the operation of separating and putting apart so as to mark distinctly the borders between kinds, thereby making a *decision* regarding these limits and thusly explaining what something means. From that point on, it is as if they have forgotten, or abstracted away from, the very point from which they began—namely, *knowledge*, and, in particular, cognitive knowledge. Here we see the typical pattern of Platonic comedy which, as elaborated in the previous chapter, consists of a movement of abstraction and (self-)forgetfulness.

Second, there is a comic disregarding of differences between the human and the merely animal. We see this especially in the story of the cranes, who shift the boundary such that humans are lumped together with all of the animals except the cranes. We see this even more starkly toward the end of the divisions, when the human comes to be determined as an animal without feathers or horns—that is, in terms of animal traits that are lacking.

Third, an equally ridiculous picture of the statesman comes into view as the divisions proceed. Having failed to distinguish properly between human and animal—that is, having abstracted comedically from this difference—the statesman is ludicrously drawn closer and closer to the animals. At the point where animals first arrive explicitly on the scene, he is pictured as resembling the horse feeder and cattle feeder. He is then later depicted as the shepherd of a herd of hornless animals. Finally, the statesman is shown as running along with his herd of pigs.

Fourth, in the initial course that the divisions take, (young) Socrates makes an error in dividing "nurture of animals": namely, he fails to divide this into

---

14. With this mention of pigs, there is an implicit reference to the *Odyssey*, in which Circe turns Odysseus's followers into swine (*Od.* X).

"tame" and "wild' before going on to differentiate between "single-animal nurture" and "herd-nurture." Once the divisions are finished (or appear to be), the Stranger runs through all of them, gathering them into the λόγος that has thus unfolded, weaving together the determinations that have been delimited:

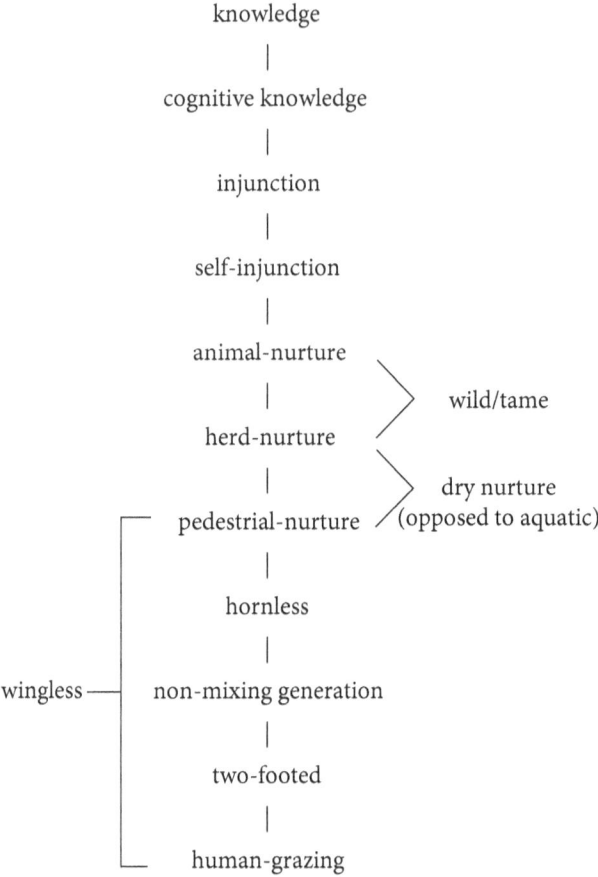

What is remarkable is that, when he finally runs through the entire course (along the straight path to the statesman), the Stranger himself omits the difference between "tame" and "wild," leaving the same gap that he previously criticized (young) Socrates for leaving.[15] This could suggest that, no matter who does the dividing, there will always be such gaps. It could also suggest that the division between "wild" and "tame" is not a proper division between distinct kinds, but

---

15. The Stranger's additional omission of "dry/aquatic nurture" removes from the λόγος the foreign animal scene—that is, the one scene that depicts the distance, difference, between human and animal. This is a distance such that its scene is withdrawn from the experience of (young) Socrates (and perhaps even of the Stranger).

rather that, as the example of the dog shows, there are things that can be both wild and tame. (The difference between "tame" and "wild" will have a special significance in what is to come.)

Fifth, even before he pulls together the would-be complete (but in fact not complete) λόγος, the Stranger actually calls attention to the comedic character of their undertaking: "And besides these, Socrates, do we catch sight of some other thing that has come to be, in what we have divided, which might have earned us a fine reputation for provoking laugher [γέλωτα]?" (*Stat.* 266b). (Young) Socrates remarks that they have indeed come up with "a very strange result" (*Stat.* 266c).

* * *

Just before he gathers up and reiterates the λόγος reached by the longer way, the Stranger lays out the shorter way. It is very short indeed:

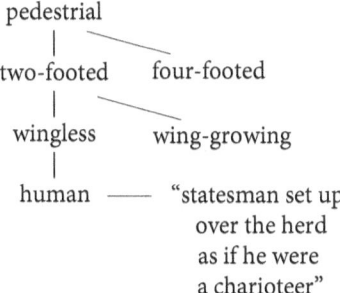

The question is: Why does one need to traverse the longer way? Why not just take this shorter way?

After he reiterates the λόγος of the longer way, the Stranger remarks that it has not been perfectly produced. Then he explains that, alongside the statesman, there are many others who would claim to be the herdsmen of human beings—for example, merchants, farmers, food makers, trainers, and physicians. He says, indeed, that there are thousands who would dispute whether or not the statesman is the only such herdsman, and who would "raise the counterclaim of a joint grazing with him" (*Stat.* 268c). In the face of this result, the Stranger concludes: "So we have to proceed again from a different beginning on some other way" (*Stat.* 268d). It turns out that this other way could hardly be more different: for the way now to be taken is a way of *myth*.

4. The Myth of Cosmic Revolutions (269a–276e)

THE COMEDY HAS run its course—at least for now. The conclusion of the comedy is marked by the Stranger's injunction that they must proceed from another beginning (ἀρχή)—that is, that they must return to the beginning and make another beginning. This other beginning is indeed quite other than the dialectical procedure of division employed up to this point. In setting out upon this other beginning, the Stranger says that they must make use of a large part of a great myth (μῦθος). Thus, not only is this other beginning a myth—indeed, a great, long, weighty myth—but it is explicitly called such by the Stranger.

How is this turn to myth to be understood? What is involved in the Stranger's inserting a "great myth" into a philosophical, even *dialectical*, discourse (λόγος)? There are two points that should be observed. To begin with, the myth is introduced here as another beginning (ἀρχή). But in the tradition of Hesiod, myth is primarily concerned precisely *with* the beginning, with how things developed from the beginning. One could say, then, that beginning anew with myth is a way of beginning with the beginning. Indeed, we will see that the myth tells of a kind of golden age out of which the present age began and developed, but also departed.

Second, and by contrast, one cannot but wonder about the appropriateness of such myth-telling to philosophical discourse. It would seem that philosophy begins (i.e., arrives at its proper beginning) by giving a different sort of account from those given in myths—namely, by giving a λόγος in distinction to μῦθος. Indeed, in the *Sophist* (and so earlier on the same day as the *Statesman*), the Stranger criticizes many of the earlier philosophers for *merely* telling myths, referring explicitly to Parmenides and all others who seek to determine beings: "Each of them appears to me to narrate to us, as if we were children, a kind of myth [μῦθόν]; one saying that beings [τὰ ὄντα] are three, and sometimes some of them are, in a sense, at war with one another, and sometimes they become friendly and make arrangements for marriages, births, and the sustenance of their offspring; another says two, liquid and dry or hot and cold, and he has them keep house together and offers them in marriage" (*Soph.* 242c–d). He goes on to mention Xenophanes expressly, and further alludes to Heraclitus and Empedocles (*Soph.* 242d). It is then in opposition to such storytelling that the Stranger launches the investigation of being and not-being that forms the heart of the *Sophist*.

And yet, rather than simply concluding that myth is pre-philosophical or even entirely opposed to philosophy, there are other considerations. Clearly, what the Stranger is criticizing is not myth *as such*, but rather the accounts of *being* in terms of human matters that take place in certain myths.[1] Such an account of being is largely absent from the myth that the Stranger tells in the *Statesman*. As regards myths as such—or rather, as regards the relation between μῦθος and λόγος—everything depends on how the relation of language to being is understood. If λόγος is taken to correspond to beings—that is, if λόγος is to say beings as they are—then clearly μῦθος will fall short of this: that is, it will fall short of the truth of beings. But if, instead, language is taken as *revealing* beings, which is precisely how dialectic has been portrayed, then we can suppose that μῦθος is yet another way, alongside λόγος, in which beings can be revealed.

Yet, in the *Statesman*, there will be not just myth but, as the Stranger says, a *mixture*: specifically, the Stranger says that the way (ὁδός) leading from the mythical beginning will be a mixture, one, he says, that is like *play* (παιδιά). Thus, the Stranger will make use of part of the myth, but will mix with this some dividing as he was employing before—a mixture, then, of myth and dialectic, a compounding of μῦθος and λόγος. It remains to be seen how this way, this mixing, is like *play*.

The Stranger begins with three ancient stories (μῦθοι). The first story regards the strife between the brothers Atreus and Thyestes, sons of Pelops, who had come into conflict with one another regarding who was to be king. Hermes placed a golden ram among the flocks of Atreus, and possession of the ram carried with it the kingship. Thyestes seduced Atreus's wife and through her came into possession of the ram, and because of this was banished by Atreus.

When the Stranger mentions the story of Atreus and Thyestes, (young) Socrates guesses that he is referring explicitly to the golden ram. However, the Stranger vehemently denies this, saying, "No—not at all" (*Stat.* 269a). He then goes on to say that what he has in mind is the change in the setting and rising of the sun, as the event by which the god testified for Atreus. This refers to one version of the story. Advised by Hermes, Atreus offers to let Thyestes keep the throne until the sun turns back in its course. Thyestes agrees—but then Zeus makes the sun turn around. However, there is another version of the story that goes unmentioned within the *Statesman*. After Atreus banished Thyestes, he pretended a reconciliation and invited Thyestes to a banquet. Meanwhile, Atreus killed his brother's two small children, had them cut up and boiled, and at the banquet served the flesh to Thyestes. In horror at this event, which is utterly contrary to

---

[1]. This is the anthropocentric fallacy that Xenophanes had already attacked (see fragment B 16).

nature, the sun turned back in its course.[2] This unmentioned version of the story links the reversal of the sun's course to an event so extreme as to run contrary to nature; indeed, as to make nature run contrary to itself.[3]

Interestingly, in this act of serving Thyestes the flesh of his own children, Atreus is repeating the actions of his grandfather Tantalus. Tantalus was a mortal son of Zeus who was so honored by the gods that they allowed him to dine with them. However—for reasons that no poet ever tried to explain—he had his only son Pelops (father of Atreus and Thyestes) killed, boiled in a great cauldron, and served to the gods. But before eating, the gods realized what he had set before them, and they punished him by setting him in a pool in Hades where he suffered tormenting thirst. Moreover, they restored Pelops to life.[4] Thus, behind the unmentioned story of Atreus and Thyestes, there is a still more ancient and unmentioned story. In other words, before the beginning—of which the Stranger tells—there is another, more ancient beginning.

The second story has to do with the kingdom ruled by Cronus. Cronus was the son of heaven and Earth, a Titan who ruled over the Titans. He was later overthrown by his son Zeus; thus, the age of Cronus was followed by the age of Zeus. Cronus's rule is associated with the golden age, a time of great peace and happiness. One sees this, for example, in Hesiod:

> First of all, the deathless gods who dwell on Olympus made a golden race of mortal men who lived in the time of Cronus when he was reigning in heaven. And they lived like gods without sorrow of heart, remote and free from toil and grief: miserable age rested not on them; but with legs and arms never failing, they made merry with feasting beyond the reach of all evil. When they died, it was as though they were overcome with sleep, and they had all good things; for the fruitful earth, unforced, bore them fruit abundantly, and without stint. They dwelt in ease and peace upon their lands with many good things, rich in flocks and loved by the blessed gods.[5]

This is the story according to which "those before [i.e., in the age of Cronus] grew up earthborn and were not generated from one another" (*Stat.* 269b). So, according to this story, those in the age of Cronus were born from the earth and there was no procreation or sexual reproduction. In other words, there was no ἔρως.

One can already see what the above-mentioned stories link together: namely, nature running in a direction contrary to itself, a golden age of happiness and plenty for humans, and the absence of ἔρως. These stories also pose the prospect of an end to the golden age that would be marked by the reversal of the

---

2. In Euripides's *Orestes*, Electra calls this deed "Thyestes' feast of horror" (1008).
3. [Editor's Note: See Cary (1949), 117.]
4. [Editor's Note: See ibid., 661 and 878–879.]
5. Hesiod, *WD*, 110 ff.

previous course of nature and by the inception of the operation of ἔρως. The Stranger declares that all of these stories, as well as many others that are even more wonderful (θαυμαστότερα), stem from the same affect or event (πάθος). He goes on to say that no one has yet stated this affect that is the cause (αἴτιον) of all of these things, but now this must be said—for it will prove to fit in with the showing-forth (ἀπόδειξις) of the king.[6] Thus, in what follows, the Stranger will tell the myth behind the myths—the master myth—and this will fit in with making manifest the character of the king.

He begins by distinguishing between two directions in which the heaven (or cosmos) goes around. At times, the god conducts it, turning it in its circling around. Then, when a certain measure of time has been achieved, the god just lets go, at which point it turns in the contrary direction (with nature thus running contrary to itself). As the Stranger says, "Then of its own accord [αὐτόματον][7] it turns backward in the opposite direction" (*Stat.* 269c–d). The Stranger offers, still as a myth, some account of this reversal of motion. He says explicitly that the cosmos is a living being (ζῷον) and has obtained a certain intelligence (φρόνησις) from the one who fitted it together in the beginning: namely, the god.[8] The Stranger then draws a distinction between the most godly things, which are always self-same and in the same way (i.e., the completely selfsame and self-identical, like the *ones* of arithmetic, or the *kinds* treated in the *Sophist*), and the nature of body (σώματος φύσις), which is not utterly selfsame. Because the heaven or cosmos has a share in body, it is not utterly selfsame—that is, it is not exempt from all alteration. However, it comes closest as possible to being such, for, though in motion, its motion is revolution (i.e., rotation) in the same place, and its deviation from this is the smallest deviation possible (namely, reverse revolution). This reverse revolution is what happens when the god turns the cosmos loose and lets it run on its own. This is the greatest of alterations, and it is difficult for living beings in the cosmos to endure it, for it brings great destruction of humans as well as other animals. From that decisive moment of reversal, everything—and not only the circling of the cosmos—is *on its own*.

Next, the Stranger tells what happens when the cosmos suddenly begins to turn in the direction contrary to that in which it turns in the present:

> First of all, the age, which each and every animal had, came to a halt, and everything that was mortal stopped its advance toward looking older, but, in altering, each genus grew back in the contrary direction, younger as it were and suppler. And the white hair of the elders was getting black, and the cheeks of

---

6. Μῦθος thus operates here as *revealing*, as *de-monstration*.
7. The word αὐτόματος means "spontaneous," "unhidden," "self-moving"—hence, a ζῷον.
8. This god is later called a δημιουργός. Here the *Timaeus*, which elaborates upon these themes, is in the background.

those with beards were, in growing smooth, becoming what they were in their previous period of bloom, and the bodies of youths in growing smooth and in becoming smaller day by day and night by night were going back toward the nature of the new-born child, getting to be similar to it both in terms of the soul and in terms of the body. And from that point on they began to wither away and vanish utterly and completely. (*Stat.* 270d–e)

Thus, with the reversal of the motion of the cosmos, the course of animate life also undergoes a reversal, owing to the fact that *time itself* is linked to the motion of the heavens,[9] such that a reversal of this motion is a reversal of time itself, and hence also of the temporal course of life. The Stranger links this reversal, through which nature as a whole runs contrary to itself, to the earthborn character that those of long ago are said to have had: as the elders become younger, those who are dead and lie in the earth get put back together again and come to life. In this manner, they are born out of the earth, and, initially old, they get younger and younger until finally they vanish completely. Thus, this reversal of which the Stranger speaks is also a reversal of birth and death. It is precisely this reversal that displaces procreation and excludes the operation of ἔρως.

(Young) Socrates asks about the time when Cronus ruled, and wonders to which period of revolutions it belonged. The Stranger identifies the time of Cronus's rule with the previous period (i.e., when the course of nature was reversed), and adds that during this period the god ruled the circling of the cosmos. Thus, the golden age of the reign of Cronus corresponds to the period when the god piloted the cosmos and when life and the heavens followed a course opposite to that of the present time. Moreover, not only did the god guide the cosmos as a whole, but various other gods were also distributed to various parts of the cosmos. As the Stranger says, "And, in particular, gods had, like divine shepherds, distributed the animals by kinds and herds, each one of whom was by himself all-suffering for each of the groups that he himself grazed, and as a consequence there was neither anything savage [or wild] nor any act of feeding on one another, and there was no war at all or sedition either"[10] (*Stat.* 271d–e). One could say, then, that the gods carried out a sort of originary division, "distributing the animals by kinds." Hence, if later—after the gods had withdrawn and disorder set in—one were to carry out divisions like those that the Stranger has carried out, they would be imperfect imitations that would re-mark the lines of those originary divisions.

It should also be noted that there is an allusion here to the definition of the king at which they arrived through the dialectic divisions: namely, a shepherd

---

9. This is the manner in which time is determined in the *Timaeus* (37c ff.). See Sallis (1999), chap. 2.
10. In other words, there was no *violence* during this time.

over a herd of tame animals. This becomes even more explicit as the Stranger goes on to describe the Arcadian state of those humans shepherded by these gods:[11]

> A god was himself in charge and grazed them, just as human beings now, being another more divine animal, graze different genera inferior to themselves. But when the god was grazing there were no regimes or possessions of women and children either, for everyone came alive again from earth without any memory of those before, but things of the sort were absent. And they had abundant fruits from trees and woodlands of many different sorts, which did not grow by farming, but the earth sent them up spontaneously. And they were grazed much of the time outdoors, naked and without bedding, for that which characterized their seasons was a mixture that gave no pain, and they had soft beds when an abundance of grass grew up from the earth. You've heard, Socrates, of the life in the times of Cronus [. . .] (*Stat.* 271e–272a)

The Stranger proceeds to speak of the end of the golden age of the rule of Cronus. How did it come to its end? Why did it not continue indefinitely? Earlier, the Stranger merely said that the god who was steering the cosmos turned it loose; now, he hints that its coming to an end had to do with a certain exhaustion in the order of generation: "[. . .] when each soul had rendered back all its generations, once it had let fall into the earth as many seeds as had been prescribed for each" (*Stat.* 272e). Thus, these souls—these distinctly *unerotic* souls—ran out of seed, and "it was precisely at that moment that the helmsman of the all, just as if he had let go of the handle of the rudder, stood apart and withdrew" (*Stat.* 272e). It is at just this moment that, according to the Stranger, a fated and inborn desire (ἐπιθυμία)—that is, a previously dormant ἔρως—reversed once more the movement of the cosmos.

Once the god withdrew, many of the beasts became wild and savage,[12] and human beings, themselves weak, were devoured by beasts, for the spontaneous nurture characteristic of the golden age had exhausted itself, and yet humans had not yet acquired the τέχναι by which to provide for themselves and for their own protection. This, the Stranger says, is the source of stories about how, long ago, the gods bestowed upon us certain vital gifts with the help of which we were able to survive: namely, fire from Prometheus, τέχναι from Hephaestus and Athena, and seeds and plants (presumably from Demeter). In this vein, the Stranger concludes, "And everything, all that has arranged human life, has been from these"—for "they through themselves had to manage their way of life and their own care for themselves" (*Stat.* 274d). This means that human beings, now operating in the age of Zeus, had to rule over themselves. Thus marks the beginning of politics.

---

11. It also becomes explicit that the operation of ἔρως was absent.
12. One sees now how crucial the difference between tame/wild becomes.

* * *

Against the background of the myth, the Stranger now identifies the two mistakes made in their determination of the king or statesman. Regarding the first mistake, the Stranger says that they asked for the statesman of the *present* revolution (i.e., the age of Zeus), but instead spoke of the shepherd of the human herd from the previous age (i.e., the age of Cronus). Yet, this shepherd was a god, not a mortal. This entails three consequences. First, the previous identification of the statesman, precisely in conflating human with animal, has also conflated the human (specifically, the statesman) with the divine—that is, it mistook a god for the human statesman. Second, the statesman was determined with regard to an age in which humans were merely to be grazed, an age in which there was no wildness, strife, or violence. The statesman in the present age, by contrast, deals with wildness, contention, strife, and the struggle for domination and power—that is, he deals with violence in its manifold forms. This was only remotely alluded to at the end of the mathematical comedy of animals, when it turned out that there were others (e.g., merchants, farmers, food makers, trainers, physicians) who would lay claim to what the "shepherding statesman" claims to do. Third, the statesman was determined with respect to an unerotic age, a time when all the complications and disruptions brought about by sexuality, procreation, and the birth of humans from other humans were entirely lacking.

The second mistake is, as the Stranger puts it, of "briefer compass" (*Stat.* 275a). The Stranger says that they "did not articulate in what manner he [the statesman] ruled" (ibid.), for in the present age, and for a mortal (rather than godly) king who must deal with all that comes about through violence and the workings of ἔρως, ruling can hardly consist in just grazing, nurturing, and shepherding the herd.

One could say, then, that what the myth makes manifest are those mistakes made in the determination of the statesman by way of the divisions. In the positive sense, it shows how the statesman must now be redetermined from this other beginning. This brings us back to a point that we passed over earlier: namely, the fact that, as the Stranger prepared to tell the myth, he said that the way they would follow was "near to child's play [παιδιὰν]" (*Stat.* 268d). At that point, he emphasized this playfulness by repeating the word twice: "Well, then, pay very close attention to my myth, just as children playing [οἱ παῖδες] do. It is in any case not many years since you've fled from child's play [παιδιάς]" (*Stat.* 268e). Now, one could take this statement as simply saying that the myth is playful, fanciful, invented, and so is not to be taken in the strict, serious way that a λόγος would be taken. As such, it serves to make manifest something about the failings of the previous λόγος. And yet, there is also a deeper sense in which the myth is "near to play." In the passage just cited, the Stranger tells (young) Socrates that he should listen to the myth, just as children playing do. But how, exactly, do children play? Children listen to a story, and then they *enact* it—they *play* at it. What we need to consider, then, is how, in relation to the myth, the myth is enacted—or, more precisely, how in the very telling of the myth, the myth is also enacted and played out *in deed* (ἔργον).

At several points in the myth, the Stranger describes the turn in which the direction of the revolution of the cosmos is reversed. Close examination of these descriptions shows something quite remarkable: namely, the fact that sometimes he describes the turn as leading from past (the age of Cronus) to present (*Stat.* 270a, 271a), but almost as often describes it as a turn from present to future. For instance, the Stranger states that "whenever it [i.e., the all] goes into the turn that's contrary to the one which obtains at present [. . .]" (*Stat.* 270d). (In other words, what it would "go into" from the present is the future.) Additionally, he speaks of how, after the time when there is disharmony, destruction, and violence (i.e., the present age), the god "once more takes his seat at the rudder" (*Stat.* 273d) and twists things around into the revolution in the opposite direction. Furthermore, there is alteration between descriptions oriented toward the past and those oriented toward the future. In this way, the *telling* of the myth itself enacts a series of reversals between temporal opposites, between past and future. Thus, the telling of the myth—like the cosmos described in the myth—turns from one pole (back to the past) to its opposite (the future). This, then, is how the telling of the myth enacts, imitates, and plays out *in deed* that of which the myth tells. The relation between what is told (i.e., the reversal of cosmic motion) and the telling itself (which consists of a reversal between temporal modes) is secured by the connection between time and the movement of the cosmos (that one finds set out, for example, in the *Timaeus*). One could say, then, that the form of the myth corresponds to, and plays out, the content of the myth: the form mirrors the content.[13]

According to the Stranger, one of the things accomplished by the myth was to show how the shepherd served as a paradigm (παράδειγμα) for the statesman. The Stranger's next step in moving toward the redetermination of the statesman is to mark the limits of this paradigm. This paradigm led them to speak of the statesman as engaged in *nurturing* (τρέφω: nourishing and feeding) the herd. Although shepherds are indeed engaged in this task, the statesman is decidedly not: he does not feed the herd of human beings. In other words, the mistake was to apply the name "nurturing" (τρέφω) to him. Thus, what is needed at this point is a name for what is common both to shepherds and to the statesman. This common kind is designated by the word "tending" (θεραπεύω), but also by the word "herd-grooming" (ἀγελαιοκομική);[14] finally, it can be designated as the τέχνη of

---

13. From another perspective, what connects the two temporal poles (past and future), such that in the future the god will again take charge and presumably there will then be a repetition of the age of Cronus, is that in the age of Zeus, the initial remembrance of the previous age decays: that is, *forgetting* sets in, and there is degeneration to such an extent that that the god *must* again take control.

14. I.e., the τέχνη of breeding and keeping cattle. Here the word is being given a more general sense.

"caring" (ἐπιμελητική). The Stranger says that these names encompass both the statesman and the various kinds of shepherds who nourish and feed their herds.

Yet, even before he introduces these corrections and refinements, the Stranger renews the division. More precisely, since he is reiterating the divisions previously made, he simply follows the straight path, without including the turnoffs. He begins with the following:

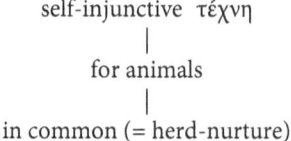

self-injunctive τέχνη
|
for animals
|
in common (= herd-nurture)

So far, the dividing follows the path previously laid out—except, remarkably, that it omits the division between "wild" and "tame," just as (young) Socrates had done (*Stat.* 264a) and then later, though he had reprimanded (young) Socrates for it, the Stranger did as well (*Stat.* 267a–c). This distinction, it seems, is easy to forget—though the relation to wildness (or violence) is previously what was lacking in the determination of the statesman as the shepherd of the human herd. What then follows is a kind of parody of the previous divisions, and a mixing-up of the terms:[15]

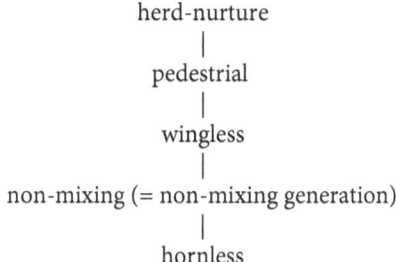

herd-nurture
|
pedestrial
|
wingless
|
non-mixing (= non-mixing generation)
|
hornless

In this parody, the terms are all mixed up from how they previously appeared. To begin with, "hornless" and "nonmixing" are mixed up, having been interchanged. Additionally, certain other terms are left out entirely: namely, "aquatic"/"dry-nurture" and "four-footed"/"two-footed." Finally, a term is added—namely, "wingless"—that does not even occur in the earlier divisions. This, then, is a parody of the divisions—or, one could say, a comedy of the comedy. It is almost as if it really does not matter how these terms are laid out. This becomes all the more evident when the Stranger abruptly abandons these divisions for the sake of the two differentiations that fall quite outside the divisions. First, the Stranger says that the kingly

---

15. One recalls here the earlier reference to mixture (cf. *Stat.* 268d).

τέχνη is the care of an *entire* human community (unlike all those others who challenged him at the end of the earlier divisions).[16] And second, the Stranger says that it is necessary to differentiate between two kinds of care: "forcible" and "voluntary." This allows him then to distinguish between the statesman or king, whose care is voluntarily accepted, and the tyrant, whose care is forcibly imposed.

After all of this, the question remains: What exactly is the care (that is, the "herd-grooming") practiced by the statesman? That is, what sense does the word "care" (ἐπιμέλεια) have other than that which it derives from the paradigm of the shepherd? Granted that *royal* care is not nourishing (i.e., feeding), and granted even that, despite the term "herd-grooming," it is not breeding, what is it specifically? In other words, in what way does the statesman (or king) care for an entire human community?

---

16. One notes especially that the Stranger now refers not to "herd" (ἀγέλη), but rather to "human community" (κοινωνία).

5. Paradigms (277a–291c)

As the middle part of the *Statesman* opens, (young) Socrates expresses his opinion that the showing-forth (ἀπόδειξις) of the statesman is complete. The Stranger, however, does not agree: "The king does not yet appear to have for us a perfectly complete figure [σχῆμα]"[1] (*Stat.* 277a). When (young) Socrates wants to know just where this figure remains incomplete, the Stranger replies by speaking of the difficulty of knowing such things. Thereby, he introduces a "methodological" discussion that will extend throughout the middle third of the *Statesman*.[2] This part of the dialogue will thus serve as a methodological reflection on the first determination of the statesman and as a preparation for the second determination.

The Stranger makes two points in his reply to (young) Socrates. First, he says that it is difficult to show forth sufficiently any of the greater things (μείζων) without the use of a *paradigm* (παράδειγμα). Now, of course, a paradigm proves to have been tacitly operating from the very beginning: namely, the paradigm of the shepherd. By means of this paradigm, the statesman was delimited through the initial divisions as the shepherd of the human herd. However, as we have seen, several things served to mark the limit of this paradigm, most notably the comedic character of the divisions in which it was operative (underscored by the parody of the divisions following the myth). In light of such a marking of limits, it has become clear that, unlike the shepherd, the statesman does not nurture, nourish, or feed his herd, but rather, in more generic terms, cares for them or tends to them. Yet, it still remains undetermined just what the specific caring or tending is that is distinctive of the statesman: that is, it remains unclear how precisely, if not in the manner of a shepherd, a statesman rules.

Second, the Stranger explains why we must rely on paradigms: "For it's likely that each of us knows everything as if in a dream [ὄναρ] and then again is ignorant of everything as it is in waking" (*Stat.* 277d). Yet, how are we to understand *dream* here? One finds a succinct indication of its meaning in the *Republic*, when

---

1. The word σχῆμα means "shape," "form," "outward appearance," or "look." One notes again the mathematical language being employed.

2. The word μέθοδος means, in a broad sense, the road or way (ὁδός) by which one goes after (μετά) something, pursuing it.

Socrates says to Glaucon (in the form of a question), "Doesn't dreaming, whether one is asleep or awake, consist in believing a likeness of something to be not a likeness but rather the thing itself which it is like?" (*Rep.* 476c). This suggests that, in the dream, one takes an image to be the thing itself of which it is an image—that is, one fails to distinguish the original from the image, hence failing to recognize an image *as* an image. To awaken means, then, *to double the image*, to apprehend it as an image of something else, a double of the original, and so to understand it in terms of, and by reference to, the original. The Stranger is thus saying that such a doubling is *always* necessary, and that in order to understand something we need to set over against it, or alongside it, a paradigm from which it can be understood. In this manner, παράδειγμα is to be taken quite literally as the setting alongside (παρά) in such a way as to show or demonstrate (δείκνυμι) something about something.³

The Stranger applies this need to know by way of a paradigm to the knowing of what a paradigm is—that is, he gives a paradigm of paradigm, one that has to do with the way in which boys who are just learning their letters can be brought to recognize the letters in various syllables. Suppose that such boys recognize the letters in some of the shortest and easiest syllables; in order that they might learn to recognize them in longer, more complex syllables, they should take as a paradigm those recognized in short syllables and set these beside the syllables in which they are not recognized. Then the boys can compare them, differentiating other from other and identifying same as same.

Owing to the fact that, in presenting the paradigm of paradigm, the Stranger does not differentiate between written letters (graphemes) and letters as they would be sounded in speech (phonemes), it is instructive to introduce this distinction. In the case of written letters, recognition of those unknown (by comparison with the paradigm) would be relatively simple—indeed, perhaps all too simple. But in the case of speech, the letters are *woven* together such that recognition requires greater effort. (In fact, the Stranger refers both to the paradigm, and to that which it lets one understand, as *weaving* (συμπλοκή) (*Stat.* 278b).) But then, in the paradigm of learning letters, one would discern not only what a paradigm is, but also the paradigm that would be applied to the statesman (i.e., weaving). It is also worth noting that the paradigm of paradigm consists of sets of *letters*—that is, elements of λόγος. This reflects the fact that showing by way of a paradigm is to take place as, or through, λόγος.

Now, just as a paradigm can function in the knowledge of the elements of λόγος (i.e., letters), so it is likewise when it is a matter of the elements of

---

3. The word παράδειγμα derives from the verb παραδείκνυμι, which means "to show by setting alongside."

things—even, it seems, of great things such as kingship. Here, too, a paradigm is needed that, by comparison with the great thing, can lead us to recognize the latter's elements (στοιχεῖον).

By the time of Aristotle, στοιχεῖον had come to refer to the "elements" (of things)—i.e., earth, air, fire, and water (in Latin, *elementum*). But, until Plato, it meant "elements" of λόγος, such as letters of syllables. Empedocles called earth, air, fire, and water not elements (στοιχεῖα) but *roots* (ῥίζωμα). The transformation of the meaning of στοιχεῖον occurs in Plato (especially in the *Theaetetus* and *Timaeus*). It is a decisive transformation from the thinking of earth, air, fire, and water as the roots from which things grow, come forth into the light, and are sustained—that is, thinking of these "things" in terms of their manifestation—to thinking of them as the ultimate constituents out of which all other things are composed—*just as* (in λόγος) letters are the constituents of which syllables and words are composed.[4]

In the face of the need for an appropriate paradigm, and at the center of the methodological discussion, the Stranger proposes another paradigm to replace that of the shepherd. In accordance with the double sense of the word,[5] this paradigm will serve both as a *model* for understanding statesmanship (πολιτική), and as an *example* to be set alongside statesmanship as that from which it is to be understood. The Stranger proposes as this paradigm the τέχνη of weaving (ὑφαντική)—or, more specifically, the weaving of cloaks or outer garments (ἱμάτιον) from wool (ἔρος).[6]

The Stranger proceeds immediately to a series of divisions aimed at delimiting weaving:

---

4. During his description of the production of the cosmos, Timaeus introduces the four elements and insists on the proportionality by means of which they form a unity, which is indissoluble except by the god himself. The proportionality is as follows—fire : air :: air : water :: water : earth (*Tim.* 31b–32c). Following the chorology (i.e., his discourse on the χώρα), Timaeus explains how the four elements are generated from out of two kinds of triangles (right isosceles and half-equilateral) (*Tim.* 53e–56b). See Sallis (2016), 52, *et al.*

5. The word παράδειγμα primarily means "pattern" or "model." For example, in the *Timaeus*, the pattern to which the god looks in making the cosmos (i.e., the pattern in imitation of which he makes the cosmos) is called a παράδειγμα (see *Tim.* 31a). However, if a model is used in order to understand something else that is greater (or more general), then we today would sometimes call it an *example*. One could say, then, that παράδειγμα is, in Hegel's sense, a "speculative" word, as it combines (or hovers between) two seemingly opposite meanings: model (archetype) and an example of an archetype.

6. There is an important play on words here that bears upon the investigation underway. The word for wool—ἔρος—sounds almost indistinguishable from the word ἔρως (desire). If one observes this play, one could say that it is a matter of the τέχνη by which the outer covering (i.e., the appearance, the look) would be woven from ἔρως—that is, from desire.

Cloak-Making (*Statesman* 279c-280a)

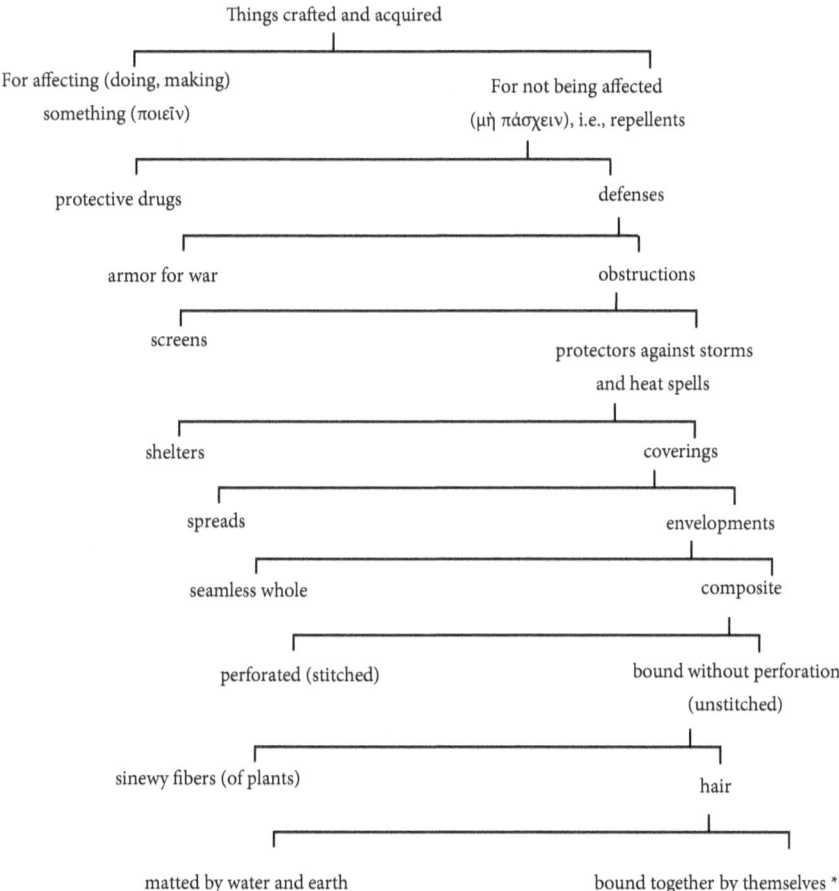

* These things are cloaks, and the τέχνη that produces them is cloak-making
(ἱμάτιον / ἱματιουργική)

The Stranger then asks whether this cloak-making is the same as weaving, and (young) Socrates says that he thinks that it is. But the Stranger retorts that one could think this only if one had not distinguished the τέχνη of cloak-making or cloak-weaving from all the others that are akin to it (συγγενής) or that work together with it (συνεργέω). The Stranger then proceeds to distinguish two groups of τέχναι that are akin to that of weaving cloaks out of wool. He first distinguishes the τέχναι that are akin to it but that were cut off from it in the course of the division. In order to do this, he goes back over the divisions, proceeding more or less from the end back to the beginning. In the prior divisions, they cut off:

- composition of spreads (*from* that of envelopments: i.e., casting under from casting around)
- manufacture out of flax, grasses (i.e., out of sinewy fibers of plants) (*from* manufacture out of hair of animals)
- making felt (i.e., binding or matting hair together by water or earth) (*from* binding together by themselves)
- composition by perforation and stitching, as, for example, in shoemaking (*from* composition involving no stitching)
- making of whole coverings, as from animal skins (*from* making of composite coverings)
- τέχναι of shelters, e.g., housebuilding, carpentry (*from* those of coverings)
- τέχναι that supply obstructions (screens) against theft and violent action, e.g., lid-making, making of doors and bolts (*from* those that make protectors against storms and heat spells)
- making of armor (*from* making of obstructions)
- magical τέχνη of protective drugs (*from* those that produce defense)

The Stranger then distinguishes other forms of τέχναι that are akin to the weaving of woolen cloaks. These are the τέχναι that work together with weaving in such a way that they are indispensable to it, and yet are nonetheless distinct from it. The Stranger begins with the broad distinction between those τέχναι that make the tools by which the thing is made (i.e., the co-cause of the becoming of the thing) and the τέχναι that produce the thing (i.e., the cause). Then he distinguishes the various causes—that is, the τέχναι actually allied with weaving in producing the cloak:

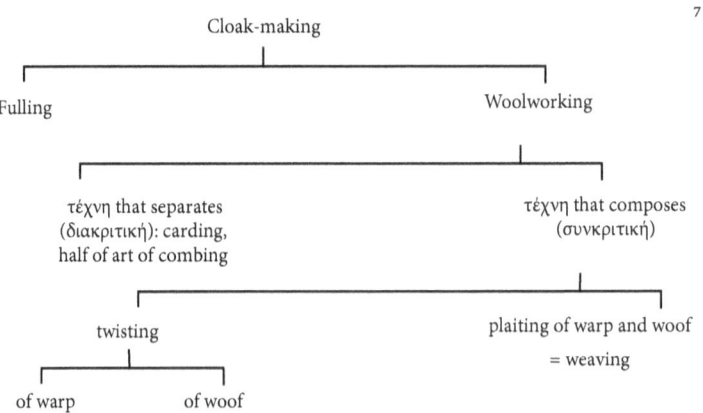

[7]

---

7. "Fulling" refers to the cleaning, shrinking, and thickening of cloth with moisture, heat, and pressure. "Carding," for its part, refers to the act of running a card through the wool for the purpose of cleaning it of extraneous matter and preparing it for spinning.

The Stranger emphasizes the way in which this is a paradigm for the configuration of τέχναι related to kingship. We saw that, when kingship is determined as nurturing or even as tending (i.e., caring for) the human herd, there are many other τέχναι that contend with the king, maintaining that they too nurture or care for the human herd. Thus, in the case of the paradigm of weaving, "all these will dispute with the capacity of the art of weaving about the treatment and the coming-into-being of cloaks, granting it the biggest part but reserving for themselves big parts too" (*Stat.* 281b).

Following the analysis of weaving, the Stranger sounds a note similar to that following the great myth: "Why did we not answer straight off that weaving was a plaiting of woof and warp, but [instead] went around in a circle distinguishing very many things in vain?" (*Stat.* 283b).[8] These self-reflexive queries regarding the excessive length of his speeches provide the occasion for asking about excess and defect in general. Now, in order to judge whether something—for example, a speech (λόγος)—is excessive or defective (i.e., too long or too short), one must apply to it a measure (μέτρον). Indeed, the Stranger says that what deals with length and brevity is the τέχνη of measurement (μετρητική). He goes on to explain that there are two kinds of measure—that is, two ways in which length and brevity can be measured. The first is what could be called "mutually relative measure" (*Stat.* 283e), where large is measured relative to its contrary, small. In this case, something's being large consists in its being larger than something else (which, relative to it, is small). In such mutually relative measure, there is no reference to a measure or standard outside of the relation between contraries. In the second case, there is measure relative to the mean (τὸ μέτριον)—that is, measure with respect to the fitting, the appropriate, the needful. In this case, the mean provides, from outside of the mere relation of contraries, the measure by which to measure the largeness (i.e., excessiveness) or smallness (i.e., defectiveness) of something. A λόγος, for example, is too long if it is longer than is appropriate for that which it would accomplish (namely, a showing-forth). Yet, while the μετρίον is outside the mere relation between the contraries, it is not merely formal or arbitrarily imposed, but is itself determined by the context in which the measurement is being carried out. For example, the appropriate length of a λόγος is determined by what the λόγος is aimed at making manifest—more precisely, it is determined by the manifestation that it aims to bring about.

Only in the second case is there genuinely a measure (μέτρον), a mean (μετρίον) in reference to which measurement can be carried out. The Stranger says that all τέχνη requires measure in reference to a mean—that is, in all τέχνη, a close watch is maintained over the making (or doing) in order that it adheres to the mean. This is something difficult, according to the Stranger, and

---

8. As the Stranger said earlier, "We raised up an amazing bulk of the myth" (*Stat.* 277c).

is possible only through the skill of the artisan.[9] Such measurement is required in all τέχνη—and, in particular, the Stranger says, in πολιτική and its paradigm, weaving, and perhaps above all in dialectic.

Appealing to the paradigm of the paradigm (i.e., letters being learned), the Stranger suggests that the search for the statesman is ultimately—or at least also—for the sake of becoming more skilled in dialectic as such (*Stat.* 285d). But dialectic—that is, division and whatever else must come to aid it—is the process by which, beginning with a name, one unfolds a λόγος through which the thing named (i.e., the thing itself) becomes manifest. And yet, one might ask: How is it that such λόγοι are needed? How is it that certain things need to be made manifest by λόγος? The Stranger's answer is that it is because there are things that cannot become manifest through an image fitted to the senses. Indeed, he says that this is so for the greatest things:

> There has been no image devised as plain as day for human beings in the case of the biggest and most honorable of the things which are, by the showing of which, whoever wants to fill up the soul of the inquirer, will adequately fill it up by fitting it to one of the senses. It is for this reason that one must practice to be able to give and receive an account of each thing, for the bodiless things, being the most beautiful and the greatest, are only shown with clarity by speech and nothing else. And it is for the sake of them that all the present remarks are said. (*Stat.* 286a)

The length of a λόγος is to be judged relative to τὸ πρέπον—that is, to the fitting, the suitable, the appropriate, but also (as the word itself says) the manifesting, the letting be manifest.[10] Thus, in compounding these two senses, it can be said that the length of a λόγος is to be measured by what is fitting for making manifest what the λόγος would make manifest. As the Stranger goes on to say, it is always a question of whether a λόγος of a certain length makes us "more capable of dialectic and more capable of finding the way to make manifest by λόγος the things that are [τῆς τῶν ὄντων λόγῳ δηλώσεως]" (*Stat.* 287a).

* * *

We turn now to the opening of the final third of the dialogue. The Stranger returns to the question of the statesman—specifically, to the task of delimiting statesmanship (πολιτική) or kingship (βασιλική) by applying to it the paradigm of weaving. We have seen in the delimitation of weaving that two different operations are involved. First, there is the cutting off of all the τέχναι that are akin to, but different from, weaving. This is what the Stranger did in the divisions in which he cut off

---

9. For example, in tuning an instrument, the musician must take care (i.e., ensure) that the strings are tightened neither too little nor too much.

10. [Editor's Note: πρέπω principally means "to be clearly seen" or "conspicuous"—it refers to that which shines forth in such a way as to show itself. Only secondarily does it come to mean "fitting" or "befitting."]

from weaving all the other kinds of production, such as the production of armor for war, of protective drugs, of shelter, etc. This procedure is a matter of sealing off the byways in the dividing that leads to weaving. Second, there is the distinguishing of the τέχναι that are akin to and work together with weaving, being indispensable to it—namely, carding and the twisting of warp and woof. Presumably, the delimitation of statesmanship will also involve these two kinds of differentiation.

In any case, the Stranger proceeds to cut off various τέχναι that are distinct from statesmanship (or kingship). He notes first that the king has already been separated from all the τέχναι that deal with herds. This refers to the differentiation of the king from the shepherd that emerged at the end of the first part: the shepherd nurtures (nourishes, feeds) his herd, whereas the statesman cares for his herd, which is thus not a herd (of animals), but rather a human community. But now, as if leaving the shepherds in the countryside, the Stranger turns to the city (πόλις) itself. He proceeds to distinguish the various kinds of τέχναι (that is, the causes and co-causes) in the city, and to distinguish them from πολιτική or βασιλική. Yet, just as he is about to begin these divisions, he inserts a remark about the character of the dividing itself—namely, that it is difficult to cut them into *two*: "Well, then, let's divide them, as if it were a sacrificial victim, limb by limb [κατὰ μέλη τοίνυν αὐτὰς οἷον ἱερεῖον διαιρώμεθα], since we're incapable of doing it in two, for one must always cut into that number that's as near as possible to two" (*Stat.* 287c).

Now, throughout the divisions, and even still, the Stranger insists that proper dividing is done down the middle, in two. But here it is as though something comes into play that complicates and renders uneven and nonuniform the division, such that the natural points where the knife is to be applied are more like those of an animal body. What is it, then, that produces this effect on the divisions? It is precisely *the body* that produces this effect—not, however, an animal carcass, but rather the *human* body, for virtually all the τέχναι have to do with supplying the means of satisfying the needs or desires of the body. These needs and desires, and the means of satisfying them, do not divide neatly into pairs. As a result, the Stranger says they will divide them like a sacrificial victim, cutting them off, or tearing them apart, *limb by limb* (κατὰ μέλη).[11]

The Stranger proceeds to distinguish from statesmanship (or kingship) the various τέχναι practiced in the city. First, there are those τέχναι that produce tools. These are the kind of τέχναι that are referred to as "co-causes," for, while they do not directly produce things that satisfy human needs, they are presupposed by the τέχναι that produce such things. The Stranger notes that separating

---

11. In the expression "limb by limb," one can hear a further allusion—namely, to the votaries of Dionysus, the Maenads, who in the wilds of the forest would seize a sacrificial animal and tear it apart limb by limb. It is as though, in the very midst of the dialectical dividing into kinds, there is an awareness of such an erotic and ecstatic force of life as is displayed in the figure of Dionysus.

this kind of τέχνη from the others is difficult (χαλεπόν), owing to the fact that almost anything can become a tool or instrument for producing something else.[12] Moreover, because it is difficult, this division is likely to be imperfect. This kind will likely transgress borders and contaminate the purity of the other kinds, of those that would seem simply to use tools in order to produce something else.

The second type of τέχνηαι practiced in the city are those that produce vessels (ἀγγεῖον) for the safekeeping of things. The Stranger observes that this "does not really belong to the τέχνη being sought" (*Stat.* 288a), and so is to be separated from statesmanship. The third kind of τέχνη the Stranger states as a kind of puzzle: "it is pedestrial and in liquid, it roams far and wide and does not roam at all, it is honored and dishonored, but with one name, because all of it is for the sake of some kind of propping in its coming to be on each and every occasion as a seat for someone" (*Stat.* 288a). What it produces, in other words, is a support or vehicle (ὄχημα).[13] Such things are not the work of statesmanship, according to the Stranger, but of carpentry, pottery, and coppersmithing.

The Stranger has begun enumerating, and now asks about, the fourth kind of τέχνη, which includes garments, armor, and walls (including envelopments of earth and stone). He sums up by calling this kind "defense [πρόβλημα]."[14] He further notes that these things are not produced by statesmanship, but rather by housebuilding and weaving. It is crucial to note that, with this fourth kind of τέχνη, the Stranger has separated from statesmanship the very paradigm that has been, and later will again explicitly be, used for statesmanship—namely, weaving.

The fifth kind of τέχνη includes ornaments (κόσμος), painting (or writing: γραφική), and the imitations (μιμήματα) produced by using these along with music—in other words, the fine arts, including dramatic poetry. This kind of thing, the Stranger says, may be called "plaything [παίγνιον]," as it is done not for serious intent, but rather for play (παιδιά). (We are to assume that this kind of τέχνη is separated from statesmanship, though the Stranger does not explicitly say so.)

The sixth kind of τέχνη is that which supplies bodies (σῶμα) out of which all the other τέχναι produce their work—for example, gold, silver, wood, and wool. (One sees, then, that the paradigm of weaving is still being carried along). The Stranger distinguishes this τέχνη from kingship, and then calls it "the first-born and uncomposite possession for human beings" (*Stat.* 288e).

The Stranger then adds the seventh kind of τέχνη, called "nourishment," provided by hunting, farming, etc.[15] He then reiterates the seven kinds; however,

---

12. One can illustrate his point with the following example: A metal worker uses his tools (e.g., hammer, forge, anvil) for producing the chisels and other tools that the violin maker uses in order to produce a violin. In turn, the musician uses the violin as an instrument for producing beautiful music.

13. Ὄχημα refers to that which bears or supports something, such as a carriage, chariot, or ship.

14. A πρόβλημα is anything held before one as barrier or defense (such as shelter, armor, screen, or a cloak).

15. This move marks a return to the country, but only in terms of what it provides to the city.

as he does so, he reorders them, putting this "first-born" kind first. It is first, of course, in the sense that it supplies the material from which the other six kinds of τέχνη produce their works. But it is also first in that it points to a certain limit of τέχνη, a limit that limits and delimits τέχνη. Whatever is made by τέχνη is made from something, a something that may itself be made by another τέχνη. But if one continues in this regression back through the hierarchy of τέχναι, one eventually reaches a point where the product is made from something that is *not* in turn made, but is rather taken from nature. In this sense, all τέχνη refers back to φύσις, to bodies that occur without our having made them. In other words, all τέχνη refers back to φύσις as its source and limit.

Following the enumeration of these seven kinds of τέχνη, the Stranger mentions "the look of coinage, of seals, and of every kind of stamp" (*Stat.* 289b). He says that these do not have "any big genus," but have to be "dragged [...] by force" into some of the kinds already laid out (*Stat.* 289b). In other words, the τέχναι that produce these kinds of things do not fit into the kinds that have been delimited and distinguished from statesmanship. Here, then, the *nonuniformity* that inheres in the divisions comes explicitly to be identified. These are τέχναι left over, extras that merely hang out, contaminating the purity of the divisions. This is precisely like what happens when an animal is torn apart limb by limb: what is produced is not a clean cut of meat, as uneven shreds of flesh will adhere to the limb that has been torn off.

* * *

So much, then, for those τέχναι that are to be separated from statesmanship—a separation that is by no means absolute, given that all of these occur together alongside statesmanship *in the city* (as co-causes). The Stranger turns next to those who more directly work together with the statesman and yet are distinct from him. These are identified in general as slaves and servants, but the pertinent sense is that they are those whose work has a certain proximity to that of the statesman, who serve the king as the carder and spinner serve the weaver. These are the ones "who dispute with the king about the web itself" (*Stat.* 289c)—that is, who dispute whether the king (i.e., the weaver) is the one who produces it, or whether, like the carder and spinner, they do not also have a part in producing it. These are also the ones who, precisely because of the proximity of what they do to what the genuine king does, can be confused with the king. For the same reason, they are also the ones who can most easily usurp the authority or role of the king. The Stranger mentions several such kinds. Dismissing slaves as having no pretension to kingship, he turns to silver exchanges, merchants, owner-captains, and retailers, asking (young) Socrates, "They won't, will they, lay any claim to statesmanship?" (*Stat.* 290a). (Young) Socrates replies, "Perhaps to commercial statesmanship" (ibid.). The Stranger appears to leave this possibility open—namely, that merchants, etc., might lay claim to or usurp the part of statesmanship having to do with commerce. All the Stranger insists on is that laborers (i.e., those hired for wages) lay no claim to kingship.

The Stranger next mentions heralds, scribes, and others who perform various jobs involved in the art of ruling. (Young) Socrates objects that these are servants, not rulers, and the Stranger agrees that it would be strange to find in subservient positions like these the ones who lay claim to kingship. Still, the Stranger thinks they are somewhere hereabouts, working in some proximity to the king.

He turns next to diviners (i.e., interpreters from gods to humans) and priests (who know about offering up sacrifices to gods). He observes that, because of the magnitude of their undertakings, diviners and priests get swelled up with pride and come to have a solemn reputation—indeed, to such an extent that in Egypt one must be a diviner or priest in order to be able to be king. The Stranger notes that, among the Greeks, the greatest sacrifices of this sort are in the hands of the greatest rulers, and then says pointedly, "They say that whoever gets to be king here by lot has been assigned the most august and particularly ancestral of the ancient sacrifices" (*Stat.* 290e). The reference is to the King Archon, the one before whom, on the previous day, (old) Socrates had appeared in order to be indicted for the charges brought by Meletus, the one, therefore, who had decided to go ahead with the trial that will lead to the condemnation and execution of (old) Socrates—who, we assume, is still standing silently by, listening to all of this. The Stranger says, "We must examine [σκεπτέον] these lottery kings" (*Stat.* 291a).

However, suddenly the Stranger says that he has caught sight of something "strange [ἀτόπους]" (*Stat.* 291a): namely, a very large crowd of people that has just come into view. As he says, "Their kind is of all sorts [or tribes], as it appears on just now examining them. Many of the men bear a resemblance to lions, centaurs, and others of this sort, and a very large number to satyrs and the weak and wily beasts, and they quickly exchange their looks and their capacities [δύναμιν] with one another" (*Stat.* 291a–b). Curiously, although he says he has just discerned who these are, the Stranger does not *say* who they are. Regardless, we note that his vision of them brings animals back upon the scene, and especially creatures that mix up the human and the animal.[16] Yet, these are *men* who put on these appearances and who can quickly exchange one look for another—that is, who can constantly change their appearance.[17] The Stranger calls them "the greatest enchanters of all the sophists" (*Stat.* 291c). Are these, then, just the sophists as such (as delimited in the previous day's conversation)? Or are they something else, something other, something more particular? In any case, they are, according to the Stranger, very difficult to remove from those who are genuinely statesmen.

---

16. For example, satyrs (which are part goat, part human) and centaurs (which are half man and half horse).

17. Such as Proteus, to whom Socrates, as he waited before the porch of the king on the previous morning, had compared Euthyphro (*Euthyph.* 15d).

6. The Weaver of the Πόλις (291d–311c)

Having finished separating out the various τέχναι that operate within the city that are different from statesmanship, as well as those that work together closely alongside that statesman and yet are distinct from him, the Stranger abruptly changes the direction of the discourse toward the topic of political rule (ἀρχή).[1] He begins with three kinds of political rule or constitution, which correspond to rule by one, rule by a few, and rule by the many:

1. Monarchy (rule by one)
2. Oligarchy (rule by the few)
3. Democracy (rule by the many)

The Stranger then introduces, as further determining factors, three pairs of contraries: namely, forcible/voluntary, poverty/wealth, and law/lawlessness. He then applies these to the three forms of rule so as to generate five altogether:

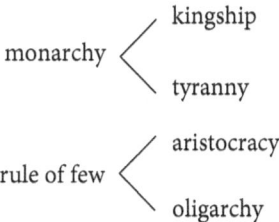

In the face of all of this, the Stranger raises the following question: "Do we believe any of these regimes [πολιτειῶν] to be the right [ὀρθήν] one?" (*Stat.* 292a). Specifically, the Stranger wants to know whether the right regime may be determined by delimiting it in terms of the following factors (or limits):

one/few/many
wealth/poverty
forcible/voluntary
with (written) laws/without (written) laws

---

1. The word ἀρχή primarily means "beginning" or "origin," but also has the sense (as here) of "rule," "power," or "sovereignty." The ἀρχή is that which, as the principle origin of a thing, rules over it, governing its character. In speaking of political rule (ἀρχή), the Stranger also uses the word πολιτεία here, meaning "constitution" in the sense of the way in which a πόλις is made up, structured, and constituted with regard to the exercise of power and authority.

The Stranger then strikes—and says that he is striking—a dissonant note, one that sounds against the assumption regarding the delimitation of the right regime. In a sense, he reaches all the way back to the beginning of the *Statesman*, back to that from which the initial series of divisions proceeded—a beginning that, despite all of the modifications and displacements, has remained in play. That beginning was *knowledge* (ἐπιστήμη, or τέχνη), and so now the Stranger says, "We said, I believe, that the royal rule is some one of the knowledges [τῶν ἐπιστημῶν εἶναί τινα]" (*Stat.* 292b). What really matters, then, and determines whether a regime is the right one, is not whether it is ruled by few or many, nor whether voluntarily or forcibly, nor in some reference to poverty or wealth.[2] Rather, what matters is whether its rule is determined by knowledge, specifically by the royal knowledge, "knowledge of the rule of human beings [ἐπιστήμη . . . περὶ ἀνθρώπων ἀρχῆς]" (*Stat.* 292d). The Stranger notes that such knowledge is "pretty nearly the hardest and greatest to acquire" (*Stat.* 292d).

On this basis, the Stranger easily dismisses democracy, as it would not be possible for the multitude to acquire this knowledge—thus, the ruling that occurs in a democracy cannot be by way of knowledge. He then draws a comparison with physicians. What accounts for being a physician is not the willingness or unwillingness of the patients, nor is it whether the physician proceeds in conformity with what is written, nor whether he is rich or poor. What accounts for being a physician is only that he presides over and carries out the treatment with medical τέχνη, and that means with τέχνη governed by the appropriate knowledge. Likewise, the only thing that counts with respect to a regime is whether it is ruled with πολιτική governed by knowledge. The Stranger intimates that the rule will then be one of justice and one that makes better, and that, furthermore, all other regimes will be only imitations of such a regime:

> And so regardless of whether they purge the city for the good by killing some or maybe exiling, or they make the city smaller by sending out colonies somewhere like swarms of bees, or they increase it by importing some different people from somewhere or other outside and making them citizens, as long as they are employing science [ἐπιστήμη] and the just and, in keeping it safe, make it better from worse to the best of their ability, we must state that this is the only right regime and in accordance with definitions of this sort. And all the rest we speak of, we must say of them that they are not genuine and in their being are not, but they have imitated this one, and some, which we speak of as with good laws, have done it with more beautiful results, and all the rest with uglier. (*Stat.* 293d–e)

While the Stranger was speaking of this right regime, he referred to the rulers as ruling with laws or without laws. (Young) Socrates picks up on this and

---

2. The Stranger does not mention laws here.

asks about this situation of ruling without laws. To (young) Socrates's surprise, no doubt, the Stranger replies that ruling without laws is what is best: "Although it is manifest that, in a way, legislation [νομοθετική] belongs to kingship [βασιλικῆς], the best [thing] is not for the laws but for a man—the king with intelligence [φρονήσεως]—to have power" (*Stat.* 294a). In other words, rule by an intelligent king is better than the rule of law. This is owing to the fact that, as the Stranger says, law can never comprehend with precision the best for each person at all times, and owing further to the fact that law is simple, whereas human affairs are never simple. Because of the enormous range of dissimilarities between human beings and their actions, and because human things are constantly changing, the rule of law is never as effective, according to the Stranger, as the rule of an intelligent king.

And yet, if law is so poorly fitted to human affairs, how is it that laws come to be made in the first place? The Stranger explains their origin by introducing the paradigm of the gymnastic trainer.[3] When there is a group of young men to be trained, it is not possible for the trainer to work in minute detail on each individual, prescribing the exercise needed for each unique body. As a result, the trainer simply prescribes group exercise irrespective of particular bodily differences. The very same situation obtains with the legislator. As he supervises the human community, it is not possible for him to prescribe exactly what is suitable for each particular person. Consequently, he is obliged to set down the law, which prescribes what is best "for many and for the most part" (*Stat.* 295a). Because the legislator "will never become competent enough, in giving orders to all of them collectively, to prescribe precisely what is suitable for each one [. . .], he will prescribe, in his writings and without writings—when he legislates by way of ancestral usages—that which is for the many and for the most part, and it's in just this way that he'll set down the law for individuals in a somewhat coarser way" (*Stat.* 295a).

There are three points to consider regarding the Stranger's discussion concerning law. First, we note immediately that there is something *arithmetical* about law (νόμος). Law considers each *one*, not with regard to what is suitable to and particular about that *one*, but rather as merely a *one* among many—that is, as one among many *ones*. From the point of view of the law, these *ones* are essentially indistinguishable: they are like the identical (yet distinct) *ones* that can be counted. The Stranger hints at the arithmetical character of law when he says that the legislator cannot prescribe precisely what is suitable "for each one [ἑνὶ ἑκάστῳ]." He could simply have said *for each*, but he conspicuously includes the "one [ἑνί]." Granted the arithmetical character of law, it is not surprising that

---

3. One recalls that the entire conversation takes place near a gymnasium where, at the beginning of the *Theaetetus* the day before, Theaetetus and (young) Socrates had been exercising.

what caught the attention of (young) Socrates the mathematician was the Stranger's reference to rule without law.

Second, the difficulty—if not the impossibility—of prescribing for each one is also expressed by the Stranger in a somewhat different way: "For how could anyone, Socrates, ever be so competent as to be always sitting beside each person throughout his life and to order with precision the suitable [τὸ προσῆκον]?" (*Stat.* 295b). Most remarkably, the Stranger goes on to suggest, though hypothetically, that one who has royal knowledge would indeed be capable of doing just this. And yet, one cannot but wonder: How could any human, no matter how knowledgeable, be capable of such a thing? How could anyone, regardless of their knowledge, attend absolutely to every particular in all of its particularity at all particular times?

Third, the Stranger notes in passing that there are two ways in which laws can come about: they can be legislated in writing, or they can be merely extensions of traditional beliefs (i.e., "ancestral usages") that can perhaps remain entirely unwritten. But even in this latter case they are passed along *as if* written, as if inscribed in the memory of every citizen. One could say, then, that to the extent that there is here a critique of law, this critique converges with the Platonic critique of writing as such.[4]

Against this background of what he has said about law, the Stranger comes around again to the king's superiority to law, saying that if someone had the τέχνη of ruling (i.e., βασιλική), and if such a king could order with precision what is suitable to each one, then "he would hardly ever put impediments in his own way by writing these so-called laws" (*Stat.* 295b). Rather, he would simply rule without laws. As before, the Stranger again makes use of a paradigm: actually, in this case, the two paradigms he previously mentioned, the physician and the trainer. If one of these were planning to go abroad and was concerned that the sick (or the gymnasts) would not remember his orders in his absence, he might write down some reminders for them.[5] Suppose, however, that the physician or trainer should return sooner than expected: to suppose that he could not then order things contrary to what he had written down would be laughable to the extreme.

Thus, for one who has the τέχνη of ruling—for one who rules by means of knowledge—it is irrelevant whether what he orders is in conformity with, or contrary to, what is written down. Indeed, almost everything else usually thought to be important—namely, whether he persuades his subjects or not, whether he

---

4. [Editor's Note: See especially the *Phaedrus*, 274b ff.]

5. One observes here the connection between writing and memory: writing is for the aid of memory. Were it not for the limits and weakness of living memory, there would be no need for the dead letter of writing.

is rich or poor, etc.—is irrelevant. Rather, what counts is only that he "does what is advantageous" (*Stat.* 296e) for all, and this he will do if he has βασιλική, the knowledge of proper ruling.

The Stranger concludes: "Mustn't this [i.e., doing what is advantageous by ruling with knowledge] in these cases too be the truest limit [τὸν ὅρον] of the right [ὀρθῆς] arrangement [i.e., governance] of a πόλις?" (*Stat.* 296e). Here, limit (ὅρος) means that which delimits and thereby renders manifest. As the truest (ἀληθινώτατον) limit of the right arrangement of the πόλις, acting with knowledge toward what is most advantageous is that which most properly delimits, and so renders most distinctly manifest, the πόλις.

The Stranger continues employing paradigms, now that of the sea captain and the physician, saying that the captain does what is proper for his ship and sailors not by writing down laws, but by supplying his τέχνη as law. Here, the strength of the τέχνη is mightier than the laws. The Stranger then embarks upon an extended and highly ironic speech in which he presents a sort of genealogy of democracy, at least of the democratic regime that was current in Athens at the time of Socrates's trial and execution. He asks (young) Socrates to suppose, as a hypothetical exercise, that the people were suffering at the hands of the physicians and captains. He then asks him to suppose that the people decided to arrange things so that these τέχναι could no longer rule on their own authority. He asks him to further suppose that the people gathered into an assembly (of all the people, or of the rich) and then let everybody, regardless of their τέχνη, contribute their own opinions about sailing or about illness. In such a scenario, whatever came to be agreed upon by the multitude would then be written down as law. From that point on, conformity with these laws would have to be maintained in making sea voyages and treating the sick. Each year, some from the multitude would be chosen by lot as rulers, and then they would rule as captains of the ships and healers of the sick. The Stranger finally asks (young) Socrates to suppose that there is someone who, contrary to the writings, is seeking the τέχνη of piloting and of healing: "First of all he must be named neither a skilled physician nor a skilled captain but a talker about highfalutin things, a kind of garrulous sophist, and then, in the second place, on the ground that he's corrupting different people younger than himself and convincing them to engage in piloting and medicine not in conformity with laws, but to rule with their own authority the ships and the sick, then anyone who wants can and is permitted to draw up an indictment and haul him before a—what do you call it?—court of justice" (*Stat.* 299b-c). It is of course perfectly transparent that the figure being described is Socrates—that is, *old* Socrates, who just the day before had appeared before the King Archon to hear the indictment against him by Meletus. The Stranger even calls the name "Socrates" shortly after this depiction (*Stat.* 299d). It is thus perhaps not accidental that Socrates—that is, young Socrates—makes one of his most insightful responses at this point: "It's plain [δῆλον]: all the arts [τέχναι] we have would completely perish, and they would never come to be at a later time on account of this law that forbids their search. And hence life, which even now is hard, would prove to be altogether unlivable throughout that time" (*Stat.* 299e). With the collapse of the τέχναι, humans would return to the condition that prevailed just after the god let go of the cosmos, that condition in which, with the outbreak of wildness and violence, they faced the prospect of utter destruction.

Thus, on the one side, there is rule by the king who rules through knowledge and not by means of laws; on the other side, there are all of the other regimes. The Stranger now grants that in these regimes, the laws have been laid down by much trial and error and must be obeyed, referring to this situation as a "second sailing" (*Stat.* 300c).[6] In the absence of true kingship, there must be recourse to law and a demand that the law be obeyed. If these regimes are to imitate the true regime—that is, if they are to rule through the τέχνη of ruling—they must require obedience to laws. And yet, the Stranger then says that as they "write up writings [. . .], they run after the traces [ἴχνη] of the truest regime [πολιτείας]" (*Stat.* 301e). (We shall return to this point below.)

The Stranger concludes this entire discussion by sketching the typology of regimes—that is, of the *incorrect* regimes—in terms of their lawfulness or unlawfulness, saying that, though all six of these regimes are difficult (χαλεπόν), some are less difficult, some more so. He places them in order, beginning with the least difficult:

Kingship
Aristocracy
Lawful democracy
Unlawful democracy
Oligarchy
Tyranny

Regarding democracy, he says that it is weak and has no capacity for any great good or evil, because the rule is distributed to so many people: "Accordingly, though of all regimes that are lawful it has proved to be the worst, it's the best of all that are unlawful. And though to live in a democracy wins out over all that are intemperate, of those that are in due order, one must live in this least of all" (*Stat.* 303a–b). It is best to live in a kingship—at least if one excludes the seventh regime (that is, the right regime, the regime of the intelligent king who rules not by law, but by τέχνη), which is ultimately the very first: "It is by far the first and best to live in the first regime, except for the seventh, for one must of course separate that

---

6. [Editor's Note: See *Phaedo,* 99d ff.]

out from all the rest of the regimes as a god from human beings" (*Stat.* 303b). (We shall also return to this issue below.)

At this point, the Stranger introduces yet another paradigm. As he puts it, in gold ore from which earth and stones have been removed, there remain other impurities (e.g., copper and silver) that are more difficult to separate. Likewise, in the case of the statesman, there are others who are difficult to distinguish from him because of their proximity to him. Then, weaving *music* into his analysis in a very remarkable way, the Stranger draws a distinction between the learning of music and the question of whether or not we should learn music. He then develops an analogous distinction with respect to those τέχναι that are close to statesmanship but to be distinguished from it—namely, that of rhetorician, general, and judge. The point of the distinction is that the statesman must not himself act, but must rule over those who have the capacity to act—like the rhetorician, the general, and the judge, but also, by extension, all the τέχναι practiced in the πόλις. But how, precisely, does the statesman rule over the τέχναι? The Stranger answers this by putting in play, once again, the paradigm of *weaving*: "But that which rules over all of these and the laws, cares for all the things throughout a city, and weaves them all together most correctly—should we comprehend its power by the designation of the common, we would address it most justly, it seems, as political [πολιτικήν]" (*Stat.* 305e).

Finally, the Stranger applies the paradigm of weaving by identifying those moments in the πόλις that correspond to the warp and woof of weaving. He uses the traditional names "courage" (ἀνδρεία) and "moderation" (σωφροσύνη), but extends their scope far beyond their traditional sense so that they apply to two opposed moments that are inherent in all human actions and thought (and thus both in what is bodily and what is soulful). Thus, the statesman weaves the web of the πόλις, the web of politics—the web that consists of an ordered totality of τέχναι animated by the opposition and intermixture of courage and moderation (as moments in all human action and thought).

* * *

In the figure of the right (i.e., *truest*) regime and of the statesman who would rule by means of knowledge, the major moments of the entire dialogue are gathered up. First, in determining how the statesman rules—namely, that it is by knowledge (or τέχνη)—the Stranger reaches all the way back to the starting point of the initial divisions, knowledge. Furthermore, this knowledge is determined as "critical and supervisory" (*Stat.* 292b). With this determination, he returns to the very point where the divisions first went wrong: namely, that point where with the division of "cognitive" knowledge into "discrimination" and "injunction," the further divisions followed the side of "injunction." Now, returning to that point, the Stranger retains both sides. Second, the myth—especially its telling of the moment when the god let go of the cosmos—has determined the entire further course of the dialogue, since this is the very moment in which politics begins, the moment in which all that the rest of the dialogue analyzes first comes into play. (Additionally, and more specifically, the distinction between the right regime and the other six regimes mirrors the separation between the age of Cronus and the age of Zeus.) Third, the analysis of paradigm (i.e., the paradigm of paradigm) releases a series of paradigms in the analyses that lead to the determination of the statesman: physician, sea captain, trainer, gold ore, music, etc. Furthermore, the right regime proves to be the political paradigm in that all other regimes are imitations of it. Fourth, the analysis of weaving is carried over directly to the determination of the statesman. Fifth, the analysis of measure comes into play in several ways—most notably, in that the statesman rules with right measure (for example, in his interweaving of courage and moderation). Sixth, and finally, all the divisions in the final part serve to distinguish the statesman from those who practice other τέχναι, and thus these divisions are all taken up into the determination of the statesman.[7]

* * *

What remains to be said, then, of the one true statesman—the one who would rule through knowledge in the seventh regime? There are three decisive passages that bear immediately upon this question. The first passage occurs during the Stranger's discussion of the various regimes: "There is no king that comes to be in the cities, as we in fact assert" (*Stat.* 301e). Thus, the true king, the true statesman, is not to be found in any of the six regimes that are ruled by law. The second passage extends this notion, suggesting that those who take part in governance of any of the six regimes (that are not based on knowledge) "are not statesman but partisans," going on further to state that they are nothing other than counterfeits and "the sophists of sophists" (*Stat.* 303b–c). The third passage, occurring just prior to the previous one, refers to the seventh (i.e., the correct) regime: "One must of course separate that out from all the rest of the regimes as a god from human beings" (*Stat.* 303b). Thus, the true statesman is not to be found in any of the six regimes, but only in a regime that is removed from these as a god is separated from human beings. And yet, gods do not show themselves to humans except

---

7. Moreover, in the determination of the right regime and the statesman who rules in it, the entire dialogical trilogy of *Theaetetus*, *Sophist*, and *Statesman* is gathered up in many ways. Here it suffices to note only two general ways in which this is so. To begin with, in the *Statesman*, it is determined precisely what knowledge is, at least in the realm of the political. Such a determination is precisely what the *Theaetetus* attempted, but managed to accomplish only in a very general manner (namely, in the account of the κοινά). Second, in the weaving together of courage and moderation (as described in the *Statesman*), the blending together of kinds, in the account of which the *Sophist* culminates, is represented.

on certain occasions when they intervene in human affairs, and even then, they soon withdraw. One could say, then, that the true statesman *withdraws*. He is like the doctor and trainer who go away and leave some writings behind (as laws) as a guide until they return. But the true statesman never simply returns—and was never simply there in the first place. The Stranger says that those in human regimes "run after the traces of the truest regime" (*Stat.* 301e), and so after the traces, and not the full presence, of the statesman.

Yet, how do they pursue these traces left, or granted, by the true statesman as he withdraws? The Stranger does not say. However, we might venture to say that one can pursue these traces, and so imitate the withdrawing statesman, only by engaging in that very withdrawal—that is, only by letting oneself be drawn along in the withdrawal.

As to what such engagement requires—this remains an open question.

Editor's Afterword

THIS VOLUME CONSISTS of two lecture courses delivered by John Sallis: the first, on Plato's *Symposium*, was held at Boston College during the fall semester of 2011; the second, on Plato's *Statesman*, was held at Boston College during the fall semester of 2014. Although other versions of both lecture courses had been given in previous years at other institutions, the present volume is based on the handwritten manuscripts as they were prepared for the above iterations. Sallis touches on the *Symposium* and the *Statesman* in other published contexts, but the present volume represents his longest and most sustained engagement to date with either text.

I have stayed as true as possible to Sallis's handwritten manuscripts, adding elaborations, references, and amplifications only where the text absolutely demanded it. Most notes are Sallis's own; however, some have been added for purposes of clarification or elaboration, and have been marked as "Editor's Note."

Owing to the fact that Sallis moves more or less linearly through the Platonic texts, and owing also to the fact that his analyses and interpretations remain firmly grounded in the texts in question, citations of Plato's texts are given only where there is a direct reference to, or quotation of, the dialogues. The general range of Stephanus numbers with which a particular chapter deals are provided in the table of contents and at each chapter's heading.

For the sake of fidelity to the Platonic text, and in keeping with Sallis's own custom, the Greek has not been transliterated. Additionally, the diagrams that appear throughout the volume are of Sallis's own design.

I had the good fortune of being present for the 2011 *Symposium* course in its entirety. Although I am in possession of extensive personal notes from that course, the precision and specificity of Sallis's own manuscripts made it unnecessary to consult them. I hope that the present volume brings something of the *wonder* of Sallis's classroom to those who have never experienced it, and reminders of such wonder to those who have.

S. Montgomery Ewegen
Middletown, CT
Spring 2021

Bibliography

Aristophanes. 2000. *Birds, Lysistrata, Women at the Thesmophoria*. Cambridge: Harvard University Press.
Aristotle. 1950. *Physica*. Oxford: Oxford University Press.
———. 1957. *Metaphysica*. Oxford: Oxford University Press.
———. 1965. *De Art Poetics Liber*. Oxford: Oxford University Press.
Athenaeus. 1854. *Deipnosophists, or Banquet of the Learned*. Translated by C. D. Yonge. London: Henry Bohn.
Bury, R. G. 1909. *The Symposium of Plato*. Cambridge: W. Heffer and Sons.
Cancik, Hubert, and Helmuth Schneider, eds. 2004. *Brill's New Pauly Encyclopedia of the Ancient World*. Leiden, Netherlands: Brill.
Cary, M., J. D. Denniston, J. Wight Duff, A. D. Noch, W. D. Ross, H. H. Scullard, eds. 1949. *The Oxford Classical Dictionary*. Oxford: Clarendon.
Diogenes Laertius. 1925. *Lives of Eminent Philosophers*. Translated by R. D. Hicks. Cambridge: Harvard University Press.
Euripides. 2007. *Dramatic Fragments*. Translated by Christopher Collard and Martin Cropp. Cambridge: Harvard University Press.
Hamilton, Edith. 1942. *Mythology*. Boston: Back Bay Books.
Heidegger, Martin. 1977. *Sein und Zeit* (GA 2). Frankfurt am Main: Vittorio Klostermann.
Hesiod. 1970. *Theogonia, Opera et Dies, Scutum, Fragmenta Selecta*. Oxford: Oxford University Press.
Homer. 1961. *Odyssey*. Translated by Robert Fitzgerald. New York: Doubleday.
———. 1990. *Iliad*. Translated by Robert Fagles. New York: Viking.
Hopkins, Burt. 2011. "The Unwritten Teachings in Plato's *Symposium*: Socrates' Initiation into the Ἀριθμός of Ἔρως." *Epoché: A Journal for the History of Philosophy* 15 (2): 279–298.
Klein, Jacob. 1968. *Greek Mathematical Thought and the Origin of Algebra*. Translated by Eva Brann. New York: Dover.
———. 1977. *Plato's Trilogy*. Chicago: University of Chicago Press.
Lycurgus. 1962. *Minor Attic Orators*. Vol. 2. Translated by J. O. Burtt. Cambridge: Harvard University Press.
Nietzsche. 1887. *Morgenröthe: Gedanken über die moralischen Vorurtheile*. Leipzig: E. W. Fritzsch.
———. 1907. *Geburt der Tragödie*. Leipzig: C. G. Naumann.
Pausanias. 1914. *Description of Greece*. Translated by W. H. S. Jones. Cambridge: Harvard University Press.
Plato. 1901. *Parmenides, Philebus, Symposium, Phaedrus, Alcibiades I and II, Hipparchus, Amatores*. Edited by J. Burnet. Oxford: Oxford University Press.
———. 1907. *Minos, Leges, Epinomis, Epistulae, Definitiones*. Oxford: Oxford University Press.
———. 1986. *The Statesman*. Translated by Seth Benardete. Chicago: University of Chicago Press.

———. 1995. *Euthyphro, Apologia Socratis, Crito, Phaedo, Cratylus, Sophista, Politicus, Theaetetus.* Edited by E. A. Duke. Oxford: Oxford University Press.
———. 2001. *The Symposium.* Translated by Seth Benardete. Chicago: University of Chicago Press.
———. 2003. *Respublica.* Edited by S. R. Slings. Oxford: Oxford University Press.
Rose, Gilbert. 1985. *Plato's Symposium: Commentary.* Bryn Mawr, PA: Bryn Mawr College.
Sallis, John. 1975. *Being and Logos.* Bloomington: Indiana University Press.
———. 1994. *Stone.* Bloomington: Indiana University Press.
———. 1999. *Chorology: On Beginning in Plato's Timaeus.* Bloomington: Indiana University Press.
———. 2005. "The Flow of φύσις and the Beginning of Philosophy: On Plato's *Theaetetus.*" In *Proceedings from the Boston Area Colloquium in Ancient Philosophy* 20, edited by J. Cleary and G. Gurtler, 177–193. Leiden, Netherlands: Brill.
———. 2008. *Transfigurements*: On the True Sense of Art. Chicago: Chicago University Press.
———. 2012. *Logic of Imagination.* Bloomington: Indiana University Press.
———. 2014. "Plato's *Sophist*: A Different Look." In *New Yearbook for Phenomenology and Phenomenological Research* 13, edited by Burt Hopkins and John Drummond, 283–291. Oxford: Routledge.
———. 2015. "The Span of Memory: On Plato's *Theaetetus.*" *Epoché: A Journal for the History of Philosophy* 21 (2): 321–333.
———. 2016. *The Figure of Nature: On Greek Origins.* Bloomington: Indiana University Press.
———. 2017. *Plato's Statesman: Dialectic, Myth, and Politics.* New York: SUNY Press.
Schleiermacher, Friedrich. 1836. *Introduction to the Dialogues of Plato.* Translated by William Dobson. Reprinted in 1968. *Great Thinkers on Plato.* Edited by Barry Gross. New York: Capricorn Books.
Thucydides. 1998. *The Peloponnesian War.* Translated by Steven Lattimore. Indianapolis: Hackett.
Xenophon. 1923. *Memorabilia.* Translated by E. C. Marchant and O. J. Todd. Cambridge: Harvard University Press.

Index

Achilles, 22, 37, 51
Admetus, 21–22, 51
Agamemnon, 18, 37
Agathon, 5, 7, 13–14, 16, 18; and Apollo, 36–38; and ascent, 34, 41; and comedy, 43, 67; and contributions to tragedy, 35n11, 36n12; and Dionysus, 18, 35, 37, 60, 64; and Gorgias, 42; and hubris, 18–20, 34, 41, 60; and order, 36; and Pausanias, 25, 27, 44n6; and self-ignorance, 43; and shame, 35
Alcestis, 21–22, 51, 60
Alcibiades, 14–16, 59, 60n3; as embodiment of Dionysus, 60–61, 63; and mutilation of the herms, 15–16; and Socrates, 9, 14, 17, 19, 60–66
(the) all, 84, 115–117
Ammon, 86
animals: comedy of, 98–110, 116; and the cosmic reversal, 113–114; and the divisions, 98, 105–106, 129; and eros, 27, 41, 50; and the human, 101–102, 106–107, 116, 127, 130; and the king, 114–115, 127; and the Maenads, 4–5, 127n11; and natural joints, 96; and Socrates, 62–63
Aphrodite, 10n17; and Ares, 38–40; birth of, 26, 46–47 and Dionysus, 29; Uranian and Pandemian, 24–26
Apollo, 5; and Admetus, 21–22; and Agathon, 36–38; and Aphrodite, 40; and Apollodorus, 5–6, 17, 59n1; and the Delphic Oracle, 5; and Dionysus, 6, 10, 22, 33, 37, 59–61; and Ephilates and Otus, 31; and Eros, 10, 36–40; and Hermes, 40; and Socrates, 20, 33, 54, 61, 63, 67
Apollodorus: and Apollo, 5–6, 17, 59n1
Apology, 5, 6, 20, 33, 46n11, 77, 83
Ares: and Aphrodite, 38–40; and Ephilates and Otus, 31
Aristodemus, 11–13, 16, 17–19, 23, 27, 43, 67

Aristophanes: and Apollo, 33; and comedy, 27–28, 30, 32, 34, 43, 67; and Dionysus, 29, 33; and hiccups, 3, 27–28, 30, 59; meaning of name, 29–30; and tragedy, 32, 43, 67
Aristotle: and Agathon, 35n11, 36n12; and logic, 3, 74n10; and number, 87; and στοιχεῖον, 122
arithmetic, 96, 103, 106, 113; comedy of, 94, 99; in the divisions, 91, 93–94; and kinds, 88–89; and law, 131–133; and Plato, 87. *See also* ἀριθμητική; *See also* mathematics
ascent, 8, 22–23, 26, 31, 34, 41, 47n13, 56, 60; and Agathon, 34, 41; and the beautiful, 56n29; and comedy, 43; and descent, 60, 64, 74; and hubris, 41; and interruption, 43; and self-forgetfulness, 57–58; and Socrates, 60. *See also* ἀνάβασις
Athena, 41, 46n12, 72, 115
Athenaeus, 13
Atreus, 111–112

banquet, 4, 8n14, 47, 111
beauty: and Aphrodite, 24; and Dionysus, 37; and eros, 21, 38, 41–42, 49, 53–54; and excess, 58; and μοῖρα, 50; pure beholding of, 56, 60; and Socrates, 17–19. *See also* καλός
beginning: and myth, 109–113, 116; of politics, 115; and the *Timaeus*, 4. *See also* ἀρχή
body: and disorder, 28–30, 127; and eros, 49, 53–54; and immorality, 51; and medicine, 27; Pythagorean theory of, 28; and statesmanship, 80; and τέχνη, 28, 80; and φύσις, 51n21
Bury, R.G., 42n3

care, 115, 119–120, 123, 127, 137. *See also* ἐπιμέλεια

145

cloak-making, 122–125, 128n14
comedy: and Agathon, 43, 67; and abstraction, 95; of animals, 98–110, 116; and disorder, 28, 29; of the divisions, 118, 120; and forgetfulness, 77n18, 97, 107; and ignorance, 30, 43, 95; mathematical, 94–110, 116; Platonic, 29–30; and self-ignorance, 30, 43; and tragedy, 32–33, 67
counting, 84, 86–88, 93n16, 94, 96, 103, 106, 133. *See also* ἀριθμέω; *See also* arithmetic; *See also* καταριθμεῖν; *See also* mathematics
courage: and Agathon, 34; and Eros, 36, 38, 40; and Socrates, 65–66; and statesmanship, 137–138. *See also* ἀνδρεία
cranes, 100–101, 105–107
Cratylus, 29, 77, 95
Cronus, 26, 112–117, 138

daimon(s), 4, 47n13; and Eros, 46; and Socrates, 46. *See also* δαίμων
death, 32–33
Delphic Oracle, 5, 30, 33, 51–52
democracy, 131–132, 135–136; and Alcibiades, 15
descent, 3, 8, 74; and ascent, 59, 60; and Socrates, 60, 67. *See also* κατάβασις
dialectic: and Dionysus, 127n11; and division, 89; and experience, 101; and mathematics, 88; and measurement, 126; and myth, 110–111. *See also* διαλεκτική
Dionysus: and Agathon, 35; and Alcibiades, 60–61, 63; Aphrodite, 26; and Apollo, 6, 22, 37; and Apollodorus, 6; and Aristophanes, 27, 29; and disorder, 27, 29, 59, 66; and eros, 26, 29, 33, 37, 40, 47; and the flute, 20; and Maenads, 4–5, 22, 127n11; and Socrates, 18, 20, 33, 62–64; and wine, 4, 59, 61–62
Diotima, 43–44; and self-forgetfulness, 57–58
discrimination, 96–98, 102–104, 107, 137. *See also* κρῖναι
disorder: and the body, 28–30; and the cosmic reversal, 114; and Dionysus, 29, 59, 66
dogs, 106, 109

Eileithyia, 50
Eleatics, 81, 84
elements, 121–122
Eleusinian Mysteries, 15–16, 60n3
Empedocles, 28n28, 110, 122
eros: and animals, 27, 41, 50; and Aphrodite, 10n17, 24, 47; and Apollo, 10, 36–40; and beauty, 21, 38, 41–42, 49, 53–54; as between, 45–48; and the body, 49, 53–54; as daimon, 46; and Dionysus, 26, 29, 33, 37, 40, 47; and excess, 31–33; and the good, 34, 46, 48–50; and Hera, 9; in Hesiod, 10, 20–21, 24; in Homer, 9; and human temporality, 47, 50; and ignorance, 47–48; and immortality, 47–48, 50–51, 53–54; and law, 25, 28, 32; and medicine, 27, 40–41; Pandemian, 24–26; and philosophy, 48, 54; as poet, 40–41; and ποίησις, 48, 52; and pregnancy, 49–50; and selfsameness, 47–48, 53–54; and Socrates, 62–63; and the soul, 24, 27, 37, 49, 52, 54, 115; and τέχνη, 27–28, 32, 41; Uranian, 24–26; and φύσις, 30–32, 51n21. *See also* ἔρως
Eryximachus, 5, 16; and comedy, 28, 30–33; and Dionysus, 28; meaning of name, 28; and Phaedrus, 44n6
Euripides, 4, 26, 35n11, 112n2
Euthyphro, 76–77, 130n17
excess: and Alcibiades, 59; and beauty itself, 58; and eros, 31–33; and hubris, 5, 18n4, 41; and measure, 125; and Socrates, 61

flute: and Dionysus, 20, 37, 59–60, 62; and Marsyas, 63
flute girl, 4, 20, 26, 37, 59
forgetting, 57–58; and comedy, 77n18, 95, 97, 107; and the cosmic reversal, 117n13; and the Stranger, 118

going up, 7–8, 11, 22–23, 26, 35, 56, 59n1, 74. *See also* ἀνάβασις; *See also* ascent
golden age, 46n10, 110, 112, 114–115
(the) good: and Agathon, 18–20, 41; and eros, 34, 46, 49–50
Gorgias, 42

Hades, 3, 21, 22, 26, 31, 33, 42n2, 60, 74, 112
Hephaestus, 32, 39–40, 115

Hera, 26, 50; and eros, 9
Heracles, 22; and Socrates, 6
Heraclitus, 72n3, 110
Hermes, 15, 31n7, 40, 111
herms, 15–16, 60n3, 62
Hesiod: and Ate (Ἄτη), 37; and δαίμων, 46n10; and eros, 10, 20–21, 24; and the golden age, 112; as immortal, 52; and myth, 110
hiccups, 3, 27–29, 59
Homer: and Aphrodite, 38; and Ate (Ἄτη), 37; and Ephilates and Otus, 31; and eros, 9; and the Gorgon, 42; as immortal, 52; and κατέβην, 74; substituting worse for good, 18–19; and ξένος, 81
hubris, 18, 19, 25, 64. See also ὕβρις

ignorance: and Agathon, 43; and comedy, 30, 43, 95; and correct opinion, 45; and eros; 47–48; and Eryximachus, 32; and philosophy, 45–46; of self, 30, 43; and Socrates, 64–65
immortality, 47–48, 50–51, 53–54
(the) instant, 55. See also ἐξαίφνης

kinds, 84–89; and εἶδος, 90n12, 99, 100; and natural joints, 96, 98–99, 105; and parts, 100; and φύσις, 96, 99, 113. See also γένος
Klein, J., 83, 88n7

language: Greek understanding of, 85; relation to being, 111
law, 131–133; as arithmetical, 133–134; and eros, 25, 28, 32; and writing, 134–136. See also νόμος
Laws, 4, 71
limit, 84, 89, 95, 99, 105, 107, 135; of τέχνη, 129. See also ὅρος.
logic: and Aristotle, 3, 74n10; and Plato, 3
logistics, 96, 103. See also λογιστική

Maenads, 4, 22, 127n11
Marsyas, 5, 20; and Socrates, 63–64
mathematics: comedy of, 94–110, 116; and counting, 87; and kinds, 84, 86; and law, 133–134; and philosophy, 88; and politics, 76, 120; and Theaetetus, 79

measure: and the cosmic reversals, 113; and hubris, 19–20; and λόγος, 125; and the mean, 125; and Protagoras, 78; and the statesman, 138; and τέχνη, 125–126. See also μέτρον
medicine: and eros, 27, 40–41, 59n2
Meno, 4, 45
myth, 3; and beginnings, 110; of cosmic revolutions, 110–119, 137–138; and λόγος, 110, 116; and philosophy, 110–111; and play, 75, 111, 116–117. See also μῦθος

natural joint, 89; and kinds, 95–99, 105
Nietzsche, F., 3, 35n11
number, 79n21, 84, 87–88, 96, 100, 103. See also arithmetic; see also mathematics
nurturing, 44, 51, 98–102, 106–108, 115–120, 125–127

ones, 84, 87–89, 94, 103, 113, 133. See also arithmetic
opinion, 6–7, 45–46, 99, 103. See also δοκέω; See also δόξα
Orpheus, 21–22

paradigm: and correct-opinion, 45–46; and dreams, 120–121; and εἶδος, 92; of gymnastic trainer, 133–134; and letters, 121, 126; literal meaning of, 121; of paradigm, 121, 138; of physician, 134–135; of sea captain, 135; of shepherd, 117, 120; and weaving, 121–126, 128, 137
Parmenides, 81, 110
Parmenides, 10n18, 55
Pausanias, 13, 16, 25–27
Peloponnesian War, 14–15, 60n3, 65n9
Phaedo, 6, 77, 83
Phaedrus, 16, 22
Phaedrus, 17, 47n13, 89, 96
Phaleron, 7, 9
Philebus, 30
philosophy: and the body, 80; and eros, 48, 54; and ignorance, 45–46; mathematics, 84n1, 88; and myth, 110–111; and Socrates, 33; and wonder, 3, 55, 80
pigs, 107
Piraeus, 7–8, 74

Plato: and arithmetic, 87; and graphic ventriloquy, 73; and logic, 3; and slow reading, 3, 74; and the theory of forms, 54n25, 90
play. See παιδιά
Potidaea, 14, 17, 65
pregnancy, 44, 47–52
Protagoras, 78, 80, 86
Protagoras, 4, 10n18, 25

recollection, 11–12; and knowledge, 13; and Socrates, 87–88
Republic, 4, 8, 10, 29, 71–74, 95, 99n7, 106, 120
roots: and Empedocles, 122; mathematical, 79–80, 105

Schleiermacher, F., 75
self-forgetting, 57
self-ignorance, 30, 43
shame, 21, 25, 27, 35, 64. See also αἰσχρός
shepherd, 99n7, 101, 106, 107, 114–122, 127
Socrates: and Agathon, 17–20, 34–35, 42–43, 66–67; and Alcibiades, 3, 9, 14, 60–61, 64–66; and Apollo, 5–6, 33, 54n26, 67; and Apollodorus, 6; and Aristodemus, 11–12, 17–19; and beauty, 17–19; and comedy, 43; and concealment, 62; and his daimon, 46n11; and Dionysus, 18, 20, 33, 60–67; and erotics, 20, 44, 62; and Heracles, 60; and hubris, 19–20, 60, 64; and ignorance, 64; and interruption, 35–36, 43, 56; and Marsyas, 63; and recollection, 87–88; and silence, 33, 35, 64–65; and sileni / satyrs, 19, 62–63; and tragedy, 35; and ugliness, 19, 63; virtues of, 62, 65–66; and φύσις, 65
Sophist, 75–78, 80–93, 99, 110, 113, 138n7
soul: and ascent, 21, 47n13, 57; and daimons, 46n10; and descent, 74; ensouled, 98, 102, 105; and eros, 24, 27, 37, 49, 52, 54, 115; and immortality, 51; and philosophy, 48, 80
(the) Stranger, 81–82

statesman: and care, 118–119; and knowledge, 90, 97; and nurturing, 98–99, 117–118; and the philosopher, 88; as shepherd, 98–99, 107, 109, 116–118; and τέχνη, 91; and weaving, 137–138; and withdrawal, 139; worth of, 86–87. See also πολιτικός

temple: of Apollo, 67; and the πόλις, 72
Theaetetus, 79–80
Theaetetus, 4, 10n18, 76–83, 122, 138n7
Theodorus, 78–79
Thucydides, 15
Thyestes. See Atreus
Timaeus, 4, 113n8, 114n9, 117, 122
tragedy: and Agathon, 13, 35, 43, 67; and Aristophanes, 32–34, 43, 67; and Dionysus, 5, 18, 35

violence, 36–38, 114n10, 116–118, 136
virtue, 25, 36, 38, 41, 52, 57, 58, 62; of Socrates, 62, 65–67. See also ἀρετή

weaving: and Athena, 41; paradigm of, 121–129; and the statesman, 137–138. See also ὑφαντική
wine, 4–5, 22, 47, 59–62, 64, 66, 67
withdrawal: and the gods, 114, 138; and the statesman, 139
wonder, 3, 55, 56n29, 79–80, 113

Xenophanes, 110, 111n1
Xenophon, 25

Zeus: and Aphrodite, 24, 26, 39; and Apollo, 22, 33; and Ate, 37; and Atreus, 111–112; and Cronus, 112, 116, 117n13, 138; and Dione, 26; and Dionysus, 5; and the divine banquet, 47; and Ephialtes and Otus, 31; and Eros, 41; and excess, 31–33; and Hephaestus, 39; and Hera, 9; and Metis, 46n12; and politics, 115

Index of Greek Terms

αἰσχρός, 25, 27, 28, 35. See also shame
ἀκολασία, 31–32
ἀνάβασις, 8, 31, 34. See also going-up
ἀνδρεία, 36, 137. See also courage
ἄνειμι, 7. See also going up
ἀλήθεια, 5, 60
ἀντιλέγειν, 43
ἀπορία, 34, 35, 47
ἀριθμέω, 87. See also arithmetic; See also counting; See also mathematics
ἀριθμητική, 96
ἀρετή, 25, 36, 52, 62. See also virtue
ἀρχή, 31, 80, 110, 131–132. See also beginning

βασιλική, 93, 126, 127, 133–135

γέλοιος, 29–30
γέννησις, 49
γένος, 84, 86, 89, 90n12, 100. See also kinds

διαλεκτική, 89. See also dialectic
δαίμων, 46, 48. See also daimon
δοκέω, 7, 52. See also opinion
δόξα, 7, 45. See also opinion
δύναμις, 29, 30, 46, 105, 130

εἶδος, 37, 53, 54n25, 56, 63, 90, 92, 93, 99, 100
ἐκφανέστατον, 17
ἐνταῦθα, 53, 58
ἐξαίφνης, 55, 57
ἐπιμέλεια, 118, 119. See also care
ἐπιστήμη, 27, 51, 89n9, 91, 92, 93, 132
ἐρασμιώτατον, 17
ἑρμαῖ, 15
ἔρως, 17, 19, 20, 24, 95, 112–116, 122n6

ἰδέα, 54n25, 90, 99

καλός, 17, 18, 21, 24–28, 31, 35–37, 49–50, 53–56, 79. See also beauty

κατάβασις, 8, 64. See also descent
κατεῖδον, 57
κρίνω, 96, 97, 103n8

λογισμός, 78, 87
λογιστική, 96

μεγαλοφροσύνη, 34
μέτρον, 125. See also measure
μοῖρα, 50, 58, 60
μουσική, 41
μῦθος, 28n29, 113n6; and λόγος, 75n11, 110–111. See also myth

νόμος, 28, 54, 133. See also law

ὄγκος, 94
ὅρος, 84, 135. See also limit

παιδιά, 75, 111, 116, 128
ποίησις, 40n16, 41, 48–49, 52–53, 91–92, 95
πόλις, 71–73, 78, 80, 91, 127, 131n1, 135, 137
πολιτικός, 71–73, 78, 90. See also statesman
πολιτεία, 73, 131n1, 136
πρέπον, 126

στοιχεῖον, 122
συνουσία, 4, 50
σχῆμα, 94, 120

ὕβρις, 5, 6, 18–20, 24, 41, 60. See also hubris
ὑφαντική, 122. See also weaving

φαλλός, 9
φαός, 5, 17
φιλοτιμία, 21, 51
φοῖβος, 5
φύσις, 30–32, 49, 51, 54, 65, 79, 83, 91, 96, 113, 129

χώρα, 19n7, 60, 93

149

JOHN SALLIS is Frederick J. Adelmann Professor of Philosophy at Boston College. He is author of more than twenty books, including *Chorology, Songs of Nature,* and *Kant and the Spirit of Critique.*

S. MONTGOMERY EWEGEN is an Associate Professor in the Department of Philosophy at Trinity College, Hartford. He is author of *The Way of the Platonic Socrates* and *Plato's Cratylus: The Comedy of Language,* as well as cotranslator (along with Julia Goesser Assaiante) of Martin Heidegger's *Heraclitus.*

www.ingramcontent.com/pod-product-compliance
Lightning Source LLC
Chambersburg PA
CBHW030116170426
43198CB00009B/636

PHILOSOPHY

On Beauty and Measure features renowned philosopher John Sallis's commentaries on Plato's dialogues the *Symposium* and the *Statesman*. Drawn from two lecture courses delivered by Sallis, they represent his longest and most sustained engagement to date with either work.

Brilliantly original, Sallis's close readings of Plato's dialogues are grounded in the original passages and also illuminate the overarching themes that drive the dialogues.

JOHN SALLIS is Frederick J. Adelmann Professor of Philosophy at Boston College. He is author of more than twenty books, including *Chorology*, *Songs of Nature*, and *Kant and the Spirit of Critique*.

S. MONTGOMERY EWEGEN is an Associate Professor in the Department of Philosophy at Trinity College. He is author of *The Way of the Platonic Socrates* and *Plato's* Cratylus: *The Comedy of Language*.

THE COLLECTED WRITINGS OF JOHN SALLIS, VOL III/2

iupress.org